**BOCCONI
UNIVERSITY
PRESS**

Claudio Scardovi

GEN Z AND THE FUTURE OF WEALTH

Sustainable Investing and Wellbeing for Our Next Generations

Premise by **Larissa Iapichino**
Foreword by **Cristiana Capotondi**

Cover: Cristina Bernasconi, Milan
Typesetting: Laura Panigara, Cesano Boscone (MI)

Copyright © 2022 Bocconi University Press
EGEA S.p.A.

EGEA S.p.A.
Via Salasco, 5 - 20136 Milano
Tel. 02/5836.5751 – Fax 02/5836.5753
egea.edizioni@unibocconi.it – www.egeaeditore.it

All rights reserved, including but not limited to translation, total or partial adaptation, reproduction, and communication to the public by any means on any media (including microfilms, films, photocopies, electronic or digital media), as well as electronic information storage and retrieval systems. For more information or permission to use material from this text, see the website www.egeaeditore.it

Given the characteristics of Internet, the publisher is not responsible for any changes of address and contents of the websites mentioned.

First edition: July 2022

ISBN Domestic Edition	978-88-99902-89-6
ISBN International Edition	978-88-31322-65-2
ISBN Digital Domestic Edition	978-88-238-8472-4
ISBN Digital International Edition	978-88-31322-66-9

Print: Logo s.r.l., Borgoricco (PD)

For Benedetta and Berenice,
the "alpha" stars of what will come next.

Table of Contents

A Premise from "Gen Z" for "Gen Alpha", by *Larissa Iapichino*   XI

Foreword, by *Cristiana Capotondi*   XIII

1 **The Wealth of People**   1
    1.1 Wealth of Nations   1
    1.2 Economics and philosophy   3
    1.3 What "nealth"?   5
    1.4 Gnoseology of wealth   9
    1.5 What wealth for which stakeholders?   11
    1.7 Capitalism for everybody   16

2 **Wealth and Wellbeing**   21
    2.1 Wealth and wellbeing: there is a point   21
    2.2 Wealth, wellbeing and wealth-being   23
    2.3 Gen Zero and Grinch finance   24
    2.4 Financial burden   26
    2.5 Debitization, monetization and debasization   29
    2.6 Social burden   32
    2.7 Not in my (green) backyard   35
    2.8 Green nemesis   37
    2.9 Three unbearable burdens: ecological   40
    2.10 Was Malthus eventually right?   44

3 **The Wealth of Italy**   49
    3.1 The wealth of Italian citizens   40
    3.2 Living beyond our means   52

	3.3	Are we citizens or pensioners?	54
	3.4	Equitization matrix	61
4	**The Future of Wealth**	**67**
	4.1	The Grinch generation and traditional wealth management	67
	4.2	Towards a new wealth management model	69
	4.3	The future of wealth and wealth of the future	70
	4.4	From ego-systems to eco-systems	72
	4.5	Gen X + Z: an intergenerational alliance	74
	4.6	From Gen Zero to Gen Alpha	76
	4.7	Enlarged investable universe	78
	4.8	Tell me where you invest	79
5	**Sustainable Investing**	**85**
	5.1	Sustainable capital in the 21st century	85
	5.2	A greater wealth tax or a better wealth management?	87
	5.3	Green wash: is labelling good enough?	88
	5.4	The Green bubble and flop	90
	5.5	Green in public and private markets	92
	5.6	We all live beyond our means	94
	5.7	Somebody has to pay	96
	5.8	A pension fund for the next generations	98
	5.9	Benefit corporation in private markets	100
	5.10	Sustainability in private markets investment	102
	5.11	Regulating sustainable investing	105
	5.12	From regulations to behaviours	107
6	**Private Equity for Everybody**	**113**
	6.1	Private wealth: extended, augmented	113
	6.2	Private gains, public losses?	114
	6.3	Private equity: a balanced risk/return opportunity	116
	6.4	Three ways to go private	119
	6.5	Are public markets worth a premium?	122
	6.6	Private equity: barbarians at the gate?	124
	6.7	Private equity for everybody	126
	6.8	Private equity "all-in-one"	129
	6.9	Retailization of finance	131
	6.10	Is private equity good for stakeholders?	132
	6.11	Green is good	135

	6.12	Ant or grasshoppers?	137
	6.13	Rollercoasting… and long Covid	138
7	**HOPE: A Case Study**		**143**
	7.1	The serendipity of HOPE	143
	7.2	Capitalism for everybody	145
	7.3	HOPE's mission and vision of "wealth"	147
	7.4	HOPE as a stakeholder based, benefit corporation	150
	7.5	HOPE's framework as a benefit corporation	153
	7.6	HOPE framework as pursuant of ESG	165
	7.7	Black swans and Russian bears	216
	7.8	A balanced scorecard for total sustainability	218
	7.9	Death of globalization and the return of autarky?	220
	7.10	The force of a new generation	223

A Premise from "Gen Z" for "Gen Alpha"

by *Larissa Iapichino*

Reading these pages, which also have an impact on our future as Gen Z, many themes are brought to mind.

Firstly, how sustainable is our attitude to consumption and how green are we in our daily life? As young people we would love to live in a better and fairer world, to be more sustainable, and not to waste what can be saved for others wellbeing.

Fairness means ensuring everyone has the same opportunities to grow up with equal rights in terms of learning, practicing sports and being cared for.

Via my participation in the HOPE Sicaf committee I sincerely want to represent a young generation willing to one day rule its life with strong values and I believe that today's healthy investments are the basis for this.

Wealth also needs to be used for building infrastructure which will allow an optimized, sustainable well-being, and I believe Mr Scardovi has been found a good recipe to succesfully solve this fundamental dilemma.

But also the way in which funding will be recovered is meaningful and significant: this book outlines a new way to get this done.

Reading these pages is useful for us, "Gen Z", to have an overview of the economic and financial trends which nowadays are the most urgent to be understood for our future.

I would definitely recommend reading this book to have a deeper view and to shape opinions to help us understand of our role in this world even more.

Foreword
by *Cristiana Capotondi*

In 2021 I became a member of the Sustainability Committee at HOPE, an alternative investment fund. I decided to join because I think its main objective is fascinating – to put back at the center stage of finance the Italian small and medium enterprises, and with a view of pursuing a "total sustainability" – economically, but also socially and environmentally based. The very fact that the traditionally exclusive world of finance is opening up its inner sanctum and decision making to people from the world of humanistic culture and from the new generations, signals a search for a new way of doing things and for more lateral thinking.

Certainly, there are rules that must be followed to achieve success, as there are others that we need to keep during normal times – and others that are instead required during times of great change. In fact, we live today in flux, with great transformations and challenges. During times like this, we need to be brave enough to even question Adam Smith, as indicated in the incipit of the book, and his concept of the "invisible hand." Maybe this is because his economic vision cannot be applied to times of great disruption, like ours. More specifically, the digital revolution is changing our world in new ways. The huge decoupling between those able to embrace the new digital world and those left behind will be brutal if no rules and no state intervention were in place to balance the resulting economic, social and ecological tensions. The very economic growth and wealth creation that our country has been able to sustain after WWII would be put at risk.

Because of all this, I believe there is a profound need to rethink the culture of our contemporary times, not just in economic, but also in social and environmental terms. This is the mission of my association (IoSono) that seeks to help people in gauging how much technological innovation and the core values of liberal democracies, are today at stake and endangered by top down and so called "pragmatic" policy-making; and in understating how they can in fact become sustainable only if they are nurtured by a humanistic culture.

We often speak of never-ending humanism to really mean how our never-ending soul searching should be at the basis of each of our actions. We are born to know ourselves, and to then open up – from our most inner self – to meet and know other people. We love having others to love and fulfil us and overcome that stupid and vexatious dichotomy between egoism and altruism. Adam Smith had fully understood how the wealth of nations is born out of the righteous need of individual organization and success. But maybe he had not fully appreciated or clarified how, behind the utilitarian, selfish motivation of an individual, and behind the very same idea of human being, we need to assume (and advocate) something more profound and even spiritual. As individuals, we are nothing if not understood in the context of our holistic relationships with other fellow human beings and with the larger ecosystem of Planet Earth. This is the ultimate meaning of ESG (Environmental, Social and Governance). Not a new fad or a passing fashion, but something much more profound, critical and urgent that we need to understand and act upon, to pursue a positive impact for us and our future generations and drive change, for good.

1 The Wealth of People

1.1 Wealth of Nations

In his *magnum opus* "An inquiry into the nature and causes of the Wealth of Nations," the Scottish economist and moral philosopher Adam Smith offers an analysis of what builds nations' wealth – reflecting on the economics at the beginning of the industrial revolution through a discussion of broad topics such as the division of labour, productivity and free markets. Not only has his book become one of the most influential in modern history, but its resource allocation theory has developed into one of the most substantive and dominant propositions in economics. In a regime of free markets and competition, the owners of scarce resources (labour, land and capital) use them most profitably, exchanging them through the market price mechanism, until an equal rate of return for all uses is achieved at equilibrium. In turn, this principle of focusing each owner, and each nation as a macrocosm of owners, on what they do best (and relatively better than others) optimizes the value that the global economy can create each year. For example: "the fund which originally supplies (the nation) with all the necessaries and conveniences of life which it annually consumes, and which consist always either in the immediate produce of that labour or in what is purchased with that produce from other nations," as he describes it in his incipit. In short, the relative competitiveness of what they do better allows nations to optimize the value created globally and, in turn, their own. If free markets work on the basis of industrialized production and distribution, supporting the increase in the overall productivity and the optimal allocation of scarce resources, will maximise wealth as a consequence. This overall process of wealth creation can then be addressed and solved with simple analytics and basic formulas, using a quantitative approach that creates certainty, allowing the free market to do the rest.

In short, as economic agents, we all live to own and consume more, and we produce more as a means to that end. We can do this by focusing on our comparative advantage, as individuals, companies and nations, by leveraging new technologies that, from time to time, are made available, to produce even more and hence own and consume more. Being able to own and consume more is therefore a sign of success, as producing more is an early indicator – albeit not absolute – of this outcome, as different parties in the production and distribution value chain can take a bigger or smaller share, based on the competitive scarcity (or uncompetitive abundance) of what we have on offer, based on our competitive advantage. In short, as decision makers, we can base our choices on a simple analysis of net income or return on equity, or on more sophisticated approaches based on the net present value and the discounted cash flow, or on economic value added and related market capitalization, and count on the workings of the "invisible hand" of the free market. We will all use our scarce resources prudently and optimize our economic fortunes as, through trade, we will be in a position to gain access to everything we do not have by using those fortunes and the money they can be converted into. We will use money to buy everything we want, assuming of course it is sufficient, given the market price. Assuming we, and our nation, are rich enough, almost anything will become possible, based on the polar star of wealth – financial, competitively gained and based on the sacred working of markets and on the use of money. Free markets will work out the best development path to create optimized and sustainable economic growth for the long term. Moral issues could then be addressed later on, once wealth has been maximized, through the use of taxes and liberalities that rich people (and nations) can decide to gift others.

In truth, Adam Smith also hypothesized four "maxim" of taxation – proportionality, transparency, convenience and efficiency – and was one of the first advocates of progressive taxation for the benefit of overall society and to pursue redistribution against the extreme polarization of fortunes. He also warned how any expansive role of the state can negatively impact on economic growth, which is exclusively determined by free markets and by the entrepreneurial nature of private individuals. He argues that if governments can borrow with impunity, they would be more likely to wage wars or to spend on projects that will be popular with their constituencies – what we could define today as "populism" – with the financial burden left to future generations. Leaving these points aside, Smith's main legacy remains the inner and infallible working of the "invisible hand" of the market, the extreme justification of specialization on a global basis and the straight and sometimes ruthless use of our financial toolkits to gauge the relative competitiveness of products, services, people and nations and therefore their right to survive, prosper and enjoy their fair share of wealth. Market prices, based on financial returns, or economic value added or net present value, become the ultimate archetype of our living as humankind – a primitive mental image always present in the collective unconscious that separates the winners from the losers, the good from the bad, and happiness from unhappiness. From this basis, we have been living, investing, working and consuming through the last few centuries, prospering (certainly from a financial and economic point of view) across industrial revolutions. And we have found easy answers – from macro policymaking to micro behaviours – from this set of simplifications, and defined logical solutions – to any kind of need – based on the certainties that have become mainstream after Smith's work.

1.2   Economics and philosophy

Economics begins with closed-ended simplification and needs certainty and therefore an easy way to rationalize, classify and calculate something that we use to make decisions and embark on certain courses of action. Its utility is a main, short-term driver, with usually very tangible, material ends. On the contrary, philosophy begins with open-ended questions and seeks perfection. It therefore develops a complex way to ponder, argue and elaborate something that may be useful for defining our ultimate purpose and sense of being, but rarely to make choices that have short term, tangible consequences. It is then obvious why the "dismal science" is the one we use most to gauge wealth and make decisions on its management and accumulation, deployment and consumption. It is not for philosophers to decide on investments or even to contribute to setting the policy makers' agenda for the future of our nations. It is not for them to develop an asset allocation strategy and do stock picking. Still, even Adam Smith was both an economist and a philosopher and we believe that, sharing their different perspectives, both disciplines could become stronger and, most importantly, of greater use to mankind. In our own enquiry on wealth – the wealth of nations and of people most of all – we will focus on several critical questions, developing old and new arguments that could support both the economic and philosophical development of societies with some useful answers to questions of our time:

- If, according to the fundamental hypothesis and simplifications at the base of economics we all strive to maximize our own utility and expect a very tangible pay off, why have so many imbalances developed over time, both financial and otherwise?
- Why have these imbalances left most of us deeply sorry of the extraordinary GDP (Gross Domestic Product) growth as a result of the industrial revolutions? Shouldn't we just care about ourselves and leave moral issues to the state?
- If, based on this, the scarce resources of the economy are competitively allocated and based on comparative advantages, why are there so many failed nations where people struggle to survive? Shouldn't most of them be wealthier based on their comparative advantage to trade?
- Why, even at the global level, is the global economic system and the transnational fabric of society seemingly on the verge of irreversible decline or even break up – give the depletion of rare resources, the ecological burden created, and the social tensions created by a tiny minority becoming outrageously rich with the majority owning only debts and peanuts?
- Why are we, even if as economic agents we are assumed to be almost omniscient and rationale, courting ecological and existential disaster driven by climate change? And with gender, faith and race disparity that separate our societies in few safe enclaves and wider areas of exclusion why are we getting closer and closer to global and regional deadly wars?
- If we are wealthier by any kind of economic measurement than ever before, why do we feel so unsecure, stressed and almost irremediably poor? Is money not enough to buy us happiness? We could even buy love and health, but what about our conscience of being?
- Why have many of the decisions we took, based on a profitability, economic value added, or net present value analysis, brought

us short-term abundance coupled by mid-term misery and by the long-term depauperating of the heritage we are leaving to the future generations?
- If our new generations are also driven by their own utility and expected benefits, what do they think of the current plans to "build back better" and to develop a "green economy" at their financial expense? What do they think about initiatives like ESG and "Next Gen EU"?
- And, finally, is the very definition of wealth, implicit in Smith's *magnum opus* and most modern economic theory and wealth management industry practice, sufficient to fully address these questions and support us in addressing the critical sustainability challenge we all (and future generations) face? Or is a new definition of 'wealth' required, by building on the contributions of economics and philosophy?

1.3 What "nealth"?

The world has never been wealthier, according to McKinsey.[1] Leaving aside concerns about pandemics, climate change and the risk of a global war – everything looks so rosy! In fact, based on McKinsey's research, the value of real assets – buildings, machinery, infrastructure and so forth – and of financial assets of the 10 biggest economies (not including Italy and Russia), gives a global balance sheet of $1,540 Tn, around four times as much as 2000. Net of liabilities, this wealth equates to about 6 times of global GDP (from around 4.5 times in 2000). Unsurprisingly, this greater wealth has made rich people richer, increasing the polarization of wealth postulated by the economist Thomas Piketty. In fact, most of the new wealth created – half from China and a quarter from the United States of America – has increased this gap. The top 10% in these two countries own more than two-thirds of the overall wealth and, in America, the bottom half owns just 1.5% of the total. In China the figure is 6%, albeit before the launch, by President Xi Jinping, of the Communist Party's "common prosperity" vision. For families, their wealth is split roughly in equal parts between real estate and financial assets, with Italian households owning more real estate (around 65%), almost exclusively as a result of direct ownership of a few assets, typically their first and sometimes second home. This makes their reliance on the real estate economic cycle very concentrated versus other countries, where households are also big investors in real estate, but through well diversified and actively managed funds (and often relying on rental income for a living). There are also big disparities on the financial side, with Anglo-Saxon countries usually investing more in "liquid" equities than European countries (with Italy at the bottom, with a market cap of its stock market at around €750 Bn – around 30% of its GDP). Illiquid equities (e.g. referred to private markets – corporates and other real assets not traded on regulated markets), are even less invested in by European and almost not at all by Italian households (though indirectly, via their Pension Funds and other retirement schemes; and directly, through their participation in private equity initiatives, including those recently promoted by the Government with a fiscal incentive and some level of capital protection – the so-called PIR^2 Alternative).

From a purely financial point of view, it is worth considering some of the concerns about the huge increases in wealth that have been created in the last 20 years. If the multiplier between these and the GDP has increased and keeps increasing, is this caused by higher productivity in these countries? Or is it driven by the wealth migration operated at the expense of other nations and the global population? And is it simply driven by a purely monetary phenomenon, where prices are going up but the purchasing power stays the same. In a closed economy, where Robinson Crusoe and Friday are exchanging seashells to buy the bananas and mangos they respectively produce and consume (each specializing in one only, as per Smith's thesis), there will be a price determining their respective exchange rate. But if the production of exotic fruits remains the same and a sea storm leaves an abundance of shells on the beach, they should expect those prices to increase with the relative exchange ratio of bananas to mangos also influenced by whom gets to the beach first after the storm. In fact, as we will discuss later, the lax monetary policies of the last decades and quantitative easing across the globe may not (yet) have resulted in inflation that is measured on the basis of the price of products and services, but could have resulted in asset bubbles for certain real asset classes. Take real estate for example, where countries such as France and Canada have seen their average value grow by 120% and 168% respectively (with Italy gaining a modest 7% in the same period.)[3] These bubbles may have also developed in different forms based on the final owner of that excess liquidity, with the prices of penthouse and trophy mansions going higher and higher and social housing performing more modestly, given the hypothesis of further polarization and the extreme price inelasticity of the tremendously rich. If all this seems to disregard the value and credibility of nominal "fiat currencies" (those created by the force of law, at the whim of the central bank of reference), it is also worth considering the recent trend to include cryptocurrencies (like Bitcoin and Ethereum) among the global investable asset classes that are not productive *per se* and whose "store of value" function is questionable, as they are not backed by the law and are not issued by central banks that could decide point blank to outlaw them.

In any case, finance will not be our most critical issue, as we gauge and consider, from a broader perspective, what wealth really is and what it can truly bring to nations, and more importantly to people, globally – i.e. considering the world population of 8 billion and counting – and over the long term, by taking a cross-generational perspective that poses analytic challenges for our current financial toolkit. In fact, McKinsey's very rosy description of the quantitative analysis of "wealth" could be reinterpreted as "nealth" – the nemesis of wealth – that has been generated by the financial, very tangible wealth, that was targeted, supported and then maximized by the industrial revolutions of the last few centuries with the help of new technologies and that was mostly financed by oil and by the exploitation of other non-renewable resources. This has created huge, concentrated fortunes "for the few and in the present" at the expenses "of the many and for the future" – an increasingly large share of the current population are suffering as a consequence and even more will suffer in the future. This "nealth" has produced a "secluded world," where the few ultra-wealthy live isolated from the excluded majority that cannot accept anymore the situation they are living, with global societies and entire regions lacerated by hate, violence, war and governed by increasingly autocratic states (some presented as democracies where, however, information, resources and power is controlled by a small minority). We can also think of this "nealth" as an "extinct world," where climate change has made the ecosystem so inhospitable that we are forced to live indoors or in outer space and with a sort of regressive development that turns back the clock of evolution. Because of this short-sighted definition of wealth, and the application of rational theories of maximization based on unethical utilitarianism, we are now living unsustainably and courting tragedy

Figure 1.1 The world has never been so wealthy

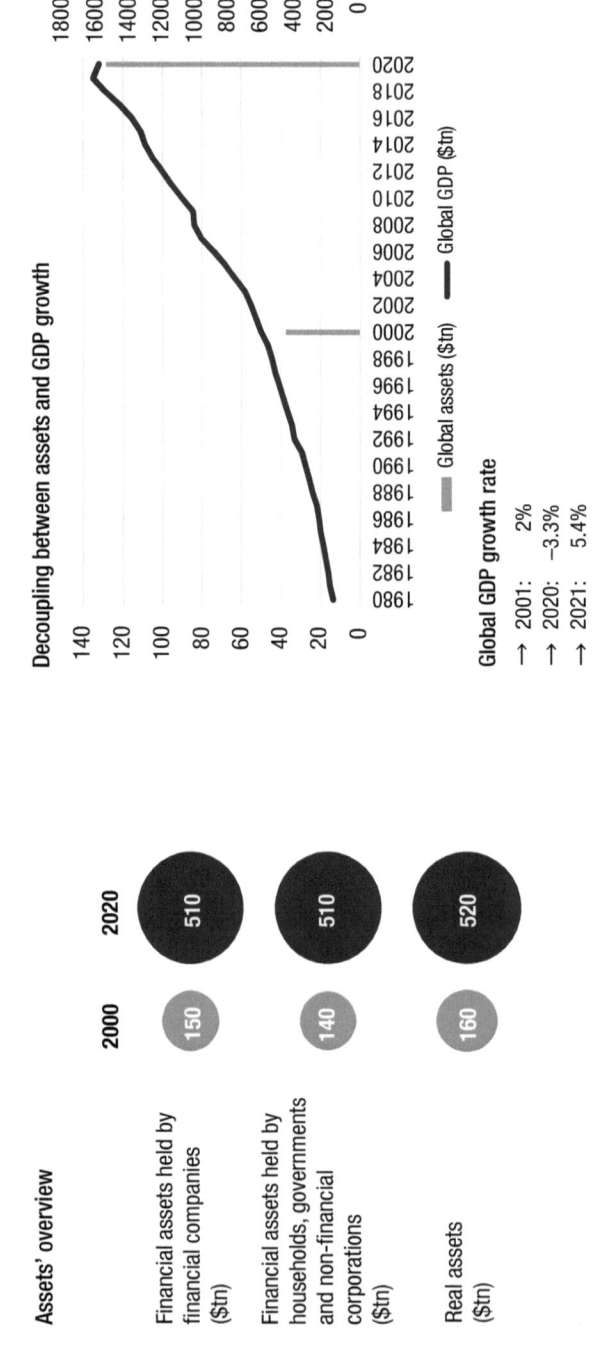

Source: McKinsey, *The Rise of the Global Balance Sheet*, 2021

Sources: International Monetary Fund, World Economic Outlook Database, October 2021; McKinsey, *The Rise of the Global Balance Sheet*, 2021

from a financial, social and ecological perspective. We are also at the brink of a cross generational disruption, where future generations will sooner or later realize they have become the big losers in the history of humankind and could potentially react in nasty ways – taking revenge to gain control of the few non-renewable resources remaining. Through this kind of revolution, they could lead the state towards anarchy or seek the creation of a dystopian world that could be as undesirable as pragmatically unachievable. Could all this become the unintended consequence of the 'Wealth of nations' that Smith postulated to lead us towards continuous growth and development? And will the current generation shoulder the responsibility of this in the next generations' memory for centuries?

Figure 1.2 The nemesis of wealth and total sustainability

Wealth is not just an economic dimension.
Wealth and **wellbeing** (**wealth-being**) should be found in the concept of shared happiness, to be achieved through total sustainability: economic, social and ecological.

"There is no value in financial and economic wealth, if we can only dispose of it in contexts of extreme creation of debt, money and inflation. If we can only take advantage of it at the expenses of the many living in poverty and segregation, under the constant threat of regional and global wars, in polluted and unhealthy cities and inside a biosphere destined to bequeath our children with eroded land, polluted water and reduced or infested animal species"

1.4 Gnoseology of wealth

A new gnoseology must inform our approach to the definition of and search for wealth. It should capitalize on the developments of economics, including a macro and a microeconomic perspective which are based on the individual living in complex societies. But it should also extend to qualifying categories that are different from finance and should include other dimensions that complement a purely utilitarian approach based on the mantra "I have (more) therefore I am (successful/ happy)." Most importantly, it should be based on our heritage and experience of the past and on the many different and pressing needs we all have in the present moment – but also include our ultimate pursuit as human beings, including our right to survive and evolve as a species and well beyond our mortal self. Extending the reasoning of Richard Dawkins, our "selfish gene" should only care about ourselves and seek merely material wealth and the satisfaction of our most basic needs that money alone can ensure. But it should also consider more intangible things, contributing to our physical and psychological wellbeing, in equilibrium with the overall ecosystem we live in; as well as other more spiritual dimensions, that can include, for example, our feeling of self-fulfilment in what we do every day, and self-realization in what we leave behind us as a memento of an existence that has been "greater than life" and extending (in a biological or spiritual form or both) to our next of kin. In fact, extending Dawkins's arguments, our "selfish gene" should also care a lot about our (direct or indirect) procreation and the continued existence of the human species, as part of a sustainable balance with the many others that constitute our current society, and the many others that will come after us. This sustainable balance should include the preservation of a hospitable environment that is benign enough for the survival of humankind and conducive to further opportunities for its advancement – and not for its means, such as machines, technology or capital – through a mix of innovation and transformation. We are caring about planet earth *per se*, praying for it as a proxy of mother earth's divinity as ancient populations were accustomed to. We care for it because it supports the life and development of mankind and many other animal species that complement and sustain our lives. If we accept that a broader and deeper gnoseology of wealth is needed, we need then to establish its starting definition and related mission, and a corresponding vision for moving from long-term goals to actions:

- Wealth could be defined as the aspirational set of goals that translate the ontological end of a human being into measurable, well-defined objectives that help them in becoming a better person and, in doing so, ensuring the survival, development and evolution of their gene/ species.
- The mission of wealth is then to inspire, guide, support and develop better people – reaching wellbeing and happiness for ourselves and others as something which is not confined to our mortal

(therefore limited) existence but can also extend to and progress through others.
- The vision of wealth could then be postulated as a more general framework that helps us, as a citizen of the world and of our country, in designing and managing our main systems of existence and co-existence – economic, social and ecological – towards total sustainability.

If we then define as "total sustainability" the sum of its financial (including its economic and governance dimensions), social (including inclusion, the fair access to opportunities and the avoidance of extreme polarization of fortunes, not to mention acts of brutal force and violence such as subjugation, terrorism and wars) and environmental (including the preservation of scarce resources and of the overall equilibrium of the biosphere), it becomes obvious why typical financial analysis is, at most, partial. If we then add to that definition the "cross generational" dimension, we can also realize how any static analysis is not just limited, but most likely wrong and at the expense of who will come after us – assuming of course our "selfish gene" cares about the survival, development and evolution of our species.

1.5 What wealth for which stakeholders?

It follows that, in order to optimize our new definition of wealth and of total, cross generational sustainability, a new gnoseology of value must be considered and supersede the current tools of financial analysis, including the universally popular and widely used alphabet soup of ROE, EVA and NPV:

- Is the ROE (Return on Equity) calculated as accounting-based net income over accounting-based equity capital invested, taking account of the different leverage of diverse companies or projects and the risks that are underwritten by them in order to achieve the expected profitability? ROE could in fact be maximized, in the short run, bringing to near zero the equity denominator, hyper leveraging the company and cutting costs as if there was no tomorrow. It could also maximize net income by embarking on all kinds of risks or mispricing them, as they would be, but probably only in the mid-term. With little regard to economic soundness, not using even basic statistics and forgetting about the future, the ROE is one of the most partial, easily manipulatable and short-sighted indicators used to gauge wealth and inform any strategy or action plan.

- Would then the EVA (Economic Value Added), calculated as the NOPAT (Net Operating profit After Tax) minus an indicator of the opportunity cost of the equity capital employed (hence measured in euro terms and not as a percentage like the ROE) provide a fuller picture of the value being created? Certainly, this indicator is more difficult to game with regards to leverage and risks undertaken (included in the calculation of the opportunity cost of capital), but would still be based on accounting rules, short term, yearly analysis and subject to significant subjectivity (hence risk of error or fraud). Its pretence to be a good predictor of future market performance has also been hugely overestimated, with even old ROE giving better predictions.
- Finally, would then NPV (Net Present Value, and the whole DCF – Discounted Cash Flow analysis, the almost religious set of dogmas on which modern corporate finance is founded) be a better yardstick, able not only to discriminate leverage and risks, but also the time value of money – the undisputable paradigm based on the equivalence between an egg today *vis a vis* a chicken tomorrow, given certain other conditions. The fact is, however, that under typical assumptions, the relevance of the future is basically forgotten after 5 years and totally killed after 10. Which is to say, better an egg today for me than tens of chickens for my children and an entire farm for my grandchildren. As the "cross generational" dimension is clearly for the very long term, NPV becomes the absolute negation of our extended "selfish gene" hypothesis.

Based on the flaws of these approaches, as economists, policy-makers, investors-consumers and simple citizens, we have taken decisions and assumed behaviours that may have been not just too selfish and utilitarian – a potential issue that is more related to justice and ethics – but selfish in the wrong way, as the obvious impact of our "wealth maximization," from the first industrial revolution onwards, has started weighting heavily on our own short term wellbeing – not to mention the impact on

1 THE WEALTH OF PEOPLE

the future generations that, as ethical humans with "selfish-genes," we should be expected to care about. But in order to define new and more comprehensive approaches inspired by "total sustainability," we need a new definition of wealth (and wellbeing, or wealth-being), that can be related to models of value that are then driven and managed optimally. That approach – we postulate – should satisfy these basic requirements:

- Our wealth-being definition should be driven by an honest, unbiased, passionate and relentless search for truth, the ontological aim that should inspire us as human beings. Each of us can then refer the ultimate truth to different philosophical or religious beliefs, but the common ground and core values shared in the journey should be enough to make it as universal as possible.
- Based on Robert Nozick[4] discussion of truth, this should be "objective enough" to make it serviceable and therefore useful for the objectives we are aiming to achieve. Targeting an absolute truth would make it unrealistic and impracticable, and being too subjective would make it debatable and easy to manipulate. Having an quick and objective truth that cannot drive decisions and actions for our own purposes would be of little value anyway.
- Following Nozick arguments, we should then build our own mission and vision around the few critical "invariances" that, although subject to some change in the long run, are sufficiently stable to be acted upon and guide our mid-term decision making and actions, with real impact on the optimization of what we have defined as "wealth-being" 1.6 Davos man and the evolution of the species

If these are the challenges that we need to overcome to set the basis, and the direction, for a sustainable wealth management of the future, in order to answer the "what is wealth?" *vexata quaestio* (that we have suggested is strictly intertwined with the "for which stakeholders" one), we need first to address another, even more critical question that is "who is going to answer these very tough ones?" In fact, the one who will have the privilege, and the responsibility, to provide an answer will also influence its fall backs and related outcomes – determining which sustainability we truly want to achieve, the chances we will achieve this and, even more importantly, who will mostly share its benefits and who will just enjoy the leftovers. One obvious answer could be, for example:

let the policymakers and the regulators decide – are they not the ones elected by the people in a democratic society? Or should we trust an autocratic but far-sighted leader or dictator to take charge? In fact, the lawmakers will certainly have an important role, but political bureaucracies are neither the most effective way to get to a result, nor guarantee the representativeness of the strategic decisions being taken. Regulators could provide constraints and rules to follow and exercise moral suasion in a number of ways, but would this be conducive to an optimal allocation of all the scarce resources needed to ensure the maximization of wealth and wellbeing? And what about a far-sighted autocrat or dictator – leaving aside the certain risk that they will become less able over time, should we trust a single person to provide a view on these gnoseological undertakings, given its implication on our purest ontological dimension – is it not better to be wrong by our own choice, than right because of the decision of somebody else? We prefer to suggest a liberal and democratic view, that is well informed and grounded on the greater conscience that each citizen should gain by living in complex societies: something that is absolutely required, to "take back our destiny in our own hands," ideally being right by our own choice. Hence, in our view markets and societies need to contribute to the definition of wealth as much as they contribute in optimizing this once a sufficiently objective definition has been developed, shared and then acted upon in a serviceable way. Aren't modern markets and societies eventually, the reasoning goes, a contemporary approximation of the competitive ecosystem where only superior species can survive and evolve through natural selection, leaving to the winners the privilege and responsibility to ensure the development of the best possible future for the next generations to live? No matter what the definition of wealth and wellbeing, the vast majority of democratic societies believe in the critical role of free markets and private societies to promote the overall welfare, leaving to the public hand of governments the task of redistributing the value that has been created. It may not be a coincidence that, right now, the business elite is the most vocal on the topic of ESG, sustainability and the necessity to convert towards a stakeholders'-based approach.

The Davos Man is likely one of the most vivid representations of these business elite that, pre pandemic, met at the beginning of each year for the weekly annual gathering of the World Economic Forum. It was in Davos that businesses went vocal on the green challenge and on the need to ESG – convert the world of finance – no matter how many private jets were flying there to discuss the topic. It was in Davos that the new stakeholders' approach, championed by US based global companies, was launched as a new initiative, no matter what the Gini Index of these few ultra-rich was suggesting in terms of wealth migration and accumulation (and forgetting that this approach has been championed in Europe for the last 50 years or so). We should at least pay tribute to these developments, no matter how much hypocrisy and paradoxes we find in it, and take it as an opportunity to develop with a more pragmatic approach. In the meantime, the world has not got any better and the urgency to act has increased. In fact, after two years of pandemics (and of Davos events on Zoom), the fortunes of the business elite have increased by $3.9 Tn according to Peter Goodman[5]. According to him, the incongruity of the fortunes of the rich (the very emblem of wealth as purely financial, exclusive, polluting and hence unsustainable), amid the mass suffering of the health crisis is no accident. Typically, getting super rich and behaving as such means that one single behaviour can use up scarce resources and damage the environment exponentially, if based (as it should be) on a "per capita" analysis. Burning the equivalent of the half a day energy of India to launch a space rocket for touristic purposes is an example of hyper privilege. But also having the average American eating as many kilos of red beef per year as a few hundred Africans is also a good example of recurrent misbehaviour played out at scale. Americans also enjoy a use of energy that is tens of times what is available in India, for example, and typically for more futile purposes – but they are now asking Indians to commit to Net Zero reduction targets that are proportionate to the current contribution of carbon-based emissions.

If the "cosmic lie" (as defined by Goodman but that is very consistent with the utilitarian approach and the "invisible hand" of Adam Smith) is that "what helps the rich become richer benefits everyone," then the prerequisite to this is that the business elite should be better placed to define the objective enough wealth target we want to achieve, and should be entitled not only to take critical business decisions – which is obvious and implied in the modern corporate governance of private companies – but even be the saviours of the world in their quest for lost sustainability (and sanctity?). Is the Davos man (not woman) when talking about wealth and wellbeing, sustainability and stakeholders, maybe trying to find ways to partially redeem himself? Or is he just looking for new ways to make more money, riding the trend of the day? If all obvious answers on the subject of the decision makers (the policy makers and regulators, the autocrat-dictator, the business elite) seem wrong, who should try and answer the questions that relate to the wealth we want? A third answer may in fact exist, which is clearly scoped and constrained (and incentivized) by policymakers and regulators alike and potentially sponsored by business people as well (without so much lobbying). The tax system that a liberal and democratically elected government can decide to adopt can make the use of scarce resources as part of the otherwise purely market-based pricing system and support investments and consumption that are good methods to recover the lost way with subsidies. A carbon tax could be applied to all kinds of activities and goods that produce, directly or indirectly, a contribution in terms of CO_2 emissions. And subsidies could be given to sustain the green conversion of entire industries and territories, lowering the break-even point of these project. Regulations can then forbid certain courses of action and constrain others. Markets can then intervene, leveraging entrepreneurs and managers, not as philosophers and saviours, but with their professional and technical capabilities. And the behaviour of private economic agents can then inform, through their investment and consumption decisions, the final outcome of the dynamic interaction between the public and private mix. For this to happen, and in order to define the real holistic subject that is needed to answer our *vexata quaestio*, a new model of capitalism needs to be developed, inspired by both total sustainability and a humanistic approach.

1.7   Capitalism for everybody

An extended definition of wealth, including the dimension of wellness and of the total sustainability targets pursued, should be the driving force at the basis of a new model of "capitalism for everybody" – where the people participation in the direct and indirect ownership of the real and financial assets of a country is promoted, supported, regulated and supervised, in order to make this conversion not just as safe and well informed as possible, but also educational and rewarding. In more detail, our model for a new, democratized and conscient, inclusive and sustainable capitalism should include:

- The ever-increasing participation of people, as a share of total wealth but also as a share of the total population of a nation, as equity-holders of the real economy and real assets of their country. Therefore, the Smithian "Wealth of nations" should be not just be reflected in the wealth of their populations, but also "owned" in the purest capitalist term, which is through direct shareholdership, with more limited recourse to public debt. This has in fact supported the financial burden already discussed and given leeway to the progressive detachment of citizens, with their limited participation in and caring for the destiny of their home country. The equity conversion (or "re-equitization") of the overall economy would address the excessive leverage and relative monetization being created in the last years and would better align the citizens economic interests with the sustainable growth of their home country. This participation should happen in a B2B2C format (e.g. with equity invested by pension funds, endowments and life insurance companies, on behalf of their individual clients), but also in a B2C format (e.g. with families investing directly in corporations and other real assets, with the support of the financial institutions taking care of their wealth management) and involve, proportionally, the whole investable "real" universe, i.e. with a much larger share allocated to private markets, given their relative weight versus the public, liquid markets.
- The ever increasing promotion and support by the global financial system towards this "re-equitization by retailization," given the important role of wholesale and investment banks in driving the access of institutional, patient capital investors to private equity sustainable funds, and investing across corporates, real estate and infrastructure mainly (and not debt, or already financialized assets); and the even more critical one played by wealth and retail banks in driving the access of private and retail (long term and not day traders) clients towards this model of direct equity-ownership. The "retailization" of private equity would not just be a "qualifier" (if we take the Italian example, of the overall €4.8 Tn of private financial wealth, around €3.8 Tn are still directly owned and managed by retail clients). But also potentially a winner because the feeling of direct ownership in the country could encourage private individuals, informing and influencing in a positive way their behaviour as workers, consumers

and citizens. In their role as global wealth advisors, banks, wealth managers and other financial intermediaries should then be strictly regulated, monitored and supervised by Central Banks and other market watch-dogs to promote transparency and competitiveness and reduce all kinds of operational risks (including mis-selling) but without "throwing the baby away with the dirty water" – a too stringent compliance, focused more on the form than on the substance, would incentivize banks to merely promote the underwriting of government bonds or money market products.
- The increasingly informed and educational role of all the players acting in the market, as institutional and (more importantly) retail investors, should develop their financial preparedness and conscient understanding of the unavoidable risk/return profile and related trade-offs involved in all kinds of investment management activities (even more so if investments are of the equity kind and pursued in private markets). This information-education should involve not just the short-term financial dimension but include the overall equity story of a company or project where the savings of the citizen are being invested. This equity story should then be ready to address diverse questions, from the more traditional "how are we going to make money from this?" to "how this is investment going to make the country more competitive and attractive?" to "how will wealth and wellbeing be created for other relevant stakeholders," to "how will the capital employed deliver an increase in total sustainability?" Investment managers should then have within their mission the key ambition for the creation of a better world. Investment fund companies should then act as living companies that are pursuing purposes that are much larger than the life of any Davos man, their founders or even a successive string of highly coveted CEOs. All of this should also be "entertaining," as there would be no way to force people to read and study equity investment management if they do not take an interest in the financial story and in the many other non-financial stories that can be found within a company or a real asset. Entertainment would be of particular relevance to inform, educate and capture the emotions and passions of younger generations, reviving their lost hopes for sustainability.
- Finally, our model of "capitalism for everybody" should put the human being at centre stage, helping them to become not just a better

investor, but also a better worker and consumer by passionately following their investment choices and behaving consistently in their everyday life. Ideally, they would then become better citizens for their country and in the globalized world. Finance – often seen as an end in itself, or interpreted as the key driver of the utility function of a rational, value maximizing economic agent – could reclaim its role as a very relevant tool that is able to educate and influence the behaviour of people. Paradoxically, the retailization of the equitization of a country (hence, technically, the development of our shareholders dimension as citizens) should ultimately drive its (and our) "stakeholderization," with more and more diverse stakeholders taking an interest in the present and future of possibilities of their economy and societies – hence influencing their investment decision and *vice versa*. And us, as stakeholders, taking a greater interest in the many non-economical dimensions being pursued by the investment. The shareholders – stakeholders would then naturally become the "who" that need to answer the *vexata quaestio* regarding "which wealth for which stakeholders?" They (we) should try and answer in an objective and serviceable enough way, to move from theory to a very pragmatic approach that makes a mark in real life. They (we) could also design a new framework of several "invariances" that would set the basis for the future development of wealth (or better, wealth-being) management. Something that would be able to take a long-term view to also reflect, beyond what is left over, the real needs of the next generations.

In fact, with all due respect to Adam Smith, the wealth of nations should be, first and foremost, the wealth of people that (if interested and capable) can make their country a greater one, through good and bad times, and should therefore be justly entitled to share a good portion of its fortunes if they leave it stronger and better for their future generations to enjoy and develop. The wealth that is relevant to people should then be defined in a more extended and balanced way and should not be just relegated to the financial dimension. It should involve multiple people in its creation and maximization and in its ownership and sharing as well – the entire process should not be entrusted entirely to private companies or individuals working on a purely utilitarian basis, but complemented and driven by a stakeholders' approach that would address and pursue different values for different interested parties, current and future. In fact, the citizen of a country – no matter how successful – should always remember their role as a *"pro tempore"* representative of humankind, aiming at getting the best out of their present, but also preserving the next generations' future to come. It is the people to which our wealth-being is ultimately destined – as we are all transient, but not in our final pursuit – that gives meaning to our species well and above our survival and development as dominant on Earth.

Notes

1 "Global wealth: asset inflation decouples rich from GDP," *Financial Times*, January 20, 2022.

2 Piani Individuali di Risparmio. They offer full de-taxation for investments of up to € 1.5 Mn and made in 5 years, for investments that are held for at least 5 years, with some insurance protection offered by the state.

3 The Economist Real Estate Index.

4 Robert Nozick, *Invariances*, Harvard Business Press, 1990.

5 Peter Goodman, *Davos Man: How Billionaires Devoured the World*, Custom House, 2022.

2 Wealth and Wellbeing

2.1 Wealth and wellbeing: there is a point

Wealth and wellbeing, is there a point? Tangible and intangible, are they intertwined? Richness and goodness, are they compatible? And moreover, is that a question for economics or sociology, physics or philosophy, to solve? The starting assumption of this book is that, as we all live in almost unprecedented times, in a post pandemic world, with a global decoupling and geopolitical tensions whose wealth (or "nealth"?) and wellbeing (or cold-hot war?) effects will reverberate for years, and with a climate changing in ways not dissimilar to the shifts between the different glacial eras of our planet and with more unexpected problems to come... the question we pose are worthy of serious consideration. Moreover, it is a question that is critical to analyse, discuss and eventually address for our own benefit – with due humbleness and starting from the assumption (or hope) that any small action and contribution counts. If we are not to face dire and deadly consequences, there are a number of pressing conundrums for our generation to solve, and for the next generation to fully address. Hence, this very existential question needs to be considered in light of a second one. For whom we are doing this? For us or for our children, or for our grandchildren? Or should we just enjoy a last dance on the Titanic? This is in fact where most of the problems lie. Wealth and wellbeing need not only to be considered as complementary and interlinked, as a Ying and Yang to be reconciled to overcome the partly unavoidable trade-off, but also conceptualized and tackled with an intergenerational perspective and a very long-term view. A view that looks forward to regaining a "total sustainability" that would give back hope to the many generations to come; but also to us – to feel less shame and prouder of the world we will leave behind. In order to do this, a new, more comprehensive definition of wealth (and wellbeing) needs to be articulated (we will call it "wealth-being"), and a new model of wealth management needs to be considered, to drive policymaking decisions at macroeconomic level, as well as investors, consumers and citizens behaviour at microeconomic level. A new investment management model needs to follow suit, with specific and pragmatic reference to the world of private markets and private equity, and to better inform and influence the development of the two former macro and micro-economic dimensions.

The ambition of this book is to discuss the reasons why all of this is necessary, urgent and critical, and which kind of wealth-being definition and corresponding wealth-being management model can better support the transition to "total sustainability." Something that can give back wealth and wellness to future generations who are the main "for whom?" for which our analysis and potential answers are meant. The ambition of this book is to make a modest contribution to our generation's approach towards wealth and investment management, to ensure a better legacy for the many to come, but also to inform and inspire upcoming generations as they get ready for their short-middle term future leadership and take stock of the many challenges they will need to face – taking action and their destiny back in their hands. Not by giving up hope or merely contributing to the many futile discussions with more words, but by getting their hands dirty with bold, pragmatic, strong actions. The journey is not for the weak of heart. Emotion, passion and lots of curiosity will be required to rise to the challenge to change, evolve and survive, and develop for the better in a competitive but also compassionate way. With a heterogeneous and open minded approach that could include elements of economics and philosophy, finance and sociology, even with the help of innovative technology and on the basis of a new humanism that is required now more than ever. We will start our discussion by offering a basic and then a better definition of wealth and wellness, before demonstrating why a "total sustainability" target is the required nexus between the two. We will then analyse why a transformation towards sustainability is urgent and needs to be tackled with the help of a new wealth-being management approach, where technical and social sciences both have an important role to play. And why investing in private markets with the equity capital (financial and emotional) of citizens is becoming an increasingly important driver for this change to be successful for Gen Zero and the many Alphas to come, and for the future of mankind.

2.2   Wealth, wellbeing and wealth-being

Wealth is defined as the abundance of valuable financial assets or physical possessions, which in turn can be converted into a form or tool that can be used for transactions. The modern concept of wealth is then of great significance in all areas of economics – the "dismal science" – and clearly also for growth and development economics, two subjects of great interest in our future discussion of "transformation." Following a narrower definition, wealth management (WM) refers to the business played by financial intermediaries as they provide services to a wide array of clients, ranging from high-net-worth (HNW) and ultra-high-net-worth (UHNW) individuals and families. WM typically incorporates wealth structuring and planning, to assist their owner in growing, preserving and protecting this wealth over time, often including financial protection, estate and succession planning. This should be included and is also of interest for our arguments. Still, of greater interest to us is the wider and more holistic definitions of wealth and wealth management, which need to comprise of values, features and embed key elements of wellness. In fact, at the most general level, economists may define wealth as "anything of value" that captures both material and immaterial dimensions, objective and subjective elements. It is also capturing the very idea that wealth itself is not be a static concept but can be very subjective, changing through time and for different generations. A more comprehensive definition of wealth is for example given by the United Nations, where "inclusive wealth" relates to a monetary measure which includes the sum of natural, human and physical assets. Natural capital, for example, can include land, forests, energy resources and minerals. Whilst human capital refers to the population's education and skills. Physical capital may include such things as durable machinery, buildings and infrastructure – of a tangible and intangible nature, e.g. related to data driven digital assets. Other definitions have more recently included other intangibles, such as the quality of life and of the environment of reference, the social infrastructure available, the safety of the place we live – hence including part of the defence and military assets – and even in its general level of perceived happiness (Finland has been named the happiest country for a few years in a row, notwithstanding the cold weather).

Based on this definition, wealth management should not become something focused just on financial value and offered to rich individuals only. It should include life ambitions and purpose. It should consider the non-financial values of the individuals or society without limiting the analysis to financial planning, even if finance is a relevant tool to drive their behaviour and achieve their goals. In fact, it is true that we usually refer to wealth by using a certain measure of money – with Aristotle, money "measures all things …, making things alike and comparable due to a social agreement of acceptance." But with Nietzsche, our fixation of measurable wealth has become a danger in itself as for him "the real purpose of all wealth has been forgotten." In fact, wellbeing or wellness is also important, as it refers to the quality of life, based on what is intrinsically valuable relative to someone. It may include physical, mental or emotional wellbeing – the one and only subject that needs to be pursued according to some welfarism. Hence our suggested definition of wealth-being, that includes wealth measurable in monetary terms as well as in other wellbeing dimensions that are difficult to quantify and can relate to the social and ecological dimensions of the world we live in. Moreover "total sustainability," including financial, social and ecological dimensions, should be considered in parallel and as an interconnected system, where a single imbalance can lead to the catastrophic destruction of wealth and wellbeing. On top of this, we need to add an intergenerational dimension, often forgotten, since the first industrial revolution.

2.3   Gen Zero and Grinch finance

We all live, or should live, for a greater aim and purpose. Something that goes beyond our individual existence as we behave for and build something that – as the saying says – is greater than life. We may be more or less spiritual, people of faith or agnostic, compassionate or cynical. No matter what the differences, most of us believe in the value of evolution and continuity of the human species and have a typically kinder heart for the generations to come. Likely, one of the most common attitudes we could assess and verify through a global referendum is that "children come first," and that we should nurture and protect them in the way we behave, and we wish to be remembered by our future generations. Is this view well meant, full of purpose and almost romantic? Or is it theoretical, unrealistically exaggerated or, even worst, almost the opposite of how we behave in the real world? We all belong to specific cohorts that, as defined by period of times, we call "generations." In modern times, following the great depression of the thirties and the two world wars, we have tended to define cohorts and entire generations by names. We had, for example, Gen WWI, those born between 1918 and 1927, and Gen WWII, born between 1928–1945. Then baby boomers, born between 1945 and 1964, followed by the Gen X (to which I belong), those born between 1965 and 1980 – the main decision makers of our times and for a few years to come (along with a few "older vintage" baby boomers). This generation is followed by the millennials born between 1981 and 1996, and finally by Gen Z, born since 1997. The latter are colloquially known as "zoomers" and likely the most impacted, in terms of lifestyle and culture, future set of values and behaviours, by the digital revolution and by other innovative technologies, not to mention climate change, the coronavirus pandemic and the Ukrainian war, with the global decoupling between western and eastern blocks impacting further on supply chain disruption.

In fact, this generation (and probably most future generations to come) could be renamed Gen Zero, as they will be left with an extended set of almost unbearable burdens to manage and overcome. By wanting a world of Net Zero CO_2 emissions and total sustainability, they could end up being Net Zero-ed in terms of financial resources (if financial public and private debt overcomes net assets, inflation overcomes productivity and wage increase and pension funds are based on ratios of 1 to 5 or 1 to 10 between contributing workers and benefitting retirees).[1] They could also become Net Zero-ed in terms of polarization of wealth (in favour of older generations) and Net Zero-ed in terms of ecological resources to exploit and support future growth and development. The massive debt to repay, the inflationary money created, the geopolitical tensions and decoupling, the polluted air, water and land, and the climate mayhem to come, would be their inheritance. Not to mention the threats from a new global cold war and the continuous risk of miscalculations leading to a third world war or to some other nuclear catastrophe. Instead of the green finance advocated by us all, almost as a mantra, has a maleficent "Grinch" finance stole their Christmas instead? Have their hopes of better futures, full of wealth and money, wellbeing and wellness and (even!) happiness, with a total sustainability, been stolen? We will look now at three unbearable burdens that we need collectively to overcome to re-gain total sustainability and hope in a greater and better wealth-being – both sustainable and sustainably so to improve the lives of multiple generations.

2.4   Financial burden

Our next generations will be left with (at least) three almost unbearable burdens: financial, social and ecological. They are all threating to undermine the "total sustainability" we are aiming to achieve as we pursue wealth-being for ourselves and, more importantly, for the future generations to come. The financial burden is driven by the significant increase in the private and public debt of nations following the global financial crisis and the coronavirus pandemic. The massive amount of public finance (i.e. financed by public debt or via the provision of "unfunded" credit guarantees provided by the state) that was introduced in 2020 was likely the right thing to do from an economic and social point of view, but it came on top of an already very leveraged global context. It is also being swiftly followed by further "debitization" that will be created to fund the massive "green conversion" needed at the global level to fight climate change and avert an unprecedented ecological disaster (however, our planet has had a few of these experiences – ask the dinosaurs). Further "debitization" is now expected from the geopolitical tensions that, following the Ukrainian war, are making a new cold war possible, with greater spending on defence (typically leading, in the best case, in a reduced productivity rate in the economy) and huge misplacement of natural resources. The structural decoupling between the US-EU led block (the so called "democratic" block) and the Sino Russian one (the so called "autocratic" one), will also further impair the global supply chain, leading to a reduction in the sustainable growth rate of the overall economy (hence impacting negatively in the ratio of Public Debt/ GDP) and to the need of further, less productive investments to sustain the independence and self-sufficiency of nations in strategic sectors (with the risk of a re-run of autarchy), requiring further public debt to make up for domestic private investors, when not available.

Excessive leverage is not just an issue for developing nations or a regional (e.g. Italian) one. The size of burden can be highlighted with data. According to Vito Gaspar, Paulo Medas and Roberto Perelli of the IMF (international Monetary Fund)[2] the overall stock of global debt (public and private) reached $226 Tn in 2020 (+28% on 2019, the steepest rise since the end of WWII), equal to around 256% of the global GDP. It went even higher, according to The Economist,[3] at $295 Tn in 2021, from just $83 Tn in 2000 – its growth was nearly two times the pace of the world's GDP growth. As a result, debt (public and private) rose from 230% of GDP to 320% in 2019, just before the next jump due to the pandemics – impacting on both the nominator and the denominator – and going up by 355% in 2021.[4] Based on our hypothesis, it is likely that we have not yet reached the top of the debt mountain due to climate change and cold war challenges. The question however is not how high this debt burden has or could become, but how sustainable it is and – eventually – if it is not, how it could be managed back on a path of mean reversion and stability. So far, these high levels of debts have apparently been easily sustainable given the low (or even negative) level of interest rates prevailing in the economy. The risk-free rate for the USA was, for example, at around 6.5% in 2000 and around zero in 2020, with benchmark rates in Europe and Japan in negative territories (which means, rather counterintuitively, that lenders have to pay borrowers to accept their money, whilst leaving them bearing both solvency and performance risks). It also follows, from a mathematical point of view, that a borrower needs to wait just long enough before repaying its debts to its creditors, in order to get them lower and lower, to the point of becoming immaterial in nominal value and, more quickly, given an inflationary scenario in purchasing power parity (PPP) terms. As a result of the state of interest rates, the world's debt servicing costs, as a share of GDP, are well below their peak in the 1980s (around €10 Tn in interest paid each year globally, according to The Economist – equal to around 12% of global GDP). Interest is also not even making up for the surge in global inflation, hence deflating the value of the overall debt when measured as PPP.

A change in the macroeconomic scenario is however in the making. With interest rates rising and with the expectation for them to rise even more in the future, the picture could change dramatically. Interest rate rises would in fact imply significantly higher costs to serve the existing debt – that could imply a greater and greater number of defaults. They could also be not particularly effective on inflation, if this is driven by further supply chain disruption and by the rational expectations of economic agents. Households would therefore be hit on two fronts: as main underwriters of public debt, they would lose big time in terms of the purchasing power of their savings. An interest rate increase would also immediately reflect in the market to market losses of existing fixed rate debt instruments. As main consumers in the economy they could suffer most because of the price hikes already happening in basic goods such as food, energy and building materials. Leaving aside the further debt that, as we have argued, could be required to finance the green transition and the (return to autarchy) self-sufficiency of most nations, the stack of debt we have indicated in our previous figures would not even be fully representative of the real status quo. In fact, initially, "debitization" was spurred by developing countries in the form of public debt and through straight financial instruments such as "funded" government bonds. For developed nations only, public debt went from 70% in 2007 (prior to the start of the GFC – Global Financial Crisis) to 124% in 2020 (at the end of the first year of the pandemic), based on "funded" financial instruments. However, these figures do not include the unfunded credit guarantees (such as those provided by SACE and CDP in Italy, for example). Neither do the figures include other short-term debt that is renewed recurringly nor the share of the EU and other international institutions' debt that will eventually need to be repaid by Italy.

2.5 Debitization, monetization and debasization

If public debt is a major issue, interestingly enough, the private debt component has had, for developed nations, just a marginal increase from 164% to 178% in the same period. This has been mostly driven by corporations: at the global level, the share of debt for corporations is similar to the public – at around 98% – with families owning just a 58% of it – around €51 Tn, with an estimated "collateralization" of residential real estate assets equal to $150–180 Tn[5] – hence well above its nominal value. Excessive public debt seems also limited to developed countries. In fact, that developing and underdeveloped countries borrowed less has been, by the way, neither a matter of choice nor virtue – in fact they had no option to borrow more even if they were in greater need – too little debitization is then the real issue for them. In fact, the net effect of the GFC and even more of the pandemic has been an even greater divergence in public debt and growth, as well as in terms of accumulated wealth (or the lack of it, as most countries still live well below the poverty line) between developed and developing countries. Most poor countries that are now asked by richer ones and their various GOP to contribute to the reduction in CO2 and in the usage of hydrocarbons, are still struggling to provide the very basics for the survival of their people, from food, shelter and energy. They are also facing the greater volatility of capital markets, with "flight to quality" that are curtailing the international capital that they need to sustain their growth, build the basic infrastructure required and reach their first "industrialization dividend." Whatever the burden created by excessive leverage (for developed countries) or by its too limited development (for developing ones), the "debitization" of global economies and societies does not represent the full picture of the financial burden – that needs to include two other factors:

- Debitization – mostly on the public debt side and for developed countries – has led to alternative ways to manage and inflate this away, through quantitative easing of the money supply.
- Monetization is then typically following and is closely intertwined with excessive public debt and the two together, along with several other factors, may lead to the the entire system losing credibility – based on "fiat money," Central Banks and regulated capital markets and intermediaries.
- Debasization is the following, and almost logically consequential, effect – with the loss of credibility starting at the level of financial intermediaries and then extending to regulators and money.

Debitization is not the end of the financial burden of our times as the other, even greater but less visible financial burden that we are leaving as heritage to our Gen Zero is the huge quantity of money that was created after the GFC and during the pandemic. The "monetization" of debt is a typical pattern that we have seen many times in history. When things go bad, the lender of last resort is the state. Its ultimate back up plan is printing money – where "fiat money" is basically the power attributed to the to create money *ex lege* and at the whim of the key decision makers. Central Banks should be designed and managed fully independent of governments. In fact, in certain circumstances, they have no choice other than quantitative easing: printing money and keeping interest rates and regulatory capital requirements for lenders as low as possible. The creation of money, according to a monetaristic interpretation, will eventually turn into higher prices in the long run – allowing more indebted governments to inflate their way out of trouble, avoiding debt consolidation or technical bankruptcies – but *de facto* "defaulting" on the purchasing power that its citizen underwriters have been entrusting in their hands by deciding to underwrite their bonds. Just consider M1 (the basic definition of money). This has grown around 5 times in the EU (European Union) in the last 20 years, from around €2 Tn in 2000 to around €10 Tn in 2020. And M2 (a broader definition including cash, deposits and the other easily convertible near money) in USA that has grown from around $8 Tn to around $20 from 2010 to 2020, whilst its velocity of circulation collapsed (hence helping to explain the low inflation of the period, as defined in the Fisher's equation where "price = quantity of money X velocity of usage"). Debt monetization is in fact the ultimate weapon of central banks and governments which have a "fiat" (*ex lege*) right to create money on demand. This creation of money out of thin air may help in sustaining the economy during times of crisis and to support growth in GDP, in nominal but also real terms, according to a more Keynesian interpretation of the power of expansive policies during a time of crisis. But if this is not followed by a corresponding increase in the productivity (because, for example, money is invested in long term technological advances) it will just end up as higher and higher inflation – a vicious circle that could get out of control if the "rational expectations" of consumers and workers get embedded into the economic structure and fabric of society, leading to higher prices and wages, lower investments and so on. Or, even worst, it could result in a "liquidity trap," where people keep accumulating "trash cash" (in the words of Ray Dalio of Bridgewater Associates), which does not translate into short term inflation but basically glutting the overall economy, from new consumption to new investments, R&D and so on.

Should the "debitization" and the "monetization" of the economy be insufficient, it is likely as a consequence that a third component of our financial burden will now be well underway. A world with too much debt and too much money becomes one where the reputation of the global financial system starts crumbling and even Central Banks and formal *ex lege* and regulated money lose credibility. Enter crypto currencies, as

Figure 2.1 Financial unsustainability

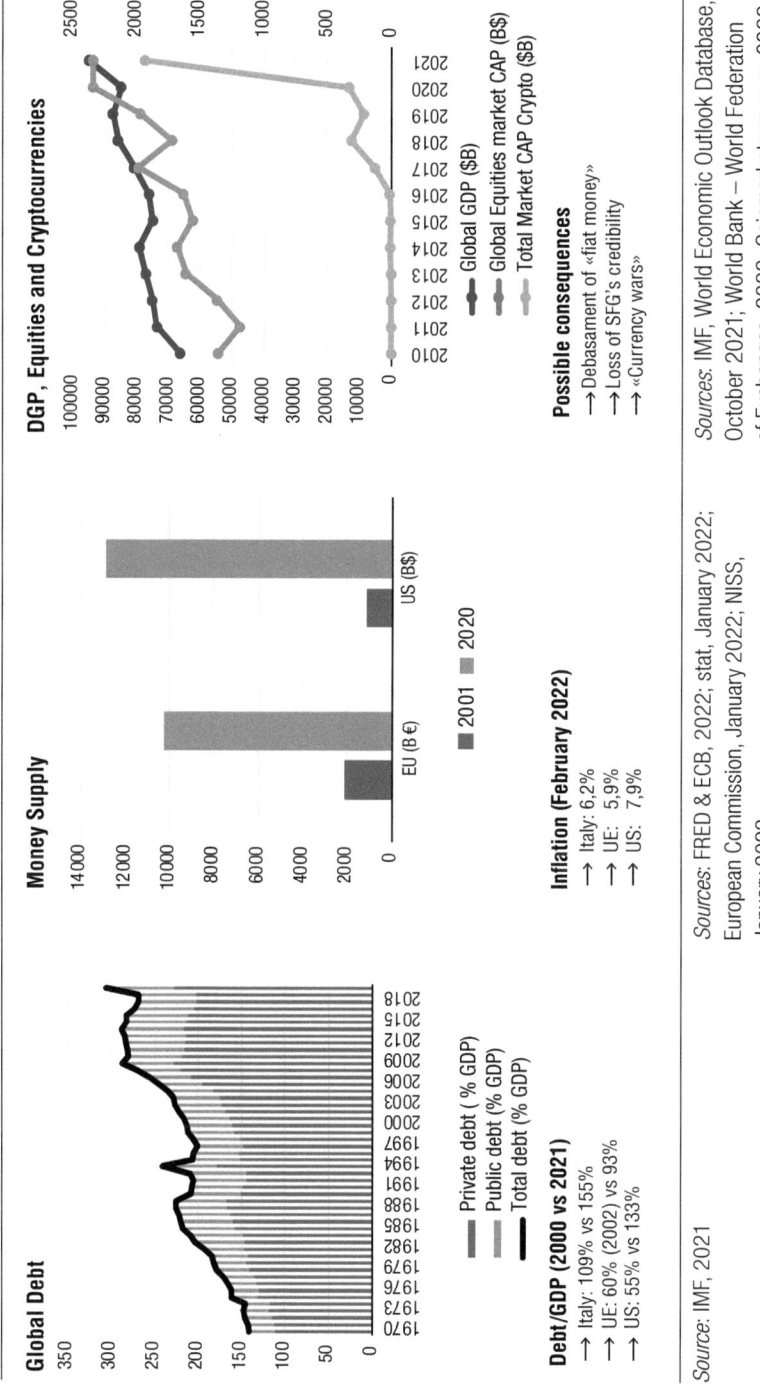

Source: IMF, 2021

Sources: FRED & ECB, 2022; stat, January 2022; European Commission, January 2022; NISS, January 2022

Sources: IMF, World Economic Outlook Database, October 2021; World Bank – World Federation of Exchanges, 2022; Coinmarketcap.com, 2022

an almost anarchic, loosely controlled (or utterly uncontrolled) means of doing transactions, investments and business. They have developed out of nowhere to skyrocketing importance, with huge volatility in between, but with increasing relevance in our lives and for financial markets. Is this an alternative form of debasement of traditional money itself? If a parallel, unofficial system gets underway and grows in value and relative importance, all else being equal, it means that the official system (money, financial institutions, stock markets and even Central Banks) become demoted, losing relevance by the day. The strategy of creating digital currencies for traditional money but Central Banks themselves can then stand as a good defence, but further debasing traditional money, financial intermediaries and capital markets, could be interpreted as a sign of weakness as much as of strength. It follows that "debitization," "monetization" and "debasization" can develop and intertwine, with exponential effects, making the financial burden increasingly unsustainable over time. What equity capital, stable monetary policy and credible, secure money will then be left to Gen Zero?

2.6   Social burden

Finance is ultimately a mere means to support the pursuit of greater purposes. People are in fact social animals, ideally compassionate and supporting each other for the greater good of humankind. Long gone is the cynic paradigm at the basis of modern economics, where each of us, as rational beings, are solely interested in the maximization of our own short term utility functions, mostly made by material objects that can be valued in dollar terms. We may certainly be driven by our search for some utility, but this is as much material as spiritual, meant for ourselves and for our loved ones as well and strongly informed by a set of core values. Otherwise, we could not explain religions and wars, arts and philosophy, friendship and love and lots of our good intentions. Even our bad intentions are driven by non-monetary components, such as hate and revenge, ego and envy. Let us refer to all these immaterial components as "social," for they mostly relate to our interactions with other human beings and could not be understood or even exist if we live in complete isolation. In fact, we often refer to "social capital" as the spiritual component of a particular group of people, including their set of values, behaviours, culture and sense of belonging to a human system which is driven by self-preservation and by the satisfaction of immediate, material needs, but also inspired by greater ambitions and the urge to develop a journey towards higher futures. Social capital is therefore a critical and scarce resource for the competitiveness of people and nations. Unfortunately, a number of social burdens are also acting as liabilities *vis a vis* this intangible capital. In an increasingly populated world, greater divides are separating the few lucky winners from the many left behind. Race, gender, sexual orientation or religious-based discriminations are certainly still very prominent with little advancement in developed countries; while most of the developing world is in a state of often overlooked chaos. On one hand, the great wealth polarization of recent years has sustained those discriminations – making the weaker parts of societies also the poorest, and *vice versa*, in self-reinforcing ways. On the other hand, the main limits to the wealth creation of the future are coming from these discriminations, preventing for example the great "pink-dividend" that could be attained if women (around half of global population) could be supported and allowed to become as productive and wealth creating (and owners as well) as men.

But other forms of old discriminations are still at play, from race-based to sexual orientation to religious faith and political affiliation. Also, new divisions are developing in favour of, for example, between the digitally connected and well-informed people *vis a vis* the web, and disconnected and "out of reach" people. Being digitally connected can also pose other threats as digital people become able to leverage Big Data (BD) and Artificial Intelligence (AI), but also control and secure their own set of information and resulting intelligence, fending-off the predatory and dominant behaviour of "big" and "bad" global tech players. In fact, exclusion in a cyber-risk dominated digital world could become a heavier burden and constraint for the development of social sustainability, with bad tech and malicious AI-animated robots making us slaves and taking charge of our destiny in a most inhuman world. Another form of discrimination could also be related to the people and countries that will be less impacted by the green conversion and by the long-term effects of climate change. Because they will be in a position to use and monetize their fossil fuels no matter what the GOP (Group of Parties) Accords and in a better position to defend themselves *vis a vis* extreme weather conditions (you could still leave in a desert if you have excellent carbon-fuelled air conditioning).

Finally, it is useful to remember that war, including terrorism, acts of violence and any kind of regional and international conflicts, is the worst enemy of social capital – creating huge levels of damage, distrust and even hate between entire populations and sovereign nations. Unfortunately, the most critical component of this social burden that we risk leaving to our future generations is the severe decoupling between the western and eastern geopolitical blocks. This new cold war, based on an economic, social and now military decoupling, is posing a serious threat to the overall international trade framework which developed after WWII. Even more importantly, it is disrupting the most critical and value adding global supply chains and pushing countries towards more autarchic strategic posture – against the very principles proposed by Adam Smith in his *magnum opus*. After the GFC, we were left with wealth polarization and the many discriminations summarized above, to the detriment of the many, as the 99% movement implied. The challenges of the pandemic, the digital revolution and climate change have accelerated and increased this polarization, with a further risk added by the Ukrainian conflict and the resulting geopolitical divide and decoupling between the leading economic blocks of the USA and China and the more extended political ones (adding Europe and the "4 eyes" alliance to the first and Russia to the second). A number of local and regional wars have been happening in recent times with more or less limited impacts on global wealth and wellbeing.

But the war in Ukraine and the chance of a more radical and long-lasting confrontation between the two geopolitical blocks is, at the very least, something to reckon with in terms of the disruption to the global supply chain. This is causing the suboptimization of both the global wealth created and the coordinated efforts to regain financial, social and ecological sustainability. It could also lead to much bleaker scenarios, should an all-in (traditional or cyber) war set in, as anticipated by the Thucydides' trap and as it has been typically observed at the end of a prolonged period of economic crisis, excessive debt creation and money-fuelled inflation. Of course, "people-based discriminations," "digital and green divides" and "geopolitical decoupling" can develop and intertwine with exponential effects, making the social burden increasingly explosive. What social capital and world will then be left to Gen Zero? Also, is it not the case that extreme wealth polarization can occur across countries (developed versus underdeveloped world), social classes (white collars versus blue collars, landowners versus capitalists and the labour force) but also across generations? And can the depletion of ecological resources happen across those same categories? And can those tensions in the fabric of societies – from wars to religious extremism to terrorism – last for a long time, well beyond the memory of the living people? If this is true, then another form of social exclusion is happening at the detriment of future generations. This has been mostly overlooked so far and it is worth discussing further.

2.7   Not in my (green) backyard

We could certainly argue that truth may be thought of as absolute and that our shared values could also be interpreted as such, as much as our passion and drive towards total sustainability. However, from a more down-to-earth standpoint, it should also be noted that our sensibility to climate change could be different if we are living in the Maldives (soon to disappear because of the Artic and Antarctic melting ice) or in Greenland (where new land could be taken back from ice and used for agriculture or urban development). Our marginal cost (or benefit) from climate change would in fact be rather different in the two cases (was not President Trump, notoriously sceptical on climate change, ready to make an offer to Denmark to buy out all of Greenland?). The same could be said if we are billionaires, and therefore able to face most of climate change nuisances and threats (air-conditioning our ski-slopes built in the middle of the desert), or making a living just on the poverty line, where a single drier season could translate into a deadly famine for us and our family (is not the next greatest and most expensive international city being built in the middle of the scorching desert of Saudi Arabia, and mostly financed with the dividends of the biggest oil producer globally, i.e. Aramco?).

Maybe because of these quite different and subjective perspectives, very diverse behaviours could emerge. In economics, we derive most of our theories and related economic modelling from founding assumptions such as "information asymmetry" (the decision making of agents is driven by how much information they have got, as they try to acquire more and in a more privileged fashion, and try to monetize any asymmetry in their favour), "moral hazard" (economic agents will risk freely and almost recklessly when the potential positive payoff is mostly for them, with

Figure 2.2 Social unsustainability

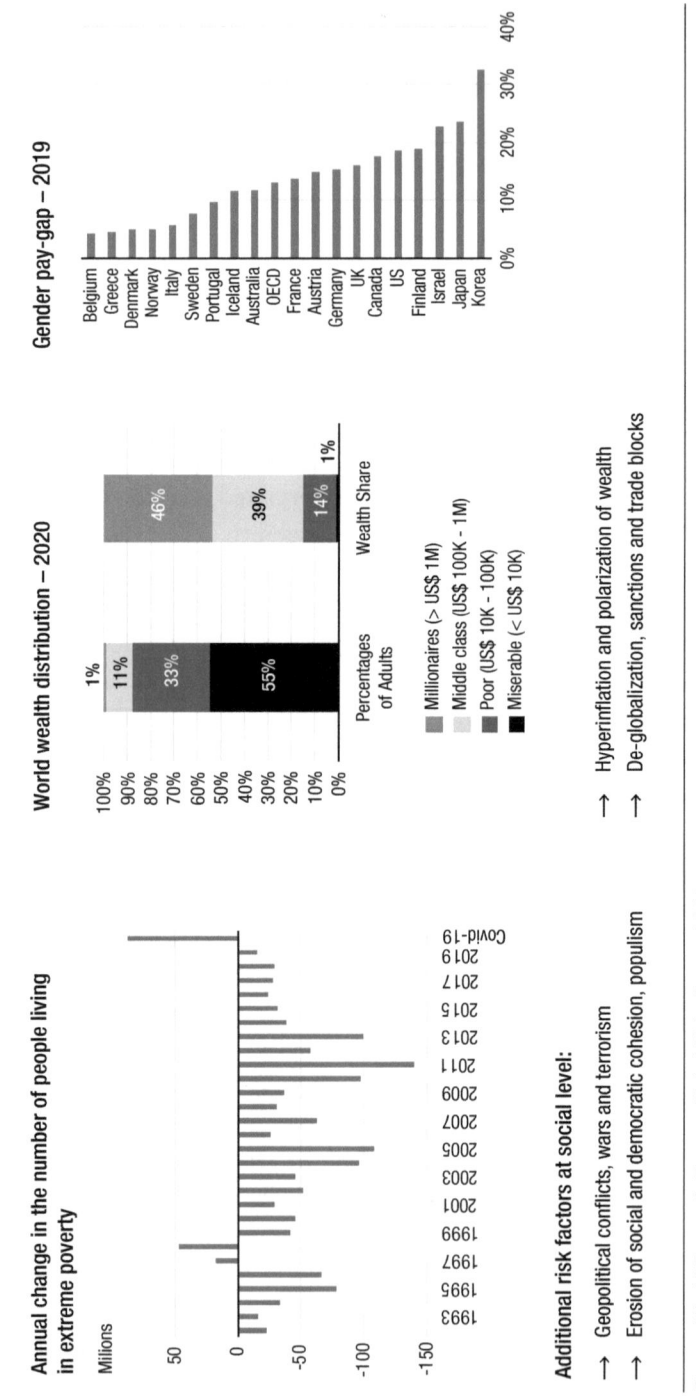

Source: World Economic Forum, *Global Risks Report*, 2022

most of the negatives going to others) and "adverse selection" (economic agents, not knowing exactly the value of a certain good or service – for lack of better information – will assume the worst for them, e.g. implicitly thinking that their counterpart to a trade, having better information, will try to game this and make them overpay). All of this especially applies to social dynamics and even more in the context of the ecological threats we are now facing, where the main issue is not so much "how would it be technically possible to address it?" but actually "who is going to pay for that, in the transition and end state, and who will profit?" There are at least a few instances that may lead to a social and market failures on this:

- The "green-wash" failure, where everybody pretends to be green and acting for the greater good, not so much to clean their soul and avoid taxes, but to use this as a marketing tool.
- The "green-bubble" failure, where big money managers, managing the money of third parties and often in passive ways, keep buying green stock, making their price inflate without reason.
- The "green-flop," where big money managers and "good companies" start dumping their heavy CO_2 producer assets in the market and "bad guys" buy them to make an easy profit.
- The "green-flation," when the transition to renewable energies and other Net Zero products is done too early and in too uneconomic ways, leading to a sudden surge in their market prices.
- The "green-fashion," where the ESG and green movements follow the destiny of so many other management fads, becoming unfashionable by the day after "much ado about nothing."

2.8   Green nemesis

We could define an overall green nemesis, where the good idea of pursuing green investments and management approaches is actually having the opposite effects, because of green-wash, green-bubble, green-flop, green-flation and green-fashion. Green wash is a serious issue with two potential fall backs. The first, which is already bad enough, is to use green (or ESG) as marketing label to achieve an unfair attractiveness and hence mislead potential investors, workers and consumers (or even the voters) to achieve personal gains, typically of an economic, reputational or political nature. However, the second fall back of green wash is potentially even worst and more damaging in the long term. As all the green and ESG labelling becomes unclear, blurred and subject to manipulation, interpretation and with limited credible third-party certification, not only do people fail to identify the posers and the lairs, but they also start to become sceptical of everybody, levelling down any green statement or proposition (as per the adverse selection phenomenon). Certainly, independent regulations can help to limit this, and third parties' analysis can also reduce the "principal – agent" dilemma. The fact is, as noted by Stefano Caselli, at the end of 2020, there were at least 40 different methods of ESG valuation, and over 450 indexes, with a limited correlation between the (mostly subjective) analysis performed and the objective impact on the social and ecological dimensions.[6]

Green bubbles are also interlinked with green wash. If big money managers are just pursuing the ESG and green labelling (regardless of representing an objective and serviceable truth) in their investment decisions, there will be a significant increase in the demand of those assets that may not be matched by a consistent growth in their supply. Hence, the imbalance between demand and supply will increase their market price and detached from any economic fundamental (even when considering the other intangibles and the positive externalities supposedly introduced in the ecosystem). A market bubble could then ensue and inflate until it inevitably bursts. Also in this case, two potential fall backs are to be considered. On one side, the irrational growth of ESG/ green asset prices could make "smart" people even more incentivized to game the rules and "green wash" – green stocks could also become so expensive in their daily trading (where no new capital is contributed to the green company, but just switching hands among the multiple private counterparts to the market trading) so as to dissuade any interest to keep shareholders investing in them through capital raises. On the other side, the inevitable burst of the green bubble could reverberate and create – apart from unjust value migrations between parties – a long term lack of confidence in the market, with people then avoiding investment in green stock or even become unwilling to support green companies as workers, consumers and voters – a completely opposite behaviour to the one we suggest.

Green flops are then a direct consequence of green bubbles and mostly driven by the different perspectives of diverse utility (and moral/ethical) functions. A risk of a "green flop" could in fact develop when cynical investors are taking stock of the many arbitrage opportunities that occur every day as unfortunate by-products of the ESG and green finance movements that are pushing key decision makers to divest in socially divisive and polluting assets. If the big investors (big money managers, such as Blackrock, Fidelity, Vanguard or Amundi) sell their stock of CO2 producing assets to pursue their ESG policies, a cynical buyer will always be on the other side of the trade to buy on the cheap and reap an easy, short-term profit: this has happened with oil and gas reserves, and with carbon mines. It could happen as well with military and defence spending, where the bad guys gain control of the most critical parts of the arms producing industry, turning these into "offensive" and to the detriment of good guys. Many examples are popular these days, even convincing in some instances retail investors to "follow the bads" (as they are more likely to make money with their savings – no questions about the "how"), with many private equity professionals, not particularly keen on ESG and green, publicly stating they cannot believe how many easy deals are available these days if you do not follow the ESG metrics. Some are even pretending to get the best of both worlds, making big money first by trading on the "bad arbitrage" (e.g. extracting and selling high methane carbon using young workers in slave-like conditions) and then making some, very well advertised donations (e.g. to save blue pandas in some unhospitable region of China). Cynical utilitarianism may not be the general rule for humankind, but cynic people do certainly exist and appear not to be in short supply in the world of finance. And they are dwarfed by the number of naïve or hypocritical people who have an even greater responsibility and that are ready to believe their tale, if this leaves a trail of dollars for them to enjoy as well.

Green flop could be the most vicious implication of ESG and green finance, but we should also not forget about "green-flation," where the transition to renewable energies and other products and services is made too rapidly, creating a strong price pressure that then impacts on the much-reduced purchasing power of people – with an overall negative effect on their wealth-being. Green transition could potentially have – *ceteris paribus* – a highly negative effect on the social burden we discussed, at least in the short run. Also, green-flation is now said to be the cause of price hikes which instead derive from the excessive money supply, by chokes in the supply chain or by the decoupling and political blockades that are a by-product of geopolitical tensions. In this case we risk "throwing away the baby with the dirty water," as the unreasonable promotion of (yet) uneconomical renewable energy investments could cause economic damage to investors, lenders and users, followed by a long-lasting rejection of the overall idea, even if new technologies become progressively available to make this economic and profitable. The correct timing is then of the utmost importance, as it is the optimal management of the transition risk, which could seriously impact entire industries and regions, if not managed well and taking into considerations the many trade-offs which are implicit in a total sustainability proposition.

Finally, there is also the risk that the discussion on ESG and green related issues becomes so diffuse, meaningless and repetitive, it become boring, pure "white noise" in the industry and, in turn, unfashionable. The green-fashion risk is also the reflection of the other risks. If green sustainability targets and action plans become so blurred and miscommunicated that the green transformation loses credibility (its direction also becomes unclear) because of "green-wash, the "green-bubble" and "green-flop" risks also develops as a result of the mismatch between a lot of good-intentioned money seeking companies, products and services, where these become irrationally inflated, and unaffordable in the short-term for the people and the environments that need them most (and, oppositely, bad-intentioned companies profit my buying bad assets on the cheap and popularizing them because of their inherent greater financial attractiveness). Even "green-flation" would impact on the social contract of weakest and poorest people making the topic less and less popular for the masses. Then, almost logically it follows that the green fashion is destined to turn into a mere management fad, with a limited shelf-life that will be parked and forgotten fairly soon, given the high number and variety of other urgencies we also need to address.

2.9 Three unbearable burdens: ecological

There is no easy way out of this potential nemesis of our well-intentioned green conversion ideas and, for sure, the ESG and green movements are still a force to reckon with in our discussion of the wealth management of the future, based on a different definition of wealth and a diverse pursuit of wealth-being. In fact, according to Bloomberg,[7] the value of investments in financial products that claim to abide by ESG rules has grown from $23 Tn to $35 in 2021, and could exceed $50 Tn by 2025. Let us remember that most individual investors take these claims seriously and buy these funds in good faith. Not only, as we discussed, is green wash rife and many claims (true or false) go mostly uncontested, but also other claims, even if made in good faith, are mostly untested. Opposite to the green-bubble and flop, caused mainly by the short-term mismatch between demand and supply of such funds and by cynical behaviour, and leaving aside for the moment the growing talk on green-flation, there is another widely popular claim is relevant to consider. This states that there is no trade-off between maximizing returns (that is, our "financial wealth" in its purest and speculative form) and ESG (a proxy for our "wellbeing"). In our view, this simplistic idea is prone to errors and could cause misunderstanding (and some potential mis-selling, even if done in good faith). In the short run, some trade-off between financial returns and green impacts could be the norm rather than the exception. And suggesting otherwise could create false expectations ("green-wash") or easy arbitrage opportunities ("green-bubbles and flops") – it should then be interpreted with extreme caution. No matter what these trade-offs will eventually be, we should expect them to impact further on the polarization of fortunes, with weaker and poorest people being impacted more negatively.

It is important to note here that social unsustainability could in the coming years be driven as much by our financial burden as by our ecological burden and required green transition. Our growing financial burden will drive the world towards a increasingly polarized distribution of financial wealth. This could be followed by increased moral, religious, political and military tensions between geopolitical blocks. It may potentially lead to new regional and global wars, both in the digital and physical realms, and involve the disruption of the fabric of society at local level. This is an already enough of a devastating scenario for the future generations to come. But what about if these events occur in an inhospitable environment, where an ecological collapse of the biosphere makes our planet uninhabitable for humankind? In fact, a number of ecological burdens need also to be considered and urgently addressed, likely compounding the two other burdens. Following the first phase of industrialization, our overall (albeit unfairly spread and even less evenly shared) high level of development and wealth creation was mostly financed by hydrocarbons and by the use of fossil fuel – oil, carbon and other gasses were utilized to produce cheap and abundant energy, used by the many and owned by the few. Great fortunes were accumulated, and oligarchic, political-military powers followed, often more by luck (of having access to vast resources of hydrocarbons) than virtue. Oil-based, hyper-leveraged unsustainable finance became the means to sustain a new economic and social order, often characterized by plutocrats that were leading socially unsustainable societies. However, these were not even the main drivers of the great unsustainability to come. In fact, the nemesis of hydrocarbons-based wealth creation and appropriation entails its devastating polluting effects for people and the environment in its ability to host life.

On one hand, polluting particles and other by-products such as CO_2 and NO_2 generated by the combustion of fossil fuels are damaging lungs and killing people in higher numbers per year than the most recent pandemics, Coronavirus included. On the other, the massive liberation of CO_2 in the air is contributing to global warming in an unprecedented fashion (at least, since the end of the glacial eras and the existential climate changes that followed), with great consequences in terms of climate change and extreme weather events that could develop in a non-linear fashion (e.g. becoming unstoppable and exponentially damaging as a certain number of extra degrees is reached). By climate change related risk, we refer in fact to two distinct economic burdens that could be potentially valued and priced in monetary terms. On one side, physical risk refers to the damage created by extreme weather events (heat waves, prolonged droughts, extreme winds etc.) to things like real estate, durable goods or entire coastal cities. It could also include the damaging accidents and health effects caused to people, whose economic costs could be estimated by the insurance premium required to cover them, or by the extra costs the health system could make up. On the other side, transition risk refers to the further business risk (therefore financial – for its equity and debt holders; and social – for its employees, customers and communities) posed on companies, as they try to navigate the green transformation challenge without losing their business in the process, because of miscalculated (good or bad) conversion intentions. It is not only oil producers that could become bankrupt if a too heavy carbon tax would make the cost of extracting oil uneconomical or was completely outlawed. But a renewable energy producer could also collapse if its green energy is so expensive it is priced out by dirtier energy sources, no matter what the fiscal subsidies provided by the state. That is why the physical risk from

Figure 2.3 Environmental unsustainability

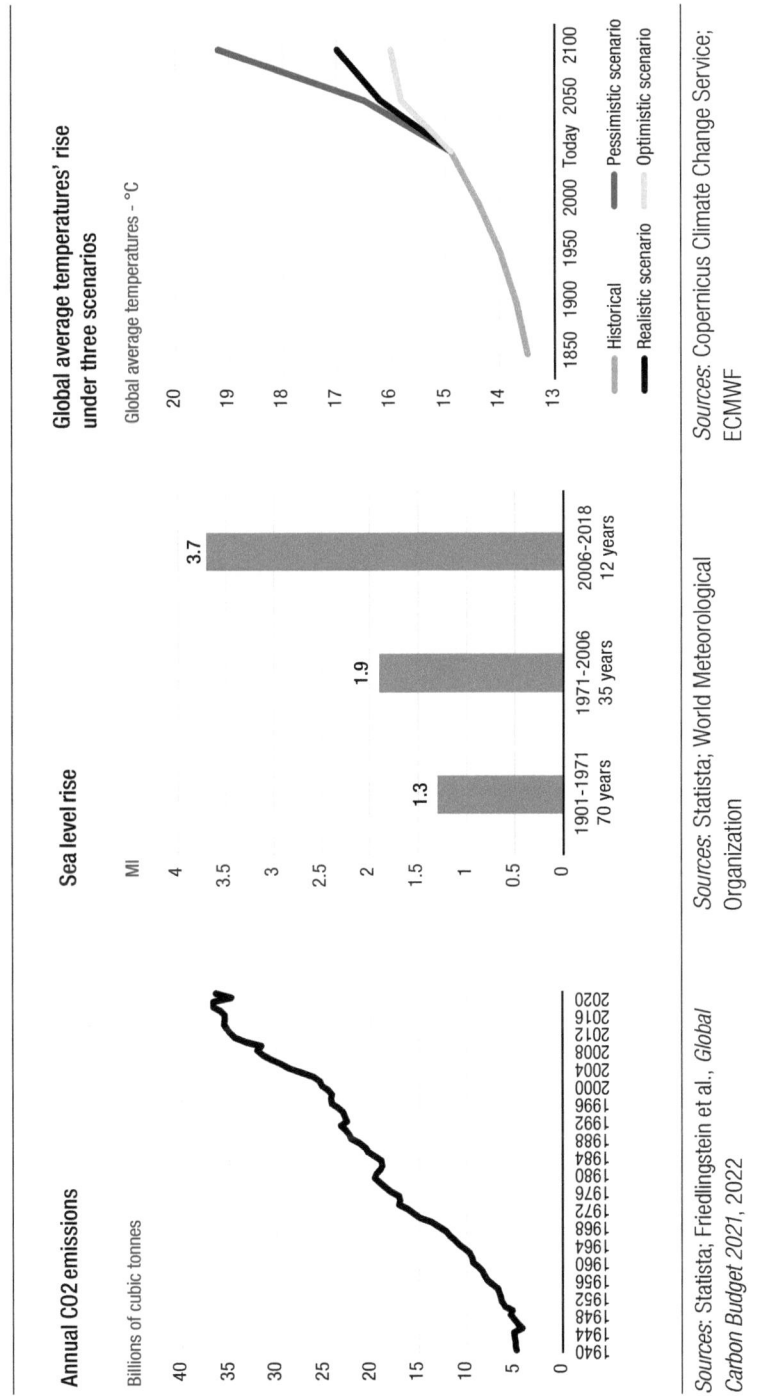

climate change is thought to be inversely correlated with the transition risk. By the time of our green transition companies need to be solvent and ideally fairly profitable.

2.10 Was Malthus eventually right?

These statistical-based definitions of climate change risks are very relevant from an economic perspective, as they are increasingly used by regulators in the financial industry to drive "green finance" through a mix of constraints and incentives. Physical and transition risks have also some correlations with the credit and equity risks banks typically face, not to mention operational risks, and with the P&C (property and casualty) and mortality and morbidity (life) risks covered by the insurance sector. But from a perspective of a holistic wealth management of the future, their overall contribution is very limited. What if the physical risk of the city I inhabit, and the transition risk of the company I work for are very limited, if the overall environment becomes so inhospitable that I need to live within fully insulated walls, in air-conditioned rooms, eating food that can only be produced far away? What if my wellbeing is becoming worst by the day, because of the heat waves and humidity? With dirty water and air particles everywhere that are damaging my organs, hence reducing my overall lifespan, even if it does not kill me in the short term? And with many millions, if not billions, of poor people that are already under the threat of death by the force of nature? And with a path that indicates how future generations will suffer even more with a great scarcity of vital resources?

In fact, a perfect climate for living is not the only critical resource at risk, as there are so many other non-renewable ones which are scarce, limited and finite in nature. Take "rare earth" for example, that are critical for electric batteries and for most other electronic devices, PCs and smartphones included. Or arable lands, that we need to use to feed the growing population. This kind of ecological unsustainability would impact on the financial health of entire countries, industrial sectors and companies. It would also likely increase wealth polarization, discrimination and the geopolitical tensions to retain control of them, for business, political or military reasons – hence increasing the social unsustainability. Many other things are also scarce and even those deem renewable are, more often than not, not fully scalable and limited in their possible uses, partly because of tiny non-renewable inputs that are required for them to operate (take for example Nickel, that is used for the batteries of electric cars). More broadly, it is not just that they are limited, or certainly re-usable but up to a point and subject to a similar nemesis that is impacting on hydrocarbons and other chemicals that were also created and mass-produced during industrial revolutions. It is also that Mother Earth can only sustain a limited population – as everything is eventually finite in the world, it is destined to reach a tipping point.

It is one thing to feed 2 Bn people, it is quite another to feed 8 Bn or 12 Bn. Whatever the productivity achieved and the use of circular economy and of renewables, it will become impossible to sustain, mathematically, if at some point, the population keeps growing *ad infinitum*, given the finite natural resources we have. There is a social issue if American people eat tens of kilos of red meat per year (for its CO_2 and methane by-products and their bad health and risk of coronary attacks) and African or Indian people consume just a few grams (with the starvation and malnutrition impact on adults and babies). But there is also an overall existential threat if the model becomes more and more unsustainable by the day because of the ecological implications. Climate change will reduce arable land and drinkable water and the overall maximum food supply until a point that too many people will be fighting for survival. In fact, Malthus could have been wrong on timing, but not on direction. And containing the future number of people on Planet Earth is unfortunately not a workable solution because it is a successful model of prosperity and development on so many fronts. As people live longer and longer, we may expect a multiplier between the young and the elderly that grows in size, with most people living off pensions and fewer and fewer people working hard to try to sustain the others. Hence, even if Mars is colonized as suggested by Elon Musk, it would not be sufficient unless a new virus that kills only the elderly people occurs and is coupled to this migration.

Notwithstanding the three burdens discussed so far, we are now facing an even bigger dilemma linked to the intergenerational arbitrage that has been unresolved for too long at the expense of future generations. We have migrated financial, social and ecological value from the future to our present, to sustain the mistakes of the past which, in turn, have led to other wrongs and more severe misjudgements. There are multiple potential explanations for this, including for example our flawed definition of wealth and our overreliance on financial modelling and techniques which measure value for the short term and make long term decisions on the basis of rather myopic key performance indicators. But the real reason may just be our tendency to have older people taking decisions in policy making as well as in investment management, hence driving the wealth management strategies at macro and micro level. However, we are now starting to realize that the situation is critical, with a growing understanding from newer generations as well. They may not count for much today, but time will pass and new leaders will join in the decision making, including investment managing. It is not well known and quite striking that, for example, by 2029 around 65% of investors will be either millennial or Gen Z. They may have not as much capital to invest as the baby-boomers, but their vote will still count in political elections, and their thoughts and ideas could count even more in the increasingly critical world of social and digital-based media. These millennials and Gen Z may already have, or develop in due time, a different attitude regarding their investment principles, on the basis of a different wealth-being pursuit and targeting proposition, with voting rights to match in the governance of companies and countries. Even in finance, and in investment management specifically, they would move the needle and change our overall direction towards better futures. In closing this first "total sustainability" discussion, it is important to remember that invested capital needs risk and return in order to create GDP growth, unemployment and subsequently the ideal setting for civilizations to thrive, also from a social and ecological perspective. If this is done well, we will have enough productivity gain to sustain our overall welfare obligations, avoiding an intergenerational default that is otherwise already on the cards. ESG and green can help achieve this and support the required change for a greater good, but using a pinch of salt, and a very pragmatic approach when seeking for the sufficiently objective, serviceable truth, that can be acted upon for the benefit of our current and of the many future generations to come.

Notes

[1] Alessandra Arachi, "L'Italia degli anziani," *Corriere della Sera*, December 10, 2021. In Italy, the ratio between babies and old people was 1.1 in 1971. It was 3.8 in 2011 and is now 5.1 in 2021 and growing.

[2] "Crescono il debito e le preoccupazioni," *Corriere della Sera*, December 23, 2021.

[3] "The global interest bill is about to jump," *The Economist*, February 5, 2022.

[4] "How high will interest rates go?" *The Economist*, February 5, 2022.

[5] The Economist real estate index and global analysis, www.theeconomist.com.

[6] Stefano Caselli, "ESG," *Corriere della Sera*, March 28, 2022.

[7] "A dirty secret," *The Economist*, February 11, 2022.

3 The Wealth of Italy

3.1 The wealth of Italian citizens

What is the wealth of Italy? And what is the wealth of its citizens that is worth considering, i.e. including some measure of their wellbeing? A wellbeing that can be measured, for example, by their positive and constructive inclusion in the fabric of the liberal and democratic society that characterizes the country? Is it the quality of life – with attractive and safe cities, an environment and climate that are hospitable, with clean air and water, good food and a beautiful landscape, both natural and as a collection of heritage and artistic artefacts created throughout its long history, in the form of architectural design, balanced sceneries – with a sense of the "sweet life"? Not even wealth and wellbeing, mixed together, would be enough to ensure that Italians reach their full happiness, pursuing successfully their ultimate meaning and sense of being. But it would be a good start, and a target sufficiently meaningful to justify the relevant contribution of economics, finance and other social sciences that are involved in determining the future of wealth. It could also be enough to develop wealth management as an industry and – progressively – as an ontological quest: to make people (and not just nations) wealthier and happier for current and future generations. If this is the task, and indeed the challenge, of wealth management we need to analyse the "financial wealth" of Italy – as a stock and flow, in its cross generational dynamics and trends – to consider the other dimensions of total sustainability that can more properly address Italian wellbeing for this generation and the Zed and Alpha generations to come. In truth, we have chosen Italy as a country and for its citizens to discuss as an example of a "new" wealth management model not only because we know it better, but also because, given its financial imbalances and high burden, there are also huge unexpressed potentials and unaddressed opportunities. It could be the perfect example of the transformation to come and a dream journey to regain sustainability and hope in better futures.

From a purely financial (and public accounting based) perspective, GDP growth in Italy has been sluggish for a long time and unable to make up for its opportunity cost of capital – not even through the risk-free rate offered by its treasury bonds for most of the recent decades. On the one hand, anaemic growth coupled with high taxation have suggested limited expected returns. On the other hand, its unstable political conditions and an overall judicial and regulatory ecosystem have also put the country consistently in the lowest quartile of the "most easy to do business with" countries. All these factors have limited the eagerness of international capital to invest in the country. A good chunk of Italian savings has also gone abroad, with the asset management industry being dominated by Anglo-Saxon money managers, and the domestic financial service players often characterized by limited innovation – coupled by a sometimes fairly naïve approach by Italian Institutional and retail investors to their strategic asset allocation and tactical trading strategies. In USD (United States Dollars) terms, Italy's GDP was $2.1 Tn in 2019, with $2.7 Tn of public debt – one of the highest levels of debt among major developed countries. Then the pandemic hit, with dramatic economic and social impacts that have still not been fully understood, set against the backdrop of a climate change crisis already in full force. Even assuming the strong recovery of 2021 will continue, Italian GDP will be back to 2019 levels around 2022–2023. It is expected to reach $2.53 Tn in 2025, still well below the level of public debt prior to the crisis. In fact, public debt exploded, as in most countries globally, reaching $ 2.9 Tn in 2020 and then $3.1 Tn and $3.2 Tn in 2021 and 2022 respectively.

Against all this, the backdrop of the Ukrainian war has introduced further uncertainty in the short term, with long term consequences that will again impact negatively on its growth rate, public debt and the overall total sustainability of its real assets. The analysis of the ratio between the stock of public debt and the flow of gross wealth produced by Italy is in fact clearly showing the extent of its first financial burden (going from 134% in 2019 to 155% in 2020). Against that, we should consider the more limited stretching of private debt[1] and of Italy's better capital-

Figure 3.1 Italian GDP

Note: Italy: Gross domestic product (GDP) in current prices from 1986 to 2026 (*projections) (in billion U.S. dollars) – ISTAT

Figure 3.2 Italian public debt

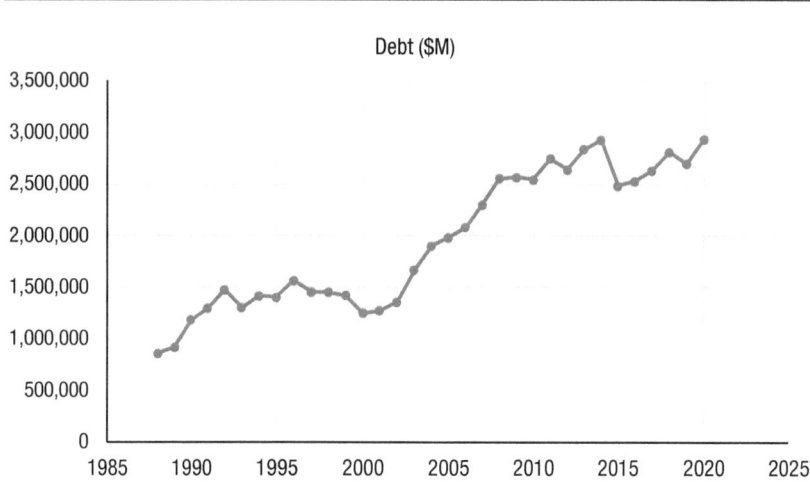

Note: Italy: Public debt in current prices from 1986 to 2020 (in million U.S. dollars) – International Monetary Fund

ized financial system and, most importantly, the very relevant stock of financial wealth of Italians (the financial assets available for investments) which reached around €4.8 Tn ($5.3 Tn) at the end of 2021. Even more importantly, we should take stock of Italy's real assets, including corporations on the stock exchange worth around €0.75 Tn, private corporations (circa €3 Tn), real estate residential and commercial assets (€8 Tn), other physical and digital infrastructure, the value of the arable land and of other natural resources – not to mention the other most beautiful intangibles of the country.

Figure 3.3 Sources and uses of the Italian budget – high level analysis

Reconstruction based on estimates, triangulations, and "back-of-the-envelope" calculations

SOURCES (BN€)		USES (BN€)		
Institutional savings	900	Real Estate	8,000	
- Pension funds	140	- Residential	6,500	
- Insurance companies	590	- Commercial	1,500	
- Foundations and privatised funds	130			
- Individual pension plans	40			
Financial private wealth of Italian households	4,800	Infrastructure	2,000	
Non-financial private wealth of Italian households (mostly real-estate)	6,200	Companies → Italian stock exchange Market cap	3,000 750	20% of the total SMEs 5% of total assets
Other (public assets, foreign savings, etc.)	1,100	Natural resources	Not assessed	
TOTAL	13,000	TOTAL	13,000	

Sources: Allianz Global Wealth Report 2020; ISTAT, Ricchezza non finanziaria in Italia, 2021; ISTAT, general data on enterprises, 2019; Borsa Italiana, monthly update, December 2021

3.2 Living beyond our means

Leaving aside the stock dimension of Italy's public debt (and of its gross and net financial and real assets worth), it is also important to consider the yearly net in- or out-flows. If we take the delta between government revenues (mostly coming from taxes) and its spending, a string of primary deficits (i.e. before the payment of interest on public debt) are showing the relative unsustainability of the financial management of the country – where a deficit means that current generations are getting more from the state than they contribute to it. In fact, as Italians we have been consistently living beyond our means for most of the last decades – leaving the financial burden for future generations to repay. If we "overspent" before the pandemics, we then had plenty of good reasons to do even more during the first two years of Covid-19 to support ailing sectors and the citizens in greater need. The impact on our finance has been brutal, with a $28 Bn deficit for 2019 going up to $157 Bn in 2020 and then to $181 Bn in 2021, with higher-than-average deficits continuing in the near future notwithstanding some barely visible mean reversion to normal. We also need to consider that in those figures we are not including the almost $250 Bn investment coming from our share of the Next Gen EU funds. These are financed anyway by debt that will need to be repaid over time with our fair share of contributions as one of the leading countries of the economic block. Given this tendency to overspend, it is interesting to note how most of this is coming from our generous approach towards "social protection," accounting for 21% of the total – of which a large share is dedicated to our over generous pension system.

Figure 3.4 Government revenues and spending in Italy from 2016 to 2026

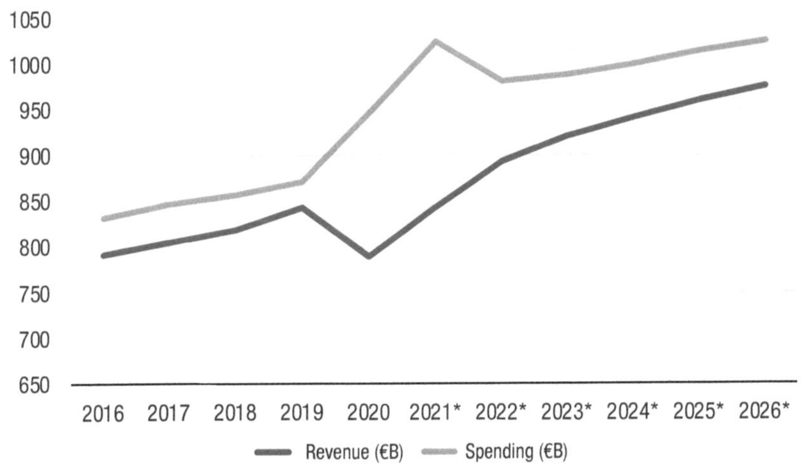

Source: IMF, World Economic Outlook Database, October 2021

3.3 Are we citizens or pensioners?

In Italy we are very proud of caring for our elderly people, through our public health structure and a fairly generous pension system. As a consequence of this, we are progressively becoming a republic of pensioners, given the share of voting citizens now belonging to this cohort – circa 16 Mn and with over 475K retired people that have been retired for more than 40 years (of which over 80% are women[2] – we think we should read this higher share as an indication of gender inequality – women choosing to retire earlier for "family reasons"). The increase in the number of elderly people is not a purely Italian phenomenon. The world population reached over 8 Bn in January 2022 according to Neodemos.[3] It was 4 Bn in 1974 and 6 Bn in 1999 and then 7 Bn in 2011, mainly due to better health care and basic living conditions in the poorest areas of the globe. As the number of people grows and they all get older, the number of pensioners will obviously increase. However, this growth is unbalanced, with most developed (and financially wealthier) countries suffering a demographic crisis, with single digit or negative growth (Italy is now in negative territory at -0.1% in the last 10 years, whilst France is at + 4.4%, the UK at +6.8%, Germany at +3.7% and Spain at +1.6%). It follows that, in the case of Italy, young generations (aged between 0–19) are just over 10 Mn on a total of around 60 Mn, with elderly people (over 60) at around 18.5 Mn. In the next 20 years, Italy's working population will decrease by around 7 Mn and pensioners will increase by same amount (the 0–14 years cohort will decrease by 3% in absolute terms and "fund" a 2% growth in the over 65 years cohort). At the global level, Europe, North America, Australia and Japan are projected to remain steady at around 1.3 Bn, with a total population reaching 10 Bn by 2050, mostly driven by growth in Asia and Africa (the later going from 1.3 to 2.5 Bn – whilst Italy is predicted to go from 60 to 54 Mn in the same period). Within Italy, there will also be huge disparities across regions, with different burdens on the cost of the pension system.

Our average pension contribution cost in terms of share of the overall deficit is equal to circa 17% (up from 14% in 2000), but with huge differences across regions, from Calabria at 24% to the Trentino Alto Adige region at 11%, potentially generating further social tension. Further social disruption should then understandably arise amongst generational cohorts for, as Italians, we are becoming progressively older – our average age was 29 years in 1950, 47 in 2020 and is expected to go up to 54 in 2050, with a increasingly smaller base of productive workers that are required to be even more productive and sacrifice their own remaining wealth to support a nation of pensioners that, in 2050, will likely have the majority of political voting rights – even if we take into account the increasing number of naturalized immigrants. If this is not enough an even more fundamental question also naturally arises. When a large population of a well-developed countries such as Italy (or Japan, also suffering from negative growth rates in its population) rationally and consistently decides to have fewer children, with no particular and sufficiently objective reasons (such as a major war, famine or overcrowding), should there be a more profound reason? Or is this an indicator that our purely financial approach to wealth maximization and basic utilitarian, narrow-minded philosophy is not really contributing to our wellbeing and happiness? What if we don't feel like having the joy of nurturing babies and the wish to dedicate work and time to younger generations, that will in time continue and evolve mankind towards higher futures and pursuits? The birth rate analysis per inhabitants (decreasing from 9–10 to 6–7 per 1,000 inhabitants) and decrease in births (from 550K to 420K) should suggest that other reasons beyond purely economic factors are at play. Apart from possibly of making Italians unhappier, this would certainly make Italy an underdog. The term "underdog" refers to the case of a looser or predicted looser in a struggle or context. This could indeed be the case for Italy from a competitive perspective and at international level, where there are issues with a huge public debt and low growth, coupled with the burden of unsustainable pension systems and a ticking demographic bomb. That Italy is losing relevance as an economic, financial wealth producing, global power is already evident from the analysis in the trends of global and Italian GDP at USD nominal value and at PPP (Purchasing Power Parity), and in their growth rates. The perception of Italy becoming inexorably a country of losers and a competitive underdog is well captured in the feeling of the young that, maybe not even considering the demographic ticking bomb, are considering the option of moving abroad to build a career and become wealthier (even if at the cost of living in countries less beautiful, more expensive and with worst weather than Italy). From 2011 to 2019, the number of people responding affirmatively to the question on whether "going abroad is the only hope for young people who want to pursue a career?" has gone up from 56 to 75%.

Figure 3.5 Government expenditures by function, with a focus on social protection benefits

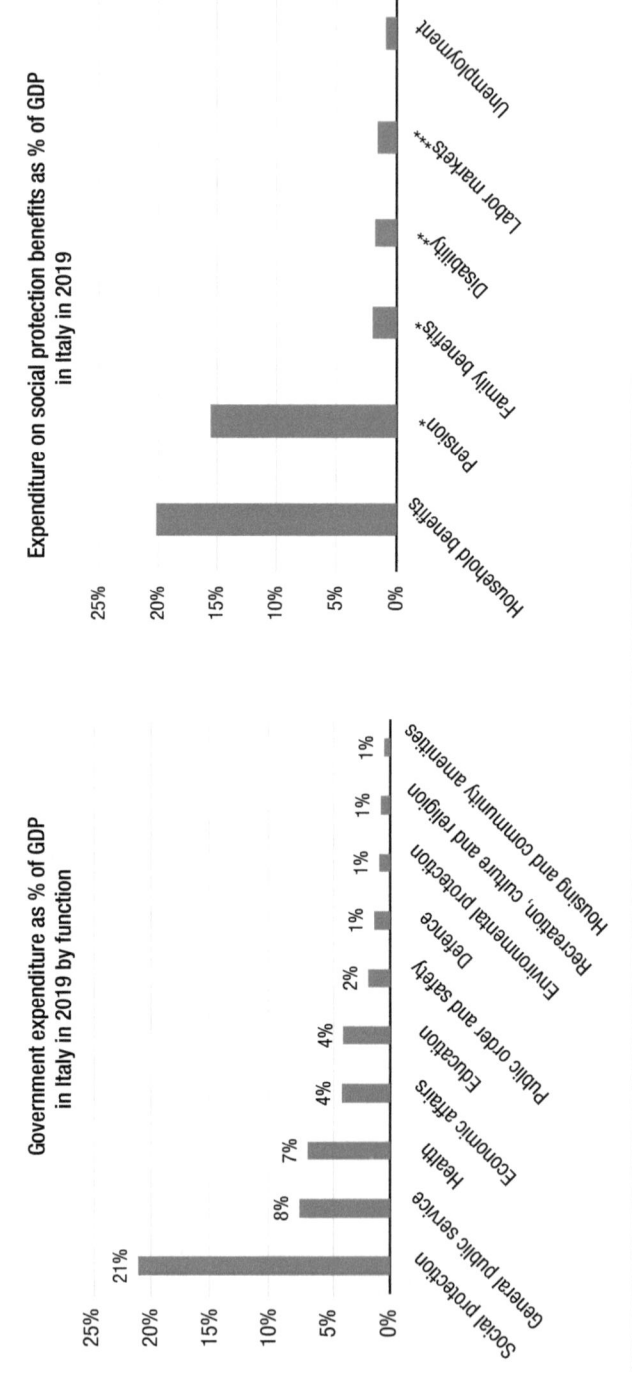

In fact, most of the young people leaving Italy are also representative of our best talents, with high level of learning, academic qualifications and training (overall, the share of young people not in education and training have instead risen from 20 to 25% from 2005 to 2020).

Figure 3.6 Spending for pensions by region

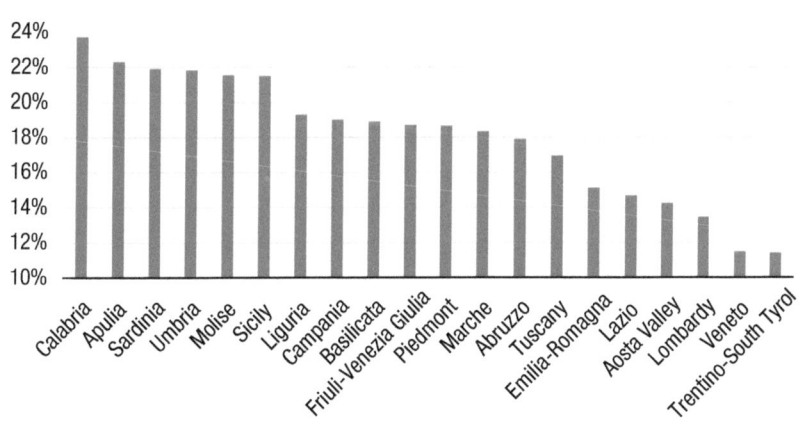

Sources: ISTAT; INPS, Condizioni di vita dei pensionati, March 2021

Figure 3.7 Expenditures on pensions as a share of GDP – evolution – 2000–2020

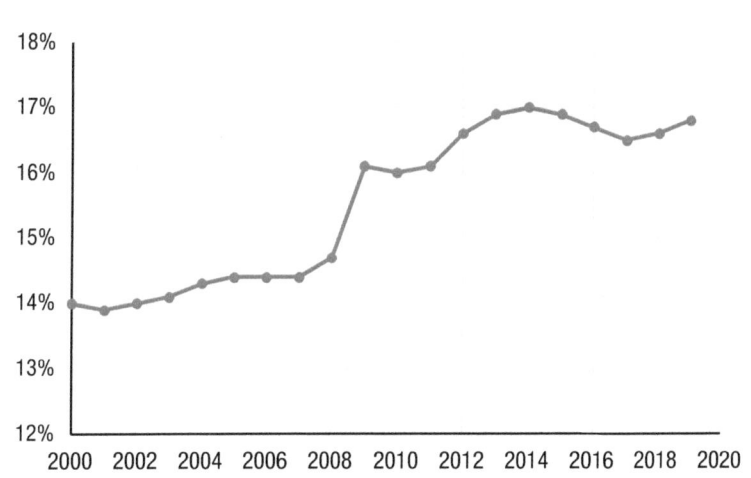

Sources: ISTAT; INPS, Condizioni di vita dei pensionati, February 2021

Figure 3.8 Population and Median Age projection in Italy

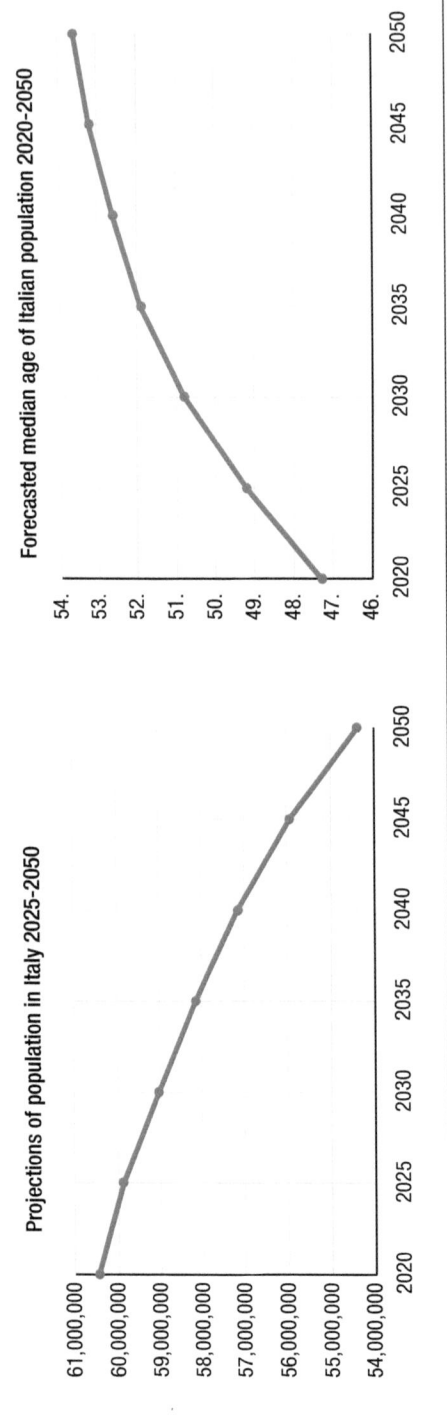

Source: Worldometer, Italy Population Forecast, November 2021

Source: Worldometer, Italy Population Forecast, January 2021

Figure 3.9 Birth rate, fertility rate and the number of births in Italy

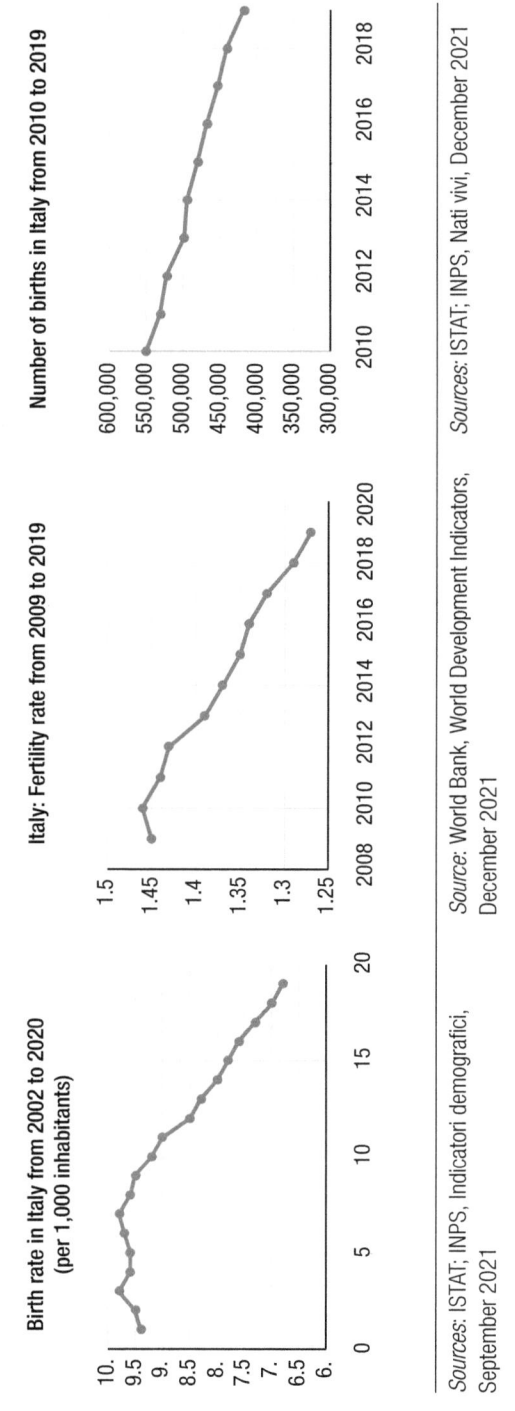

Sources: ISTAT; INPS, Indicatori demografici, September 2021

Source: World Bank, World Development Indicators, December 2021

Sources: ISTAT; INPS, Nati vivi, December 2021

Figure 3.10 Youngs: opinions on "going abroad"

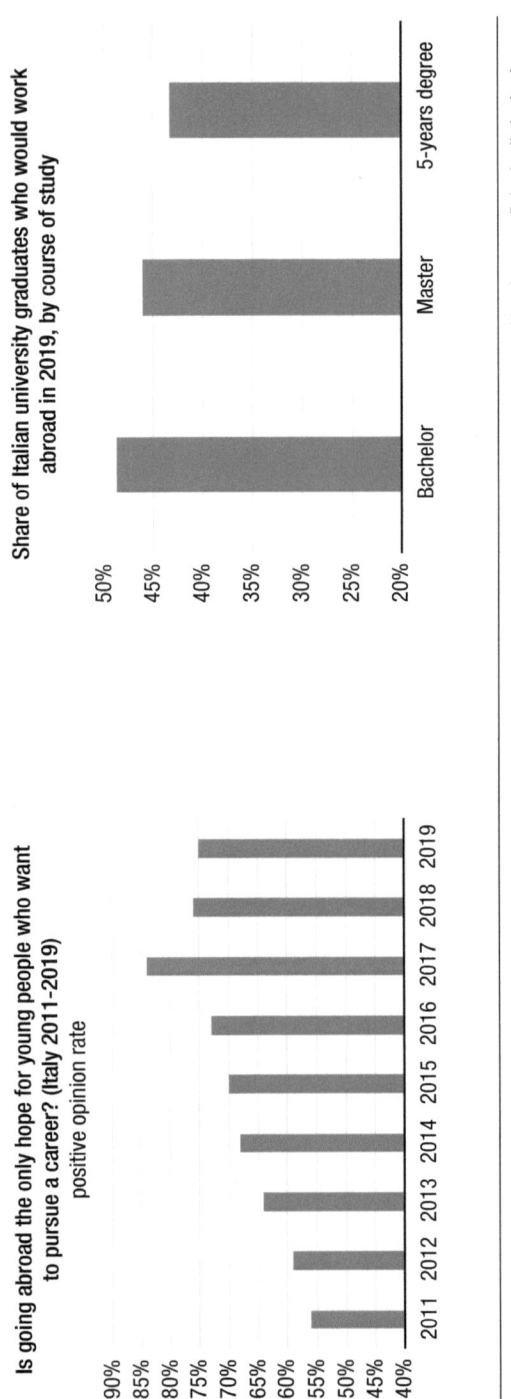

3 THE WEALTH OF ITALY

Figure 3.11 Unsustainability and intergenerational arbitrage

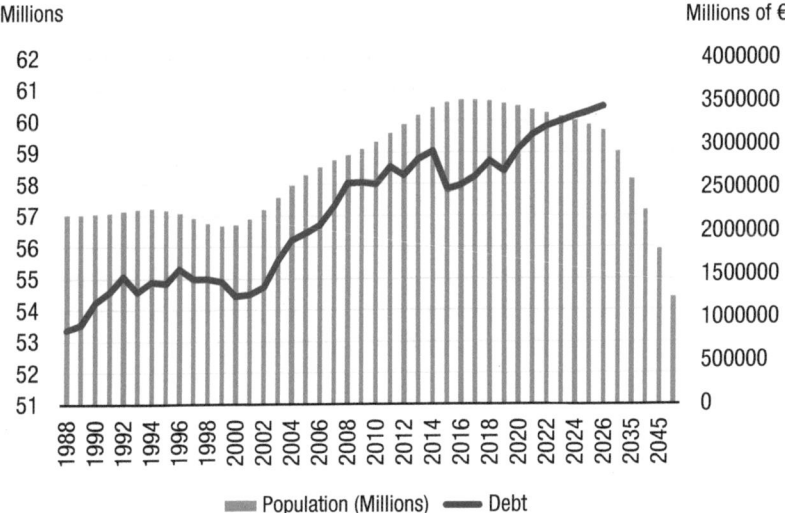

→ Italy – highest social security expenditure in the world – 16.8% of GDP
→ Retirement income is equal to 100% of the average national income
→ In 2018, 173 elderly people for every 100 young people (58 in 1980)
→ In 2047 there will be 20 million over-65s (34% of the total)
→ Risks of «green» taxonomy:
  • Green-washing
  • Green-bubble
  • Green-flop
  • Green-flation
  • Green-fashion

Sources: United Nations, World Population Prospects; Global Debt Database, IMF; Pensions at a Glance 2021: OECD and G20 indicators; ISTAT, demographic indicators

3.4 Equitization matrix

In *The Matrix* – a 1999 science fiction action film, then developed into a series – a dystopian future is depicted, in which humanity is unknowingly trapped inside a simulated reality (the Matrix). This dates back to a fictitious early 21st century era, when a war broke between humanity and intelligent machines – with the later winning the war, capturing humans, harvesting their bioelectric power and keeping their mind unnaturally pacified in a shared simulated reality modelled on the real world, known as the Matrix (and resembling the Metaverse that Facebook – now Meta – wants to create?). Whilst we are not there yet, we do feel trapped and constrained by a set of burdens we inherited from the past and with a number of recent black swans to face off – including the pandemics and inflation, the Ukrainian war and Russian related sanctions, the disruption effects of innovative technologies and the global decoupling that is further disrupting our global supply chains. Whilst with this chapter on the "wealth of Italy" we do not aim to provide a well-defined policy to address our multiple sustainability issues, we have focused instead on the definition of the baseline – the starting point of our transformative journey towards a wealth management of the future and for a greater wealth-being of Italy. In fact, our main and only suggestion has been instead to focus on the re-equitization of the country, pursued through the retailization of private equity and private markets, i.e. investing the savings of Italian families as equity in the real economy of the country and having in mind a "total sustainability target" pursued with a stakeholders based, benefit corporation approach. Equity is however scarce and even if employable savings in Italy are potentially quite abundant, their direct or indirect employment in private markets is just in its infancy. It is good then to complement and close this analysis by describing how, for the main industrial sectors, the recent black swans have impacted, mostly negatively, to further increase an equity gap that before the pandemic hit in 2020 was already large. In the following tables, an equitization matrix is describing, for the main sectors and given their relative contribution to Italy's GDP, how much they suffered as a consequence, and how much new equity is now required because of the latest black swans – on top of whatever was already required from the past, given the structural under-equitization of Italian SME *vis a vis* their European counterparts and their almost anecdotal use of regulated stock exchanges to raise capital. As for *The Matrix*, this snapshot is obviously incomplete and changes through time, and is worthy of a few sequels as for the cyber punk movie, with its Matrix "Revolution," "Resurrection" and "Reloaded."

3 THE WEALTH OF ITALY 63

Figure 3.12 The equity matrix for Italy

	Covid Impact	Russia/Ukraine war and sanctions	Inflation	New technologies Impact	Climate change	% of companies undercapitalized	Equity Gap (BN) 2020	Global decoupling (deficit-surplus Mn)	
								China	Russia
Food & Agriculture (12%)	-1.4%, reduction of loans to companies	OPEX Increase (Fertilizers), reduction of Russian and ukrainian wealth (-25% globally)	4%	High-precision agriculture, Data Analytics, Drones, Blockchain	Biotech research to increase productivity and water management	27%	8	-30	407
Automotive & Heavy Industry (6%-10%)	25% reduction in industry's turnover	Change of supplies	7%	Autonomous vehicle, Shared mobility	Electric Vehicles	7%	17	-6225	1457
Consumer Product: Fashion, Furniture (10%-15%)	Reduced impact	Strong reduction in export	1%	Novel fabrics, Blockchain	Reduction of water consumption	7%	12	-3858	1615
Energy & Utilities (7%)	Reduction of industrial use of energy	Change of supplies	28%	Solar energy, Floating wind, Green hydrogen, Smart electricty grids	Solar Energy, floating wind, Green hydrogen	11%	5	63	-6788
Healthcare (11%)	Increase in public investments	Reduced impact	1%	Telemedicine	Energy management	15%	5	229	370
Hospitality & Tourism (10%-13%)	Gap of 305 Mn tourists	Reduction of top-spender tourists	2%	Reputation management technology	Energy management	42%	10	Luxury	Luxury
Real Estate & Construction (4%-8%)	Crescono logistica e residenziale, calo retail ed entrantainment	Aumento OPEX costruzioni	4%	Building information modeling	Water efficiency, Waste reduction, Circular hospitality	7%	5	0	0
Retail (10%-14%)	Less in-store purchases	Reduced impact	3%	Cashierless store, Voice commerce	Emergence of new technologies	30%	8	0	0
TMT (5%)	Positively impacted sector	Reduced impact	-4%	Quantum computing, Quantum internet, 5g	Hardware: O&M devices (repairable systems)	8%	6	-10582	557
Transportation (5%) & Logistics (5%)	Increased costs of Transportation	Supply chain disruption	7%	Hyperloop, Delivery drones	Electric vehicles and new forms of taxation	10%	8	-73	206

About 600 Bn of equity gap, of which 90 Bn ex-Covid crisis, before the impact of Russia-Ukraine war

Low Negative · Medium Negative · High Negative · Positive

64 GEN Z AND THE FUTURE OF WEALTH

Figure 3.13 Sectors' trends caused by current contingencies

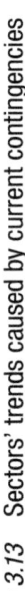

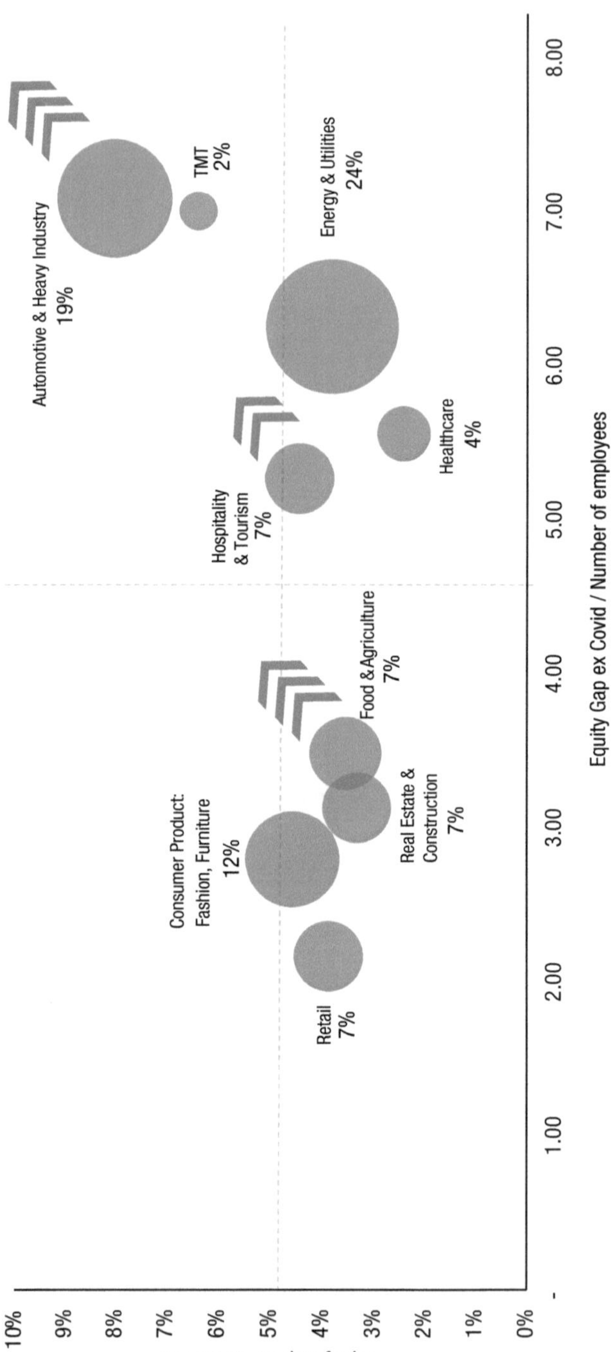

→ Arrows show the sectors' trends caused by the Russia / Ukraine war
→ Circles' dimension indicates the contribution of each sector to the total emissions of greenhouse-gasses of the country

Source: ISPRA

Notes

1 For this discussion, see the detailed analysis in Claudio Scardovi, *Speranza e Capitale*, EGEA, 2021.
2 Scenari Previdenziali, 2022.
3 "Siamo 8 Miliardi," *Corriere della Sera*, January 23, 2022.

4 The Future of Wealth

4.1 The Grinch generation and traditional wealth management

Gen WWI and WWII (to which my grandfathers belonged) were born in the worst possible years of modern history, sandwiched between two world wars, unprecedented violence and misery, social disruption and lacerating inflation – notwithstanding the short lived, joyful illusion of the "roaring twenties" in between. As my grandfather said, his biggest misfortune was to have been to be born too early. Baby boomers (to which my father belongs) were just late enough to escape war and experience the peaceful recovery of the nation, with its progressive development marked by a second industrialization era, the growth of manufacturing and of the services industries (financial services notably among them) and globalization. They have been lucky to live through one of longest periods of almost uninterrupted wealth creation and progressive democratization of societies (to some degree at global level, certainly in European, encompassing most of the "economic miracle" years of Italy). This progressive, almost irresistible liberalization of economies and democratization of societies even led political scientists such as Francis Fukuyama to proclaim the "end of history"[1] and the advent of global democracies, led by technological innovation and peaceful development of all kinds of civilizations (the theory of Fukuyama – one of the most cited, albeit to disprove it – may have lately received a fatal blow, but he is still professing an admirable optimism in his view of human history). For baby boomers, average wealth and wellbeing has been all in all pretty good, but marked by the protracted misery of the effort and sacrifices to achieve the significant but "too late in life to be good" financial rewards. In fact, a huge number of consumers are driven by the latest fashion (maybe also because of the misery they suffered, and because of the frugal education that they had in turn received – from their life in the street if not from proper teachers), and they have become big owners of real estate and big financial savers, with a significant critical mass of capital to invest.

Today my father complains that he was either too poor and hungry or too old and humble to enjoy life. In this regard, the luckiest generation has probably been the generation X, which was late enough to escape violence and misery and early enough to reap the benefits of the great economic cycles that followed WWII. Gen X barely noticed the hiccups that were happening in their formative years, such as the oil crisis. Until, of course the GFC (in 2008 and onwards), the pandemic (in 2020 onwards), the climate change reckoning (using the date of the Paris Agreement, from 2015 onwards) and the great, upcoming geopolitical divide and decoupling following the Ukrainian war– not to mention the risk of a WWIII. As Gen X (to which I belong) lived the dream of new, multiple digital revolutions (the world wide web in the nineties, big data and AI) and of globalization at its peak. Relatively speaking, notwithstanding several local and regional wars and the periodical resurfacing of terrorism, we also lived through the end of the cold war and the re-unification of Berlin – which signified a prolonged period of peaceful coexistence between east and west.

As I could now say – paraphrasing Marcel Proust – I have been neither too young to be constrained by the past nor too old to worry about the future, hence (potentially) living in best period. That is, assuming (as the "dismal science" does) that I, as *homo oeconomicus*, just care about myself, living day-to-day to maximize my utility functions, mostly driven by material things and physical needs, such as power and possession, the urge to consume and enjoy, the aspiration to live a long, easy and glamorous life. Should this be the case, wealth management would be an almost mathematical optimization of investment and consumption choices, taking into account preferences and lifestyle, the macro-economic-cycle and the micro-lifecycle and really not much else. The "wine and dine" private banking model of fortress-like global banks, usually placed in the most convenient, tax-free, no questions-asked-on-the-origin of money jurisdictions, well exemplifies this traditional model of wealth management – to which, thankfully enough for my children, I do not belong.

4.2 Towards a new wealth management model

In this traditional model, financial returns need to be maximized no matter what. Taxation is a mere nuisance without merits to be avoided at almost all costs. Discretion and secrecy (and a sense of belonging to a very limited and selected part of the society, where being rich appears almost a right that is due to particular people by virtue, and – more worryingly – *vice versa*) are also a critical part of this proposition. Even non-profit initiatives (often funded by capital which has cunningly avoided tax in its accumulation process) may become a nominal part of a very ego-centric system (as opposed to an eco-centric one, where the wealth and wellbeing of the ecosystem is the key and main driver). In this world, and counterintuitively – at least on a moral basis – the fees charged by wealth managers (as basis point of the financial assets managed) are inversely related with the richness of the clients – with poor people charged multiple times (and often being mis-sold in the process). In traditional private banking, financial risk is avoided by leveraging the clients' greater position of wealth and power, by using their close network of relationships and power broking, their access to more timely information and first rate intelligence and their right of first refusal on the best investment opportunities (what would a young talented entrepreneur do, if not seek as financial and strategic partner a wealthy family office with a King Midas brand name to match?). This is not to say, like Honoré de Balzac, that "at the basis of all great riches there are great crimes." More modestly, the point here is that is much easier to remain rich and become even more so if you are born as such, if you are provided with an average brain to drive your judgment calls and a little *savoir faire* (the latter can be taught).

But what if the "dismal science" has been imperfect in its very materialistic, individualistic and short-term definition of what an economic agent feels, and therefore how they are taking decisions and behaving as a consequence? What if, for example, Gen X, the luckiest of all, should now feel a moral duty and responsibility to address the many burdens we have described, in order to regain, at a time where statistically most of us by then will be long dead and buried, the long-lost sustainability? Even Keynes, who famously noted how "in the long term we will all be dead," formulated economic models and theories that were meant to address the long-term objective and Marshallian happiness of everybody (where optimization in society is achieved if at least somebody is better off, without anybody getting worst off). What about if even the Grinch had the chance, in a last-minute thought, to reconsider his understanding and belief of the true nature of Christmas and (therefore) his attachment to its very best, and long term, core values? What if ESG and green were in fact the Grinch finance, but after its enlightenment, conversion and re-edification? We all live, or should live, for a greater aim and purpose – as we wrote in the incipit of this book. But also, we should live, act and behave according to our main responsibilities, taking stock of the past (even if we did not live there) and worrying about the future (even if this is not destined to be ours). We, the Grinch generation, would not like to hear our children and grandchildren say how unlucky they were not to be born earlier: too young at the critical junction to be able to take their destiny in their own hands, and becoming adults too late to do something to recover the lost sustainability (and enjoy the world). This is the great challenge and the great opportunity for Gen X (or Grinch generation, for lack of better terms), to redeem itself and pay respect to Gen WWI and WWII that lived through wars and famine, and to the baby boomers, which recovered the world from the economic and social abyss to make the way for the incredible prosperity we have been able to enjoy to this day. More importantly, it is the opportunity for Gen X – Grinch generation to redeem itself and worry about future generations, fighting for the chance to give them back hope and a safer, fairer and better world.

4.3 The future of wealth and wealth of the future

What we have described is no small challenge and we should also refrain from making it too philosophical or political, as our target is to analyse and discuss the contribution that wealth management as an industry could make towards this meta-goal, and in a very pragmatic, down to earth way. A fundamentally different model of a "wealth management of the future," inspired by the wellbeing of the many generations to come – the next generations that we almost zero-ed from a future path of survival, development and evolution. In fact, the wealth management industry has already, as of today, great powers and therefore – in the words of Spiderman – great responsibilities. And our future, the future of humankind, will be marked by its strategic decisions and coherent management executions in the coming years. Never has there been a better moment to work in this industry to help it revolutionize and transform itself from inside-out, to then contribute in changing the world outside-in, addressing successfully its main financial challenges and expanding them towards other more philosophical and anthropological issues. For this change to happen, we first need to realize that there is no future for wealth (even the very tangible, material one – measurable by money) if some form of intangible wellbeing is not pursued as well. If wellness and happiness are a component of the objectives pursued, then other dimensions, including the social and ecological ones, become part of the equation and need balancing, from a financial and non-financial perspective, and with a humankind based on a long term, multi-generational perspective. Wealth-being management becomes therefore, from a macroeconomic perspective, a search for the optimization of objective wealth and subjective wellbeing, as pursued by policy makers, taking into account the different cohorts of the population and limiting the polarization of monetary fortunes. This should not necessarily imply a worst outcome for very (financially) wealthy individuals, as the wellbeing and happiness of a rich and poor individuals can both be optimised, but working more on the social and ecological dimension for the former and with a greater weight on the financial one for the latter.

From a macroeconomic perspective, policy makers should also address the emerging polarization of (financial and non-financial) fortunes between the old, new and next generations – moving from a static to dynamic point of view, e.g. even taking into consideration the unborn generations that will ensure the survival of our species. Decisions are taken, in a democratic setting by electorates, mostly middle-aged and, because of the demographic trends, increasingly composed of retired people. The explosion of public debt and of the intergenerational defined-benefit pension systems was in part driven by benign economic cycles and changing demographics. But, more importantly, by one of the main fallacies of modern democracies where "populistic policies" can sustain the governing parties if short-term expansive policies are financed by long term debt, that will be either inflated away through monetization or be born by other generations that will try to pass it over to future ones, as in the game of the hot potato. This myopic, ego-centric approach, from a macroeconomic perspective, only addresses the financial dimension – forgetting the social and ecological implications and, more importantly, ignoring how the three dimensions are closely interconnected. When minorities (either defined by gender, race, religious orientation or something else get unfairly deployed and sacrificed, short term gains in the productivity of the economic system can follow, as the measurable inputs (for example, the cost of labour) became cheaper and the rapid accumulation of capital in the hands of a few can allow more speculative enterprises and further polarization in the material outputs being created. But all of this is going to translate into some kind of social nemesis, where the disruption of the fabric of societies leads to unrest, terrorism or war and – even in their absence – results in a few "poor" and lonely ultra-rich people and a large number of desperate others seeking food and shelter.

4.4   From ego-systems to eco-systems

The myopic approach of macroeconomic policies of the last two centuries is even more evident from an ecological perspective. In fact, after the first industrial revolution, most of our material development and growth in GDP has been funded by the cheap energy we were able to attain from fossil fuels. We then built a geopolitical system that was also severely influenced by the natural resources owned by certain countries, with the support of others who had the financial capital or the military technology that was initially required to back dictators and oligarchs. As such, the cheap energy and the windfall fortunes of the small number petrol-based states have not only promoted further disparities, regional warfare for oil dominance and extended unhappiness for most of their people and for other oil-poor countries, it has also been polluting the environment in the process, contributing to the climate change challenge that we now have to face. Even before knowing the devastating effect of CO_2 and methane on people's health and on the climate and overall biosphere (long before the GOP and the Paris Accord), the trend in the depletion of natural resources was clear – as evident was the insane pursuit of unreasonable projects in inhospitable lands, and the depauperating transformation of places of natural beauty and historical heritage. Other natural resources (e.g. the rare earth) will also soon be depleted by the pursuit of renewable sources of energy (e.g. lithium for batteries) that, almost by definition, cannot be truly renewable. Where macroeconomic policies have failed to take into account, and with a cross generational view, the negative side effects of industrialization and fossil fuels on the overall society and the environment, market-based microeconomic mechanisms have often failed to include the other non-economic components that are nonetheless critical for the optimization of wealth-being and for a balanced pursuit of total sustainability.

For example, the cheap and highly productive (from an economic point of view) utilization of plastics in our everyday lives has strongly contributed to an increase in our material wealth and for a vast universe of less well-off people. However, it has created an ecological burden with a legacy that is destined to last for centuries. Market based pricing is in fact unable to take into account "public bads" and their negative effects on the environment and on the health of people. It is also very much focused on the short term, as pricing is driven mostly by the short-term matching of demand and supply, where supply is driven mostly by available inventories and very little by our long-term natural stocks (who cares if lithium is going to be exhausted in 50 years? The net present value of what comes next would in any case kill its money-based, economic implications for the so called "economic agent" taking decisions today). In fact, it is the very notion of "economic agent" (at the basis of modern microeconomics) that gives rise to the many fallacies of the market. We are egotistic people, driven by our own utility that needs to be measured with money and purchasing power. Certainly, we can include free time into the equation, or power, recognition and fame and all kinds of other short term and very material urges. But compassion, and the need to feel and behave as a social species are rarely considered in its analysis or material applications. How can you define and measure an all-too subjective passion or an emotion? How could you include values and ontological purposes into a pricing mechanism? Unfortunately, we often get the results of what we pursue on the basis of what we measure. If you use money, even in the well-meant interpretation of Aristotle, you get money-driven people that feel rewarded when they get more and more. As such they end up caring less about anything that is not translated into dollar or euro terms. The fallacy of our economic system is then a fallacy of our measurement system, which is mostly, if not only, financial, and has embedded in us an almost undisputable principle that equates what you are worth (as a person) to what you earn and own.

4.5   Gen X + Z: an intergenerational alliance

Where the utilitarian model and the very individualistic economic agent makes us all increasingly cynical (why bothering paying taxes? I can retain more for myself and eventually do some miserable non-profit donation, to cleanse my conscience and improve my image), the time value of money model makes us even more stupid, almost to the point of getting us all killed by things like climate change. In fact, the net present value approach of measuring the real value of things makes us very narrow minded – not just prejudiced *vis a vis* the right of the future generations to share scarce resources, but also myopic to the point of not even considering what is going to happen in 10 or 20 years for most of us, given the potentially snowballing, non-linear effects that are implicit in certain phenomenon. Planet earth is going to get warmer by 2 degrees Celsius. Should I swap my Italian Alps second home with the Swiss Alps – where there is going to be snow in winter anyway? Most places in the south will become uninhabitable because of scorching summers. Greenland could then become a good place for real estate speculation and a seaside resort for the summer. In short, where macroeconomics has fallen short of including intangible values, the role of public goods and bads, and a cross-generational approach, and where microeconomics has failed to make up to these shortcomings with market mechanisms, finance has then killed the matter once and for all, consigning us to the dimension of an utterly stupid, self-serving and convincing egocentrism. We only care about ourselves, and this is the best strategy for being happy. And money as a means to measure value, with economic policies and market prices and even social success and recognition there to prove it. Our societies have then become ego-systems based on cynicism and the survival of the "smartest" (not necessarily the most intelligent and best in doing something of real value to others – just smartest in caring about their self-interest in a very ego-centric way). The wealth management of the future should then aim to support the re-basing of our society as eco-system, inclusive from a social point of view and with regards to same-generation cohorts and to across-generation ones, and from and environmental point of view as well. An eco-systemic approach, driven by a "total sustainability" drive, and with a wealth-being optimization aim, should stand as our best chance to evolve, survive and keep developing – developing and capitalizing our wealth-being.

For this future of wealth management to develop, a new definition of wealth needs to be shared and agreed. A new approach to macro and microeconomics and finance should also be considered. Policy makers should include, for example, the needs and ambitions of future generations in any economic policy decision that can have lasting impact on them and where they also need to have a say. This could be based on a simple, bottom-up democratic approach but including top-down adjustments that would include solutions that may be less attractive than others but are still indispensable (we do not have referendum on taxes, but we do have taxes imposed by politicians once elected). These economic policies should then include norms and taxes, constraints and adjustments to market base prices, that then drive different patterns of investment and consumption and therefore a diverse allocation of the scarce resources available. After the two Word War generations, the baby boomers and our own Grinch generation, the next one – Gen Z – could become known as Gen Zero. It came to life during the pandemic era with a target of Net Zero CO_2 emissions that were deemed too complex and too costly to achieve, from either a technical, political or economic standpoint. They became adults with the several financial, social and ecological burdens discussed, with zero-ed financial resources (plenty of public debt and monetary led-inflation, debasement of the credibility of the official global financial system and within a context of global currencies decoupling, and with a pension fund and welfare systems increasingly unsustainable).

It also developed with zero-ed social capital (plenty of race, gender, religious and many other forms of discrimination, with richer getting richer and poor becoming more excluded), and with a growing threat of regional and global wars, either physical or digital, driven by global geopolitical tension between the US-EU and the Sino-Russian blocks. It also inherited a path towards zero-ed ecological resources (because of the climate change effects, the depauperating critical resources such as water and food, the increased level of harmful pollution and the impacts of the negative demographic dividend). This Gen Z is just getting to grips with the realization of the misery we are leaving them. An unsustainable world that is not fit for long term wealth creation and wellness and is actually at serious risk of survival and (humankind's) extinction. But they are hopefully realizing that a chance to regain an extended sustainability (financial, but also social and ecological) still exists, if their voice is heard and if their action is directed in the right way towards a common purpose with the help of the (for the time being) much more powerful Gen X (the many Grinches are now working in policy making, finance and in the most relevant industries). For this inter-generational strategic alliance (the Gen X + Z, we could write, in an almost formulaic fashion), a new more principled wealth management model would need to exist to increase its chances of success, working consistently across the public and private dimensions. Our brief critique of the traditional wealth management model does in fact show a path towards a different "wealth-being" (wealth + wellbeing) management, that is able to tap, cross and intertwine different disciplines such as macro and microeconomics, philosophy and psychology, in a more humanistic way of thinking. A thinking based on a new hypothesis for the human race that (no matter how much *oeconomicus* may be) also cares for ultimate and more intangible, even spiritual purposes, including the survival, development and evolution of its own species (the next generations). These new social sciences contributions and hypothesis will need to be captured in the future model of wealth management, for the future of the industry, the profession and of wealth itself, in a wealth-being form.

4.6 From Gen Zero to Gen Alpha

A joint effort between two quite different generations (X and Z, the Grinches and the Zero-ed) is needed to revolutionize public and private wealth management with a most radical and almost unrealistic goal in mind: giving back hope to future generations that are the many Alphas to come. In fact, even Gen Z needs to start thinking about the longer term for the many generations that will follow, as the transformation to regain sustainability will not be a challenge limited to their times. Alpha is, by the way, a quite positive term in investment management parlance, as it refers to the over performances that are uncorrelated to the economic cycle and are making investment managers that are able to master this, able to gain and beat the market no matter what, well above and beyond any macro or micro economic burden or constraint. It is the delta in the productivity of used scarce resources, tangible and intangible, that can truly create greater wealth and wellbeing. The challenge is in fact to overcome any constraint or burden by focusing on obtaining higher productivity in a holistic way: higher financial, social and ecological productivity across time. A few examples can explain the challenge to create "alpha" or, better, a number of Gen Alpha that could regain a total sustainability and bring the world back to the path of happiness. Let us consider the financial burdens first. The unsustainable weight of (mostly) public debts could be stabilized without a simplistic but inflationary way out of trouble, thanks to a real growth rate in the economy that is higher than the prevailing inflation and interest rates over the long term. Debts can be paid back without deflating their purchasing power if the output obtained by using them (and many other resources) is higher than their monetary and opportunity cost. This could happen over the very long time given the starting point we are in right now, but first a stabilization of this unsustainable financial burden could happen much faster through the re-equitization of the economy.

This is in fact one of the greatest opportunities for the wealth management of the future. Equity, in the shape of institutional and (even more) retail financial savings, does exist. The trouble sits largely in its use, as it is mostly invested in the money market and debt instruments – contributing to the liquidity trap and debt overhang we are living in. Retail financial savings could also be invested in more liquid stock markets. This would be a good thing, as there were not so many SME (small medium enterprises) and real assets (real estate and infrastructure, but also land, water and other critical commodities, such as "rare earths") that still belong to private markets. Even more importantly, if we consider a comprehensive definition of savings to include real estate, we would find that most households own too much real estate for their own exclusive use, and hence have limited flexibility for their main home should they need to change city for work or other reasons, or should they change their lifestyle or size of family as they progress in their career and make more money, or simply because they decide to live elsewhere. Even less efficiently, second and third homes are owned for very limited use through the year, with the opportunity cost of the lost rent adding to the monetary maintenance costs. Similar reasoning could be applied for real estate directly owned by corporations, which can grow in value or get smaller and face bankruptcy, with limited flexibility to the changes in business strategy and often with a suboptimized use of the value of the properties they are in (for headquarters in city centres, for example). Overall, the direct ownership of real estate by non-professional players is usually suboptimizing its gross productivity. Instead, only investors and real estate asset managers that buy properties and rent them at scale should be able to increase their productivity and best-use value.

4.7 Enlarged investable universe

In an optimized wealth management of the future, not only should a greater part of institutional financial savings be employed as equity in real assets and other private markets but also real estate, as the largest asset class globally should be owned mostly by professional investors and asset managers, optimizing its operating costs and fungibility, dynamically through time, and receiving rent in return, often through structures – then listed on stock markets – that would make properties most liquid. Similar reasoning could be developed for the social and ecological burdens to be addressed through private investments, including in real estate assets and developments, by Gen X, Z and Alpha. Aside from the return on capital, these investments should prioritise an "intangible productivity" that is higher than the "unsustainability" costs coming from the many mistakes of the past. Social rebalancing could be addressed through inclusion initiatives, such as through new sustainable neighbourhoods that are meant to reduce race, gender, pay and other forms of discrimination, or overcome divides related to the digital or climate change. As no investment in a corporate, real estate or infrastructure would be perfect but subject to many trade-offs, each investment should be considered in terms of marginal contribution, e.g. whether its social productivity is greater than the cost of the scarce resources used to acquire it, including the economic costs that could make such projects viable or not. Green conversion could be addressed in the same way, gaging its targeted productivity for the rebalancing of the biosphere's natural equilibrium and the trade-offs also implicit in the initiative to achieve a net positive effect. Many theories are in fact suggesting that a virtuous circle does exist, with socially fair and inclusive companies pursuing green offerings and products being rewarded by markets in economic terms, with easier and cheaper lending, more abundant and patient equity and even a price premium that is happily paid by the end customers. Maybe that will happen more and more and, hopefully, true enough in the long-term assuming, not only the perfect access to all information available by investors, managers and customers, but also their ideal wisdom and keen desire to behave well, no matter what short term financial gains and losses would need to be sustained as part of the transition experience. More pragmatically, wealth managers should assume a bumpy road ahead for the sustainability transformation journey, with a number of crude trade-offs to be understood, considered and managed.

It would be easy, at least theoretically, to stop using hydrocarbons and use renewable sources only – some people would not mind paying €3 K or even €10 K, instead of €1 K per month, for their electricity bill for a fully sustainable and pollution-free world of great, safe and clean mega cities. Unfortunately, the remaining 99% would have serious financial issues with this course of action and several million could die in the process, be hit by extreme cold or heat, dehydration and starvation and for the loss of their traditional jobs in highly polluting industries that nevertheless are still feeding their families and their communities. It would also be easy to ensure, in just one week, full parity in terms of race, gender and religion, but with the immediate risk of having people completely put out of place, hence prone to critical errors, suboptimal performances and therefore huge losses in productivity if not facing terminal risks. It would also be easy to cancel a large part of the unsustainable debts or reign-in the monetary supply to prevent inflation occurring at a stroke of a pen (of a Central banker). But that would again imply unjust losses for the debtholders, the destruction of governments' credibility, the almost immediate collapse of GDP with the creation of millions of unemployed people and so on. In fact, our transition to sustainability will require significant time and the optimal management of many trade-offs – good decision making in this respect will require cools heads and pragmatic judgement calls. Thinking that there is a silver lining to follow, where all good intentions get translated immediately into great returns is not just unpractical but, more importantly, untrue. My grandfather also used to say: "beware of dogs that are tied with leads made of meat." He should know better, having been born in the rosy and roaring twenties, characterized by great expectations and limitless promises, that then ended up in WWII.

4.8   Tell me where you invest

We could maybe paraphrase a famous saying: "tell me where you invest and I will tell you who you are." That is, assuming that the investment world is mostly a buy-side dominated, where investors are buying financial products, having made their decisions on the basis of a thorough financial analysis, but also on a thoughtful consideration of their core values, regret and happiness functions, and end pursuits – all well and above any economic targets they may have. Alas, if this could be partially true for the small number of highly developed and fairly professional institutional investors, the opposite is much more likely to be true for retail investors, who typically neglect financial analysis for lack of technical preparation, limited personal interest, amount of spare time, attention span and (sometimes) even because of the cosy contribution of financial intermediaries, who have an interest in keeping the industry of wealth management as one where products are sold on a relational basis to generate bigger margins. In fact, the real revolution of the wealth management of the future should start making investors, and retail ones most of all, well prepared and informed of the investment opportunities they are considering investing their personal, intergenerational savings for their best use, ideally considering not just short term financial returns but also total sustainability. A report from Credit Suisse[2] is developing a similar argument, trying to answer the first part of the question, that is: where the next generation should consider investing in an ideal (but still unreal) world of financial products to address at least the first "financial sustainability dimension."

Having been born into the most prosperous period in human history, Gen Z have much to hope for. They also have much to fear as well, with the economic consequences of the GFC and the pandemic on top of the inherited and unresolved social issues. Not to mention the impending climate change crisis, geopolitical tensions, the war driven international sanctions and global decoupling. Just from an economic and financial perspective, this could mean for them bigger rates of unemployment, lower earnings and higher taxes to pay off the huge amount of the public debt accumulated globally. On top of this, there is the less-noticed but no less serious problem regarding their zero-ed pension perspective and their overall dismal financial prospects. According to Credit Suisse, Gen Z's earnings from stocks and bonds will be significantly lower than those of previous generations. Just look at the average investment returns since 1990. The authors of the report from Cambridge University and London Business School estimate that baby boomers and Gen X have all earned average real returns of at least 5.8–7% on equities and at least

3.5–6% on bonds. They forecast what Gen Z might expect to earn in the coming decades, assuming that the real return on equities will be equal to the inflation-adjusted return on a risk-free asset (such as a government bond) which they estimate at -0.5%, plus a "risk premium" for buying equities of about 3.5%, for an overall real return of just 3%. For bonds, and not unexpectedly, they assume the current, negative real yields on the index-linked variety will remain the same in the long term. Taking a balanced view of their portfolio (say, with 70% of bonds and 30% of equities) Gen Z would get a mere 2% (less than a third of what was obtained by the baby boomers and Gen X). That is, assuming no major crisis be it from a prolonged pandemic, hyperinflation, climate change or from a major global war. If this is the perspective for Gen Z, what should it do to optimize its financial wealth and related wellbeing? The answer to the initial question would therefore become more poignant and critical. For a start, Gen Z would need to save even more, to have some hope of financial independence when they retire, and to sustain the burden of the many retirees funded by them before that moment. They would also need to take the long-term view, diversifying a lot and avoiding high management fees, according to Credit Suisse. They should exercise patience and sit out temporary shocks and turbulence. All this looks very logical and intuitive, even if not particularly revolutionary – but would this be sufficient to avoid becoming the zero-ed generation, from a financial perspective, not to mention a social and ecological one? And how do they pursue in a credible way the transformations towards the higher futures they long for?

In fact, we could also argue that (if you) "tell me which higher futures are driving your ambitions and drive, I will tell you who you are." It would then follow logically that if "you tell me which higher futures you want, for you and your children, and your children's children, and I, the ideal wealth-being manager, will tell you how to invest your financial capital and more." In our hypothesis, a more holistic analysis of the past performances from investments to include the social and ecological dimension as well, need to be considered to provide a more quantitative and objective background. For it is important to address the full spectrum of tangible and intangible objects that have a say on the regrets and happiness of the *homo oeconomicus* that is also a social animal and living in a friendly, attractive and self-sustaining biosphere. A *homo oeconomicus* that is also dominated by its selfish gene, that seeks its everlasting survival well beyond their mortal body, through the preservation of their own species and through the development of multiple generations ahead. For this, it is important to consider the many constraints and trade-offs among different targets, tangible and intangible, and across the dimensions of wealth and wellbeing, for a fuller wealth-being creation.

For example, how much of the equity returns were driven in the past by the use of cheap energy sources, the hydrocarbons that are now threatening the survival of humankind because of an impending ecological disaster? How much of these returns were driven by the unfair and morally unacceptable exploitation of women and children, people from the underdeveloped world and with a different ethnicity? How much was actually taken away through wars (as returns are mostly measured on the stock markets of the winners of history and paid by the losers), with great losses in terms of human life? How much of these returns were financed by "bad" businesses (such as gambling, tobacco or pornography) and how many good businesses produced dismal returns (not a bad thing *per se* if not leading to bankruptcy – we could reasonably and logically decide to earn less if we do a good thing instead of a bad and we feel better in the process). Indeed, we should answer the question that relates to the "which wealth and wellbeing for which stakeholders?" and keep an open mind on what financial (and non-financial) value could be a consequence of the best answer we will provide to the main question. Based on the answer to this question, we should reassess its economics, but also its social and ecological "true" and "complete" returns. What was achieved, for example, by our current generation in light of our extended "total sustainability" definition and what was missed? What was eventually the loss of wealth and wellbeing caused to the detriment of other cohorts? Based on the answers to these questions, and on the re-valuation of past performances, we should then reassess which optimal investment strategy and best allocation Gen Z, and the Alpha to follow, should consider on the basis of a long-term view based more on the eco-system and less on our own ego-system. Which investment manager should they select in order to pursue diversification, low management fees as suggested by the Cambridge– LBS experts (all of which we confirm as "good advice" anyway), but also with "total sustainability"? Aside from deciding how much equity and how many bonds to purchase on developed and developing public and private markets, we should specifically and maybe more importantly, assess which set of financial, social and ecological targets, and therefore tangible and intangible returns we should consider pursuing and optimizing, giving the intrinsic, complex and often intertwined trade-offs that typically characterize them. For, with many trade-offs our life and our well-intentioned journey is paved towards good and happiness. They maybe make us more imperfect and difficult to analyse, but likely less depressing as well.

Notes

1 Francis Fukuyama, *The End of History and the Last Man*, Free Press, 1992.
2 Elroy Dimson, Paul Marsh and Mike Staunton, *Global Investment Returns Yearbook*, Credit Suisse, 2021.

5 Sustainable Investing

5.1 Sustainable capital in the 21st century

Thomas Piketty, in his "Capital in the Twenty-First Century" (2013) has wisely focused a good part of the economic discussion on the thorny topic of how income and inequality became distributed over the last 250 years. He argues that the rate of capital return in developed countries is persistently greater than the rate of economic growth – that is, financial capital is getting more than its fair share of value creation, with other scarce resources (starting from labour) getting less. It follows that wealth inequality is destined almost inevitably to increase, as most financial capital is owned by a few rich people and whoever has a greater amount of capital can also deploy it with significant advantages. The first point may look as a syllogism, but it is not, as great wealth can be owned by many people if its is dispersed sufficiently deep and wide. Certainly, the existence of a limited number of billionaires that are getting richer and richer is something quite undisputed and characteristic of the many industrial revolutions that our civilization has experienced – look at the massive wealth accumulation of the few Big Digital players in recent years – but this could be easily addressed by way of a progressive wealth tax, operated yearly, or just as a one-off inheritance tax. But it is the second point that is of greater interest to us in the context of the discussion of the wealth management of the future. In fact, in our hypothesis, rich people have greater opportunities (and lower risks and costs) to make more profitable investments. Not only are the courted by the best private and investment bankers, happy to wave their fees to start working with them. They are also offered the opportunity to invest by the best talents and in their best ideas. They can also easily pursue lucrative co-investment opportunities and club deals as they are part of a highly influential network. They have greater access to information and can easily borrow intelligence, not to mention money, if they want to hyper leverage their own. Moreover, current regulations usually allow maximum flexibility and little oversight on family offices, whilst the remaining 99% of retail investors (and asset managers) are overly regulated and significantly constrained.

In fact, private equity and – more generally – private markets, represent the more interesting chance we structurally see at global level to invest and reach a return rate that is greater than the growth rate of the economy. Therefore, they stand as an opportunity that is almost forbidden for the masses. An affluent or mass market retailer, in order to invest even a small amount of their own wealth (say 2%) needs to prove that they have significant money (another syllogism? You could make money and leave poverty, but only if you are rich enough?), on top of a significant technical preparation (a PhD in finance, for example) and lots of experience in private markets (question: how can you get experience in investment if you are not allowed to invest?). With specific reference to Gen Zero and following the hypothesis of Piketty, we will try to prove that, in fact, investing in private markets is the best opportunity to get a superior rate of return and hence, if they are invested by the masses, this approach could be the most effective way to reduce inequality. If pursued by the Gen Z and Alpha, this could also be their best way out of the debt trap, of the monetary inflation overhang and of the pension deficit – a good way to address many financial burdens. Particularly for young people, which have long horizons of investment in front of them, it would also be a way to become shareholders in the real economy of their country, with a greater stake and a better reason to keep developing and living in their country – better, that is, than their parents' house. We will then consider the limitations imposed right now by many regulations which are, in effect, limiting the opportunity of re-equitization of the economy and of creating a capitalism for everybody. In our model of "capitalism for everybody," democratic access to the best opportunities for investment is offered to all people, no matter what their wealth is. There is also a significant contribution to the training and information on economic matters to the largest number of citizens, to improve their financial literacy and decision making on investment and life related matters.

5.2 A greater wealth tax or a better wealth management?

In fact, whilst Piketty suggested solution is focused on a progressive wealth tax to support redistribution (that is, considering accumulation and its polarization as an unmodifiable given), our solution is focused more on better wealth management for everybody, to limit polarization whilst making the overall economy more productive and sustainable (if wealth is more widespread and productively invested, it should also be better allocated to investment decisions and better used for consumption ones – avoiding unreasonable excesses and increasing people's overall happiness – given the different needs of the rich and the poor. There is however a further question that needs to be considered to address the wellness and happiness of people. This question is even more critical if we are considering the wellness and happiness of future generations that have many years of life in front of them and should consider all kinds of other non-economic factors. This question on "what else?" is however hardly discussed by economists – in western and eastern societies – and not fully addressed by the Piketty wealth tax or by our idea of private markets for everybody to spur the equitization of the economy and the "shareholderization" of Gen Z.

Political agendas designed to reduce inequality through wealth redistribution and improved welfare policies are now being discussed in most countries from the USA to Europe, including initiatives of inheritance taxes, wealth taxes and even universal basic income. More interestingly, a political agenda of "common prosperity" has now become a hot topic and mostly discussed in either very good or very bad terms. First mentioned by Xi Jinping, China's leader, in late 2020[2], it is becoming one of his country's most important objectives over the next 15 years, with the aim to reduce economic inequality by narrowing the country's stubbornly large gap between rich and poor (polarization, it seems, can also happen in socialist countries). According to Xi, China does not want to share the fate of the USA where "rich and the poor in some countries are polarized with the collapse of the middle class. This has led to social disintegration, political polarization, and rampant populism." "Common prosperity" the Chinese way is now meaning government intervention within the realm of Big Tech companies to curb their market power and break them up if useful for their cause. It is also meaning "suggested" voluntary redistributions and the promotion of government owned companies and much else. Differently from the previous years, it seems that the focus of China is now more on the definition of the 'right' shares of the pie, instead of its maximization, with not much focus given to the young and the overall sustainability.

In fact, these two remaining points are what we plan to focus on and discuss. The solutions of Piketty and our "capitalism (and private markets) for everybody" would be partial and imperfect from an economic standpoint if they are not fully focused on the "greatest polarization to come," that is between the future and past generations. Indeed, we suggest that the greatest financial divide between the rich and poor is becoming the one between old and young because of the many financial burdens we discussed: debt, inflation, debasement, the pensions gap and so on. He is calling for a property tax and pushing for wealthy people to give back more to society, with greater pensions and welfare for the poor. But also giving warnings against "the welfarist trap of encouraging the lazy" (including the idea of a minimum global salary, something that in Italy has had the side-effect of raising the rate of "voluntary" unemployment, apart from contributing further to its public debt and low productivity rate). Moreover, Xi's solution, even if extended to cover the generational divide, would be very much partial and imperfect if it were just focused on top down decisions on the reallocation of the financial pie, without considering how these decisions would not really supported by markets but enforced by the heavy hand of the government and eventually not really including the other two critical dimensions of sustainability, that are social (including in this the level of "socialization" of the decisions taken, the inclusion achieved, a fair chance offered to everybody to reach a freer and better life) and ecological (including the health of the biosphere, that is a critical and required element to support the "common prosperity" preached). We all want to be richer, but would we care if this is achieved in the context of polluted cities, inhuman urban areas and inhabitable, hostile environments?

5.3 Green wash: is labelling good enough?

All people are good at Christmas. We all feel better people during that special time of the year – or pretend to. And, most importantly, we all love Christmas and Santa Claus – except for the Grinch. Similarly, we now all feel green and very much looking towards the sustainability goals of the 2030 United Nations' Agenda and of the ESG rating system. Therefore, we all feel good and better people – or pretend to – in real life as much as in investment and wealth management. In fact, in the expectation of a Merry Christmas, we end up paving the way for the many Grinches waiting for our mistakes and our many inconsistencies, from the way we think, act, talk and behave. As a start, a lot of hyperbole has been built into the "green conversion" and ESG-related topics. When so many policy makers, businessmen and other "very important people" dedicate so much time, energy and waffle, getting together around the world, flying all over the place with their oil-guzzling private jets, you may start wondering how much of this is their "talk" and how much is their "walk." The GOP (Group Of Parties) meetings of the powerful that come together for a number of days every few years to agree a final communique that is pretty bland, usually also creates false expectations and becomes then an easy target for the cynic Grinches who complain of their non-decision making, wasting of time and resources, and inconsistencies between their huge aspirations and their modest action plans.

Even regulations may be developed with little effect if a lack of clarity make them so flexible and subject to interpretation, they become almost irrelevant. Actually, weak and opaque regulation is even weakening our motivation to be good at Christmas or pretend to be. The first threat to a real green conversion is in fact driven by green washing. Any country, company or even person can pretend to green-convert a few basic nominal actions that do not consider the full scope of their actions. The full scope of their value chain, as defined for example by the more comprehensive definition of "scope 1" (contribution to CO_2 emission by the products produced by a company), "scope 2" (also considers the energy consumed to produce them) and "scope 3" (considering the enlarged supply chain that is involved to produce the end product). If we all green wash, nothing really changes. And if green wash is effective and widely accepted, pursuing the real thing becomes a matter left to Saints if it is so easy to game the system and everything becomes unclear anyway. Why bother if we can make up some smart marketing and cunning communication?

With regards to wealth management, green-washing is encouraged by multiple sustainability-rating schemes that are mostly partial, subjective and inconsistent – and all carrying a strong incentive for asset managers and companies to mislead their investors in order to get more and cheaper capital. Fortunately, regulations are improving by the day to promote transparency and a common yardstick. Ideally, they should promote a greater sharing of information and intelligence that would allow investors, consumers and citizens to do a better job when voting with their feet, i.e. taking their investment, consumption and everyday-life decisions as free socio-economic agents. Eventually, a lot of money is needed to finance the green transition: over $5 Tn a year for the world to reach net-zero emissions by 2050[1] – or around $150 Tn in total. It follows that the great money managers will need all the information available to make the best investment decisions consistently with this ambition. A new labelling system in the process of being devised by the European Union is promising to be at the forefront of this, with a new approach that is set to define the taxonomy of the investable universe, segmented into activities that it deems environmentally sustainable, from the installation of heat pumps to the anaerobic digestion of sewage sludge. The different "scopes" already used for analysing CO_2 emissions, such as an effort to provide better clarity and with greater consistency across different jurisdictions, is certainly useful and a step in the right direction. The idea emerged after the 2015 Paris climate deal to support the initial target of defining a green-bond standard and what would therefore be required to qualify as such. This EU taxonomy hopes to end the practice of greenwashing and boost investors' faith in sustainable assets. An initial list of 11,000[2] European firms, and growing, will soon start reporting a "green asset ratio" using the labelling criteria.

5.4   The Green bubble and flop

However, in its simplistic labelling, it could lead to a purity test in which funds may focus excessively on "good" and "sustainable" assets and go for it almost barehandedly. Also, its limited coverage will be initially applied to a subset of economic activities and will let small companies (as well as private ones) off the hook. They could also exclude assets that are dirty and therefore "bad," e.g. almost un-investable. This would pose two further threats. The first, which has been dubbed "green bubble," refers to the fact that ESG sustainable companies could become over-invested, particularly by passive investors replicating ESG-compliant indexes, hence creating market bubbles that would inevitably burst sometime in the future. It is good to play the good guy role, but if too few assets are recognized as such, the mismatch between the over-supply of sustainable capital and sustainably invested assets under management ($35.3 in 2020, according to The Economist, up from $22.9 in 2016) will rapidly dislocate markets and potentially fund financially unsustainable projects that would produce even worst reallocating trajectories towards Net Zero. It could also lead to huge misinterpretations, even from an academic point of view. In fact, a lot of discussion has recently focused on the *vexata quaestio* that is "are ESG assets going to overperform the market, as the green conversion trend is there and the change in demand almost inevitable?" A number of studies have both confirmed and refuted this view. Leaving aside the number crunching answer, a couple of potentially logical solutions stand out, just apparently inconsistent between them. On one side, if the demand of investing in ESG assets overcomes (in the short term) the investable assets' universe, it follows that a series of price rises are on the cards, justifying a stock market overperformance until such rebalancing occurs, and regardless of the trends in the fundamentals of the companies invested. On the other side, if most of the institutional, highly regulated, asset managers want to own ESG companies only, then non-ESG assets and companies will become cheaper by the day and hence become an arbitrage opportunity for private investors who do not care about the public good but are quick at spotting easy gains on mispriced assets. This is in fact the second threat, which we have dubbed "green flop." It is not only investors without scruples that can take easy bets on CO_2-producing assets which are fire-sold by blue chip companies that risk falling out of favour with long-only, big institutional money managers. But they may even end up being helped or subsidized by the state if the imbalances created by a too quick and uneconomic switch towards green assets ends up creating short term problems that are bigger than the ones they are meant to solve.

The combined effect of a "green-bubble" and "flop" could become even more dangerous in light of the potential "green-flation" effect, also caused by the limited supply of renewables, unmet demand for energy during peak times and some speculation occurring during turbulent times. Green-flation that can also relate to all kinds of other products and services is one example and can be broadly attributed to the poor planning of the transition time required to convert one or more critical sectors into a green-sustainable one. We then find multiple failures and dilemmas in the market, with governments subsidizing the investment in renewable energy and taxing non-renewable ones, but then getting ready to subsidize the increased cost of gas and other dirty energy sources to overcome the period of stress, market volatility and of extreme weather, that requires even more energy. Instead, the trade-off between doing well and pursuing good intentions can be reset in an optimal and market-based way, if carbon taxes or other similar forms can include the cost of negative externalities in the price of goods and services, to align the profit motive with the imperative to cut emissions and so unleash the power of markets to reallocate capital quickly and efficiently, without generating unreasonable inflation. In fact, green-flation could also be a good excuse to kill the green movement around the world as the Davos-man inspired conspiracy aimed at stealing the purchasing the power of people, forgetting the contribution of lax monetary policies and quantitative easing to higher and higher inflation rates.

If the impact of "green bubbles" could be detrimental to ESG-keen investors and produce short-term unbalances and long-term dislocations in capital markets, the impact of "green-flation" could be even more detrimental to the poorest consumers as their purchasing power could collapse. It would also justify, not just financially but also on moral grounds, the behaviour of private investors that are trading on cheap and dirty assets, which are necessary to keep energy-related inflation at bay. In the developed world, the effect of cutting short the use of oil and carbon could in fact represent a cure that is worse than the illness it was meant to solve, with millions of people becoming unable to feed themselves or live in inhospitable territories and under extreme weather conditions. Who cares about Christmas and Santa Claus if there is no food and warm shelter anyway?

5.5   Green in public and private markets

The rise of ESG and the stigma faced by publicly listed companies (the non-renewable energy ones especially) bring an unintended side effect, as they start selling on the cheap side, gaining in market value because of the "green bubble" effects. Dirty assets are heading into shadowy private hands, with private equity companies that were able to snap up $60 Bn of fossil fuel linked assets in past 2 years from shale fields to pipelines.

That these (for bad or good) strategic assets are moving into private ownership, with private equity owned by a few institutional investors or, more typically, ultra-high net worth individuals, may also seem to contradict the model we propose, where value creation and sustainability start with shares owned by citizens. For this, however, there may be a handy solution. Institutional investors, such as pension funds, endowments and insurers could in fact behave more proactively when they push public companies to shed dirty assets by selling them to private equity players in which they are also investing – as they should consider the entire carbon footprint of their portfolios. They can become more active in the governance of alternative investment fund managers as well, and select just those committing to strong and real, well-defined ESG targets. As suggested by Larry Fink, CEO of BlackRock, the world's largest asset manager, active investors should hold on to the shares of polluting companies and support (or sack) their management in turning them around, and the same should occur when sustainably investing in private markets either directly or indirectly. This is also important because, as noted by Fink, fossil-fuel assets that are fire-sold to private counterparts not only generate unjustified, easy profits. They are also likely to be managed less responsibly and in an opaquer way than in public markets. In any case, it will be difficult to convince shareholders to give up profitable sources of business (as, in the Glencore example, driven by the extraction and sale of coal). Unless stringent rules are set, with clearly defined limits and constraints, and a carbon tax system is agreed and enforced at global level to avoid jurisdictional arbitrage, with a proper time planning for the transition required, we will see more squandering of public finances, driving further public debt, the misallocation of resources and other avoidable waste.

Fink has certainly contributed to a better definition of the challenges and potential issues related to the green transition, as addressed through the lenses of the wealth management industry. However, he has like many others, including me, contributed so much to the fashionable discussion on the green conversion to make it almost unbearably boring. This, as we already mentioned, is maybe the ultimate risk faced by ESG and by the green/fight-climate-change movement. It rapidly grew to such great momentum just before the pandemic that expectations grew even higher. It then fell short, and a number of other short-term urgencies have taken the stage. As the chaos of the many challenges we face grow higher, they both tend to fade away, becoming boring subjects and for the relatively mid-long term (at least when compared with short term urgencies which have an impact measurable in weeks, or even days). It will be for the best wealth managers to keep this movement going and deliver something tangible in due time. In fact, focusing on the most urgent issues is usually not a great strategy to survive and thrive, if other critical issues for our development and growth are simply parked and forgotten.

5.6   We all live beyond our means

Having discussed the three burdens that are fatally harming the sustainability and very existence of our species, it should not come as a surprise to say that we all live beyond our means, and this has been especially applicable in the case of the financial dimension since the global financial crisis and the pandemics and, with regards to the ecological one, since the first industrial revolution and the following exploitation of hydrocarbons as a cheap and abundant energy source (with regards to the social dimension, the unsustainability has much longer origins in history – from the use of slaves and the interpretation of women as inferior beings: this is actually the only burden which has shown some – albeit insufficient – level of marginal improvement through time). With regards to the financial sustainability, we have argued that this is mainly the result of too much debt and too much money, followed by traditional money's loss of credibility and the emergence of crypto currencies (not very ecological in themselves, but still representing a challenge and an effort to debase the value of the traditional global financial systems and of its main players, from Central Banks to intermediaries). As a consequence of "living financially beyond our means," future generations will bear a brunt in terms of unmanageable amount of public and private debt, monetary-based inflation that will erode their purchasing power and competitive devaluations and debasements among official currencies and unofficial, mostly anarchic in their essence, crypto currencies. As a notable consequence of all this, public pension systems, further impacted by the negative demographic trends registered in most of the developed countries (including Italy) will become technically unable to care for the (now) young generations, with obvious consequences on their financial security. This could cause social tensions, as future generations would feel they will need to work hard through their life to support the over-generous compensations provided to elderly people with not much remaining for them. Certainly, strikes and fights could also arise, with cross generational conflicting needs and the likely restructuring of certain public systems before it is too late. Even, social conflict and acts of terrorism could be expected, as well as regional or global wars. But eventually, as money is money, and just a means to regulate and value, transact and account, there will be a way out of this, if we take the real economy and the real asset, the real wealth and all the other intangible wellbeing elements at face value.

With regards to the ecological sustainability, the situation could become much more dangerous and go terribly wrong, undermining the very existence and survival of mankind. In fact, according to Dieter Helm,[3] we have been adding another two parts per million to the concentration of CO_2 in the atmosphere since 1990, mostly in parallel with the 26 COP (Conferences of the Parties) that happened in the meantime to discuss an action plan based on the UN 1992 Framework Convention on Climate Change. No matter what the bold statements from public and private institutions, roughly 80% of our energy demand is still met by fossil fuels. The transformation required will therefore require a lot of investment and cost a lot for taxpayers and consumers and to those who have long lived beyond their means or are just beginning to (for the new generations). Most future generations will simply need to pay for the ecological depletion caused by wasteful generations that have preceded them in the best way they can (where transformation is expensively but eventually achieved, averting an environmental disaster that could kill us all). Thinking positively – i.e. assuming a Plan B to save Planet Earth is finally agreed and executed in an effective way – we need to ensure that enough capital is provided to pursue the transformation initiatives that are just about correct and make the most polluting countries and companies pay, ensuring a geopolitical policing and strong governmental regulation and supervision of businesses. Some kind of global tax on the CO_2 produced has long been discussed, but has never really turned into something real, cross border and relevant enough to provide the capital sources needed to support the investment and, ideally, fundamentally change the decisions of corporations on whether to pursue decarbonization for real. Actually, most of the initiatives, executed more as subsidies to support good behaviours than the opposite (as in the case of the tradable "green certificates") have produced further distortions in the system, not really changing the culture or recognising the greater and more extended definition of wealth and wellbeing we all need to consider and pursue. Also, some implicit taxes, such as the higher cost of capital for most polluting public companies operated through the global asset managers and international lenders, have been easily arbitraged away through opaque private players by avoiding the green bubble of the stock markets and looking for the easy trades allowed by green flops. According to Helm, author of Net Zero, we all need to pay, as we have all lived, and keep living, beyond our ecological means, depauperating the scarce resources available from the biosphere as they are not pricing their un-renewability and negative legacy effects on future generations.

5.7   Somebody has to pay

A general outcry has followed the "green-flation" generated by rises in the cost of energy: entire sectors are being challenged by a higher cost structure that they are unable to fully reprice into their revenues. This is maybe happening not because the ecological risk adjusted new and higher price is wrong, but because end customers are unable to pay it (because of the financial burden impacting on the masses) or unwilling to do so. When private jets are used to move around rich people's pets from Asia to the US or Europe, guzzling tons of oil in the process, we can hardly argue about the high price of oil and ask for financial subsidies. For these super wealthy individuals higher and higher prices will not work and more stringent regulatory constraints should be considered. For the rest of us, higher taxes and a relevant repricing could start to have an impact and translate the new ESG Net Zero metrics into real behaviour. The challenge, we have argued, is of an anthropological nature as well. On top of taxes, we should consider information and training, and the resetting of new values, based on total sustainability and on an extended and augmented definition of wealth and wellbeing. Driving a car too much could be taxed and so should become a bad behaviour, condemned by authorities and by other people. As we are social animals, we would end up paying a higher monetary price through taxes and fines, but also a higher social one if we breach of the norms and shared values that are agreed upon by the majority of our fellow citizens. It is therefore not just a challenge for policy makers and regulators.

According to Helm, we, the polluters, do not pay and end up living consistently beyond our environmental means. If monetary (and social) top-up prices are not considered, we end up cheating ourselves (cheap energy does not mean sustainable) and, most importantly, our future generations (as they will not inherit a set of natural resources or natural assets as good as we did). The sustainability economy is therefore one where all the polluting costs are internalized and paid by producers and consumers as well, in proportion to their negative contribution and considering the long-term effects on future generations – even if they are unable to vote yet. We could for example use legally binding constraints where not even a higher pricing will work (as in the case of the private jets). The total sustainability economy is something even larger and deeper, as a concept, as it should include the financial and environmental dimensions. In a very simplified way, the richer should pay more, as they have contributed more to the polarization of financial wealth that has developed through the last decades, with the older also paying more having contributed more to the public debt/public pension imbalance. Similarly, the cohorts that have profited more from gender imbalance should contribute more, paying a higher monetary contribution and sharing a greater social responsibility to act and make amends. It is for white, old, developed country-based males to now take responsibility and share most of the pain, contributing through taxes but also with action and sharing a new idea of wealth. If, on one side, it is true that somebody has to pay for the many burdens, on the other side we are not necessarily consigned to an era of low growth or economic depression, as transformation and the many technological innovations now coming to fruition are all offering great pay offs in terms of enhanced productivity. But this higher growth and economic development need to be addressed on the basis of a different definition of wealth, comprising also of wellness, and therefore wealth-being. And avoiding what has been dubbed as "cakeism" – the generational selfishness where an egg today is better than a chicken tomorrow, or it is even better a chicken and egg today than an egg left for tomorrow. Short termism, on top of polarization, is in fact what we also need to fight, challenging well-known and widely used financial valuation approaches based on the time value of money (the Net Present Value of the investments required to leave a better biosphere for our next generation would certainly not encourage investment – but what if nobody invests and the planet becomes uninhabitable for our grand-grand-children?). The problem however is not in the modelling and the metrics in themselves (how do we challenge the Discounted Cash Flow (DCF) model that we have learnt and play every day by heart?), but in the definition of values and wealth-being goals we feed into the model to find the best way to optimize and pursue as a utilitarian, rational economic agent – but not only.

5.8   A pension fund for the next generations

An international system for a global carbon tax has long been discussed and could contribute greatly in two ways to address some of the burdens described. On one side, it could limit the supply of big CO_2 emitting products and services, as a tax applied on their suppliers, based on their enlarged scope of CO_2 emissions – from scope 1 to scope 2 – and would discourage their production and include in their pricing the negative externalities created. On the other side, making the final customers pay as well would not kill entire critical sectors in the process (ceramics, automotive and agriculture, for example) and would support the gradual shift of demand towards more sustainable ways of behaving and consuming (also including negative externalities). Informing and training the end customers through the pricing mechanism would be a first step. Pricing, for example, could be differentiated based on targeted CO_2 reduction, but also taking into consideration who is going to pay and the actual need of that product or service, given other critical needs. One option is, for example, to tax oil for the use of a multiple yacht owners which is sailing them across the ocean on their whim; another is to tax these super rich individuals for the worker that needs to drive for their job or to keep their family warm in winter. Some of these segmented pricing mechanisms are already in play. For example, if you drive alone in an oil-guzzling SUV on the motorway, you pay double in certain jurisdictions.

A global carbon tax would then contribute as a source of funding to complement the $100 Tn funds that Mark Carney has solicited (and apparently obtained, at least in principle) from the private sector, and the tax-derived funds would be used to invest in infrastructure and public good projects whose NPV would likely never be a good investment opportunity for a private investor. More importantly, part of these global and local taxes could also be used to address the other burdens described and reduce the cross generational imbalance making the future generations not just wealthier (in the most extended definition of the term) but also – crucially – more directly invested, and with a greater financial skin in the game – that is the transformation challenge towards total sustainability. Assuming the marginal carbon tax equals the changes in prices needed to encourage good decision making and the following behaviour of producers and consumers, this would imply a significant monetary in-flow as one-off but mostly as a recurring revenue through the years of the transformation journey towards Net Zero. Part of these "Net Zero" taxes could fund the public pension funds destined for our new generations, to make them sustainable on a financial and economic basis. Next generations, as current and future workers, would access the financial benefits of the public pension fund on the basis of their future contributions (based on their future salary and savings), but neutralizing the cross generational subsidization that they would need to address, given the current imbalance of defined-benefit pension funds and the increasingly negative demographic trends. In this way it would correctly incentivize future generations to contribute to GDP and productivity and hence financial wealth of the country, limiting the huge cross generational polarization of fortunes that we have accumulated.

The pool of additional funds gathered would, *de facto*, penalize the older generations more (as bigger investors in taxed companies and bigger consumers in taxed products) but they would incentivize younger people through a correct use of those funds that would be invested in the real economy. In fact, these Gen Zero, Carbon Tax financed pension funds, should be invested mostly in private markets, contributing to their re-equitization and with a clear transformation focus for any of the underlying assets towards total sustainability – the ecological one, first and foremost. And it would be fully loaded as equity, to complement (for the European Union) the Gen Zero public debt liability side that is financing the Next Generations Fund. The latter would in fact mostly pursue "public good" initiatives, whose investment is not obviously justified by their economic and financial profitability, whilst the former would strive for an economically feasible and financially profitable initiative, albeit based on a definition of a targeted wealth-being that would rebalance wealth with wellness, and short termism with the long-term view of the younger generations. These pension funds, mostly invested in real assets, would then also work as a hedge on any inflationary pressure and risk of debasement (crypto currencies, even if dominant, would eventually need to buy into the real economy and into real assets, hence investing in the same underlying system). More importantly, Next Gen, all-equity, pension funds would make the Gen Z feel more like a committed shareholder in the country, even when lacking the available financial resources to do so independently and directly through the stock-market or the democratized private equity funds that we will later discuss. These pension funds invested into private markets would make them better and more engage stakeholders as they would try to collectively and actively influence the investment strategies and the management decisions of their pension fund, to achieve a positive impact for their generation, the next ones and the future ecosystem.

5.9 Benefit corporation in private markets

The idea of pension funds fully dedicated to private markets and actively pursuing a "total sustainability" impacting investing approach may still be some years off in the minds of retail investors. However, some private equity funds targeting institutional clients are already there and an emerging wave of retail-dedicated ones are on the rise, leveraging and driving on the increased interest of individual investors (and younger ones specifically) on a stakeholders based, impact investing approach. For this approach, a benefit corporation set up may be the most well suited. In fact, private equity investment companies that are setting up as, or decide to convert into, benefit corporations are committing to act in a transparent, responsible and sustainable way – they make this commitment with regards to people, communities, territories and the environment and including cultural and social associations, entities of public interest and other relevant stakeholders. This fairly high level and comprehensive statement is consistent with the law, which defines for each relevant jurisdiction, how the company should behave (and then be monitored as such by relevant regulators). In Italy, for example, Law nr.208 of December 25th, 2015, acknowledges companies that have decided to formalize in their statutory mandate the commitment in pursuing common benefit targets, in a consistent and synergic way with the pursuit of economic goals and profitability, which are prerequisites for the realization of this commitment. On this basis, these companies are required to identify the management that is responsible for the definition and execution of such targets and are compelled to define, measure and communicate the common benefit goals pursued, and their achievements, through time and with a long-term view. As such, a broad definition of impact investing policies needs to be more clearly structured and focused on a few principles of common benefit. These principles should be supported by the company's core values and inform their investment strategies, driving them towards the wealth and wellbeing goals being pursued. Based on our analysis of the Gen Z (and Gen Alpha in the future) challenge and of the many burdens they will need to overcome to regain a total sustainability, we propose a set of core values, common benefit principles and a more granular set of objectives to benefit corporations. Based on the stakeholders' approach advocated in our previous chapters, and with the emphasis on the communities, territories, the country of origin and overall environment, our suggested guiding principles for the pursuit of a common benefit should at a minimum include:

- The creation of an enlarged and shared wealth, consistent with the definition of wealth and wellbeing given by the community of reference, that comprises of the current generations but also focused on the needs of the next ones and on their right to "total sustainability."
- The promotion and realization of value-adding solutions, with positive impacts on companies and cities, and the pursuit of a stronger real economy (more competitive companies) and more valuable real assets (more sustainable cities, more inclusive and with green infrastructure).
- The promotion of physical and psychological wellbeing for individuals and families as single entities and as social aggregates, with a greater focus on the reduction of exclusion and in the polarization of current wealth and future opportunities at an inter and cross generational level.
- The optimization in the use and deployment of the scarce resources available, to support the green transition and fight climate change, limiting physical and transition risks and the negative impacts on the other sustainability dimensions deriving from environmental change.

- Overall, from a more macro-economic perspective, the policymakers of the country would need to contribute with the necessary laws and regulations required to transform the common benefit of many groups of stakeholders into a common prosperity for the whole nation.

5.10 Sustainability in private markets investment

We have discussed how traditional financial valuation models have been mostly unable to address total sustainability targets and with a tendency to focus just on a dual, mostly dystopian, perspective:

1. Shareholders are assumed to be the "one and only" end-users of the valuation, that is mainly used to analyse and maximize their value, with more limited information also made available to debtholders. Other stakeholders are usually not considered as relevant interest parties, let alone even mentioned. Because of this, metrics such as ROE, EVA and NPV are not addressing the multifaceted dimensions of values – tangible and intangible – that may be relevant to other stakeholders but that are of little value to shareholders. All kinds of other targets can instead be considered by benefit corporations that are pursuing a stakeholders'-based approach and targeting total sustainability. For a benefit corporation it also becomes easier to consider the many interdependencies between financial targets and non-financial ones in order to optimize some of the almost inevitable trade-offs and then reflecting these in decision making and action plans.
2. Current generations are also assumed to be the only one that matters with limited interest for future generations, as any financial value that is distant enough in the future becomes irrelevant pretty soon and made irrelevant by the "time value of money." What about if DCF could be achieved by also starting from a future point of observation and going back in time to our present days, as a search of the time lost and of the better decision making that could have been analysed to pursue total sustainability? And what if all kinds of systemic interdependencies between present, future and past could have been considered in due time to leave a better present? These kinds of complementary approaches can also be more easily

considered by a benefit corporation that is looking for economic gain and non-economic impacts across generations.

A total sustainability approach, pursuing a multifaceted and intertwined set of objectives for multiple stakeholders is obviously not well served by these traditional "financial only" valuation models. For a start, they should be extended and include an enlarged definition of value – including intangibles and cutting across a longer time span. They should also include other indirect impacts caused by the invested portfolio company or real asset, across multiple value chains and include their long list of suppliers and customers, not to mention the territory and the community in which they mostly operate. They should also be designed as an *ex-ante* tool to support the strategic asset allocation and the specific investment decision of the asset management company operating as a benefit corporation and then include the management, control and reporting of the developments of such investments once made. They should define a correct set of incentives for the investment management company managers, and for the management of the portfolio companies, to drive their behaviour and strengthen their core values in full alignment towards the goal of total sustainability. Finally, they should make sure an appropriate level of information is given, in an unbiased and transparent way, to the end investors of the fund. They should have easy access to the monitoring of the multiple performances of their money, and have an opportunity to know more and "live" the equity story of transformation and conversion towards total sustainability of the companies and other real assets of which they have become owners and shareholders. Ultimately, they should feel how their "shareholder" perspective is consistently reconciled with their "stakeholder" one, with the overcoming and optimization of any inherent trade off in between. In very simple terms, a total sustainability approach to invest in private markets could include:

- A top-down selection of the sectors and territories to absolutely avoid, in order to then define the remaining investable universe. A clear justification should be given for the uninvestable universe, avoiding naïve solutions (e.g. the defence sector, because of the role of the weapons industry – could we do without defence and a way to enforce the rule of law?) and static perspectives (because it is bad, it will be forever – there is actually more value in investing in compa-

nies that need help in turning towards sustainability), not to mention manichaeistic definitions with absolute (and mostly debatable) clear cut definitions between good and bad.
- Within the investable universe, some sectors and territories may be prioritized on the basis of their larger potential for "total sustainability accretion" and on the basis of an analysis taking into consideration their critical relevance, urgency, direct and indirect effects on others and so on. Such an analysis should also be conducted in a multidimensional and multifaceted way, potentially defining a different set of stakeholders and goals for each possible investment opportunity. It is also worth noting that, if a huge "accretion" potential is possible for ESG investments, the opposite is also true. In fact, investing in already well-placed ESG companies could dilute their "total sustainability," if not at the level of the company itself (as total sustainability per euro of capital invested), at least in light of the different uses of the capital under management and given the alternative opportunities that could have been pursued.
- On a bottom up, deal by deal approach, a sustainability baseline "objective enough" should then be defined, to derive on this basis the targeted delta – the incremental total sustainability that could be attained as part of the investment proposition and pay-off, and including all the critical phases: from the underwriting and investment decision, to following the governance rules on the "sustainability compact" negotiated with the management, to the active co-management as operating partner, to the final exit – that should include a rigorous total sustainability due diligence of the future owners, to prevent all the objectives achieved being wasted.
- From a bottom up perspective, typical phases of the analysis should then include: the identification, targeting, origination, screening and selection (up to the investment decision) of the portfolio company; the engagement, goal setting and designing of the transformation plan of the invested company, along with a detailed definition of the active governance rules required to achieve total sustainability; the active management in action and actual execution of the change plan and its overall valorisation; and finally, the set up for its next phase of change and exit (as a trade sale or IPO), including the critical selection of the new owners – the best for progressing further in wealth-being creation.

5.11 Regulating sustainable investing

Assuming the simple approach described above is about right on what needs to be done to pursue a total sustainability, benefit corporation approach in investment management (specifically, in private markets), how are the current regulations supporting this desired approach and the following behaviours? In order to answer to this question, we need to briefly review the main regulations designed to support sustainable investing. We will focus on the EU's ever evolving regulatory framework, probably the leading practice globally, and then consider, *vis a vis* the optimal attributes of an ideal regulatory framework, the gaps that need to be filled, the changes that could be considered and the unintended, negative consequences that need to be anticipated and avoided at all costs – as there is a risk of good intentions resulting in even more negative outcomes and pay-offs.

As a start, a regulatory framework should inspire and incentivize the correct behaviours, without anticipating their actual feasibility too much, and to constraint and punish the wrong ones, without too many limitations that create an overall paralysis. It should also be simple to understand and communicate to the relevant parties, and sufficiently workable for them to plan, manage and control its actual application, without too many blurring of boundaries or subjective interpretations and a paraphernalia of models, tools and processes that can become so expensive it makes all the effort uneconomic, not to mention the chance of reducing any extra profitability. It should provide certainty to vague questions and flexibility to specific ones. Finally, and most importantly, it should make sure it links its principles and related developments in the real world with clearly visible and easily quantifiable benefits. It should ensure an undisputable direct link between the targeted goal, the executed action and the obtained outcome. The regulatory framework that is now at the basis of so much of the hype and interest related to sustainable finance, even if it starts with multiple good intentions, is still trying to address and qualify most of these desirable traits, but is still falling short in several respects. At a global level, the EU has consistently become a leading actor on this, as is reflected in its leading policies on sustainability. Its large ambitions have also been clearly presented in the European Commission's 2018 "Action Plan on Financing Sustainable Growth," summarizing all the measures that it intends to adopt to refocus its main capital markets towards a sustainable development model. Its targets include a greater transparency of the financial markets on ecological sustainability, the harmonization of criteria to ensure investors are better informed and incentivized to pursue sustainable investments, and the increased offering (in quantity, quality and comparability) of specific information regarding climate change, pollution, the deployment of scarce resources and any form of social discrimination. But also, they include the avoidance of "greenwashing" – the obtainment of a competitive advantage linked to the incorrect ESG branding of a financial product for commercial purposes.

At the EU level today, this framework consists of four main sets of legislation:[4]

- The NFRD – Non-Financial Reporting Directive (Directive 2014/ 95/ EU) focuses on information relating to the organization to which it applies (corporates with more than 500 employees), including information on social inclusion, moral practices and ecological impact. Specifically, article 6 of the NFDR identifies "pale green" products. These include ESG considerations on sustainability risk and how these could affect economic performance. Article 8 identifies the "light green" products that promote, among others, social and ecological characteristics but without having sustainable investments as their main target. Finally, article 9 identifies "dark green" products – they have sustainability as their key objective.
- The SFDR – Sustainable Finance Disclosure Regulation (Regulation 2019/ 2088) focuses on sustainable impacts and related risks, either linked to the organization or to its products, and it is focused and applied to the participants in financial markets and advisers. The Taxonomy Regulation has introduced in the regulatory framework the taxonomy of the economic activities which are deemed to be compatible with the ecological targets (green conversion) of the EU, given the respect of certain minimum social criteria – a detailed taxonomy is then defined and approved.
- The Taxonomy Regulation – TR (Regulation 2020/ 852) focuses on the organization and products of financial intermediaries and participants, posing quantitative targets in terms of weight (%) of taxonomy-aligned investments (and products) *vis a vis* their overall total.

- Finally, the CSRD – Corporate Sustainability Reporting Directive (still a proposal, probably starting from 2026) will be applied to large corporates, public mid-sized ones and others, requiring information on the organization and with regards to the main goals linked to ESG. Specifically, the CSRD will detail more thoroughly the targets already listed by the NFRD, extend the universe of corporations to which it will apply and consider a double perspective: "inside-out" – how sustainability factors influence performance and growth of the same organization; and "outside-in" – how the company's activities impact on society and the overall ecosystem sustainably.

The overall timeline of the implementation of these four sets of regulations started in 2021 and will be incremental and likely extend across a 5–7-year framework. Whilst large areas are still loosely defined and subject to changes in response to the feedback of the diverse stakeholders involved, it is worth considering how the current regulatory framework should develop, in order to sustain the desired behaviours and match more closely the ideal criteria set at the beginning of this paragraph.

5.12 From regulations to behaviours

Starting from a positive note, we believe the time is right for a properly designed and effectively executed regulation of sustainable investing, i.e. on investment policies and products that aim to pursue and address a "total sustainability" set of objectives, certainly including financial and economic, but also social and environmental. In fact, a wide-spread culture is already well developed in most of the largest countries globally and certainly in Europe, and a number of private initiatives in the world of finance are already well underway. The overall business case is also relevant, from an economic and larger perspective, to justify the dedication of significant political power and related resources, in order to promote regulation that supports the targeted most positive outcomes and forbids the most dangerous ones. Based on the previous discussion, the world of finance can contribute a lot to this transformation as an intermediary of lending but even more as manager of equity capital. It could do a lot by financing public companies, but even more by investing directly in private markets. However, based on our set of ideal criteria, and starting by reorganising the goodwill put into this gigantic and fairly complex effort, a number of shortcomings in the regulation still need to be fully developed and addressed. Three critical points are already the object of multiple working groups and initiatives underway, but worth summarizing and commenting on at the end of this chapter.

First, the cost of complexity and the returns from executing this. Given the many intricacies of the topic itself, a certain trial and error approach for the development of a framework comprised of multiple regulations, across sectors and jurisdictions, is obviously understandable. However, this sometimes does not help the understanding of the real drivers of the nemesis of wealth. It is difficult to communicate among practitioners and becomes an almost impossible topic for the average citizen that is also supposed to be the average investor and consumer. The burdens on policies and procedures, processes and tools, and the huge amount of reporting, is certainly contributing to the build-up of a further cost layer and of multiple compliance check points and constraints, but still with unclear pay off in terms of extra returns from these investments (apart from the access to ESG-keen pool of investors and the avoidance of fines). Not to mention that any ESG-driven effort can introduce significant operating costs, strategic and tactical constraints and also the forced waving of interesting financial opportunities would be a half-lie at least. The question, asked by so many Mifid 2 customers' surveys (required by law) regarding the preference of retail investors for sustainable investments on a *ceteris paribus* condition is logically not fully specified (preference for what? On the basis of which comparable conditions?) and almost meaningless from an execution point of view (how could we gauge that the *ceteris paribus* condition applies to future investments? We could at least argue the opposite, and limiting our investment universe is in any case reducing optionality, and putting costs and constraints is not good anyway). The first challenge is therefore to standardize and simplify by introducing objectivity and truth that may be not perfect but are good enough to be acted upon and starting from a clear statement and definition of what wealth is, for the proponent and manager of an investment, that should be compensated for their performance as measured against that target. 'his would avoid the need for a normal citizen to go through all the policies and procedures, the controlling and reporting. This extended wealth definition could be reduced to a simple scorecard, with a few dimensions (financial, social and environmental, for example), a set of 3 to 5 KPI (Key performance indicators) for each and including as much as possible the direct scope of the company (targeted directly through the economic activity) but also a few indirect ones (targeted indirectly through the activity of the portfolio companies). Key decision makers should then be rewarded on this basis, and would progress in the organization based on this simple consistency.

Second, by focusing on the good investable asset as opposed to the bad given their overall contribution to the total sustainability sought, is well meant but could lead to unintended consequences. A dichotomic world of finance would be characterized by good capital investing in a good asset and *vice versa*, with two different sub-worlds unable to communicate and interact, hence limiting the efficiency and effectiveness of the global financial system to promote and spur transformation and innovation. In fact, change can only happen in a dynamic, not static way, by using all forces of good (and some of the inevitable evil) to promote a beneficial mutation in the way we use our scarce resources, optimizing the inherent and inevitable trade-offs and avoiding Manicheism at all costs. Certain pots of good capital may be more foresighted and pursue a more holistic definition of wealth and total sustainability, but they also need profitability and economic accretion and should be rewarded on that basis as well. Otherwise, should they earn a sub-normal return on capital, not only would they be discouraged to pursue those investments but, even not considering this, mathematically they would end up becoming irrelevant in the long term, as weighed *vis a vis* the bad one. Also, investing in good, already sustainable assets is effective in sending a rewarding signal to those doing it, potentially allowing them to grow more and with more abundant and cheap sources of capital. But by not investing good capital in bad companies, we would not address the real and most urgent problems that, through change, could contribute marginally more to the achievement of total sustainability. Maybe counterintuitively, we could argue that good (equity – not debt) capital should seek bad companies first, so as to gain some relevant influence on them and contributing to switching their competitive (but un-social and un-ecological) behaviour. Finally, leaving bad assets to bad capital would open up huge almost risk-free arbitrage opportunities, with even "good" people seeking the easy and quick return first, followed by a cleansing of their soul through not-for-profit (and not-so-relevant) donations. If a lot of good capital is also competing with bad assets these arbitrage opportunities will be swept away. *Vice versa*, if bad capital is also investing in good companies (without taking control, as their sustainability stance should be ingrained in their statutory mission) this should help in propping up their valuation, hence contributing to the overall return of all kinds of retail savers investing in them.

Third, the development of so many regulations has maybe led to the proliferation of multiple acronym and terms, management fads and intellectual themes, some of them appear confusing, lose their meaning and at are risk of becoming unfashionable. In fact, a set of common values can be traced back for most of these. The CSR (Corporate Social Responsibility) theme is, for example, not dissimilar to what we now refer as B-Corp (Benefit Corporation), as a mix of the many stakeholders-based approaches which have been discussed for several decades and the new theme of "Impact Investing." Which is today that several linkages are naturally found between ESG and sustainability or, as we have dubbed it "total sustainability" and "wealth-being." In short, the contribution of these regulations could also derive in their effort to create a common ground and multiple synergies among these different approaches. They could also promote a widespread adoption linked, for example, to a statutory requirement for all kinds of companies, to make clear which kind of values they pursue and for which kind of stakeholders. And they should then promote a simple, direct way of setting up and communicating their goals to all the different counterparts involved in the life of the company. They should then report their achievement in a sufficiently objective and truthful way, and link these to the rewards and career development of its key decision makers. This third challenge is then also a mix and summary of the previous two. The first challenge to move from different regulations and metrics to diverse investment and consumption behaviours is in fact based on the simplification and clarity of the regulatory set up and supporting communication. The second challenge to support the optimal allocation of all kinds of capital in a dynamic way, to reward not only the good status achieved but also (and maybe even more importantly) its trajectory, is instead based on the consistency created among different models and approaches through multiple time horizons. The third is finally to leverage on this simplification and clarity to unify and create common ground, looking at the status but also the trajectory from multiple, stakeholders-based point of views, across extended time horizons and even generations. The ultimate target and ambition of this is nothing less than a change of paradigm in our definition and consumption of wealth, and the design of the wealth management of the future as a specific industry of the financial services sector and as an overall approach to the management of entire countries and populations at a domestic and global level.

Notes

[1] "The meaning of green," *The Economist*, January 6, 2022.

[2] "Gold standard," *The Economist*, January 6, 2022.

[3] Dieter Helm, "We are all complicit in climate change so we should all pay to fix it," *Financial Times*, January 15, 2022.

[4] For the background of this analysis, special thanks to Gentili and Partners.

6 Private Equity for Everybody

6.1 Private wealth: extended, augmented

The private wealth of our next generations will be critically driven by the multiple performances we will be able to attain in the coming decades, and not just from a financial point of view. In fact, the wealth of the future, defined by multiple dimensions and striving for a total sustainability goal, should try to promote and pursue the best transformation and innovation strategies at the level of the real assets of our economy, making every one of us – from the oldest to the youngest – a better investor, consumer and, ultimately, citizen. Therefore, the wealth of the future should be based on a wealth-being that is shared in a fair and compassionate way, while still striving for high competitiveness and productivity, and making the most of the real economy and the open societies we live in. It would pursue the public good by supporting the private maximization of sustainable wealth. In the words of Larry Fink, a new stakeholders' capitalism should be developed across the globe. It would still be "capitalism (but also) driven by mutually beneficial relationships between the shareholders and the employees, customers, suppliers and communities your company relies on to prosper."[1] This is something even Anglo-Saxon capital markets and investors are waking up to and now promoting; and well-grounded in Europe, where stakeholders' capitalism as an idea and as a practice was born and developed, long before succumbing to the excesses of the "greed is good" capitalism. For our wealth of the future, a new stakeholders' capitalism needs to develop – not as a juxtaposition to the shareholders-based version, but as its extension and augmentation of the sustainable values preached.

- It would be an extension as it should aim to reach, for the purpose of direct participation through public and private markets, the largest number of people from different geographical areas, race and genders, origins and beliefs and – crucially – from different cross generational cohorts – who would be able to democratize finance by participating as equity investors and stakeholders and by sharing a vision that is grounded in the experience of the past, the control of the key decision-making levers of the present and the long-term aspirations of humankind. In our model of "capitalism for everybody," a new model of stakeholders' capitalism becomes part of the solution, with financial intermediaries and regulated capital markets offer an easier and cheaper opportunity for citizens to become shareholders of the real economy, and also play a more direct and a larger role in influencing and pursuing their goals as stakeholders.
- It would also be an augmentation as it would need to encompass multiple values in its search for "total sustainability," as captured by benefit corporations that certainly, as in the words of Fink, are taking care of the interests of multiple counterparts, including their social and ecological, tangible and intangible dimensions – maximizing their financial wealth, but also their physical and psychological – even spiritual – wellbeing as better people. It would offer more to more people, as they are social animals and part of an *eco* (not *ego*) system. More importantly, it would offer people the opportunity to become owners of a small piece of their country and – from a cross-generational perspective – of its current and future fortunes. Being owners, with direct risk/return payoffs, should help us in feel much more in control of our destiny and our ability to influence it, driving the transformation of companies and cities towards a definition of total sustainability.

6.2   Private gains, public losses?

Financial intermediaries and regulated public markets should not only support the capital raise of innovative, competitive companies and attractive, sustainable cities looking for growth and transformation, but also make it easier for retail investors to invest a larger part of their savings into equities, not for short-term trading but for the long run.

More than public markets, a critical opportunity should then be related to private markets, including private corporates, but also real assets such as real estate and land, physical and intangible infrastructure – what our country is really all about. Private markets are also becoming a hot topic by the day, because of super-thin nominal yields on high-grade and government bonds and given the emerging inflation, with asset managers increasingly looking beyond public markets in their search for decent returns. Private markets are already sizeable at the global level, at around $8 Tn according to Schroders,[2] but their investable universe is so vast – over $150 Tn just for real estate – it makes this figure almost irrelevant. Private markets are therefore likely to represent the best available, and mostly untapped opportunity for retail investors to become interested equity investors and (almost by design) active stakeholders, promoting the re-equitization of the global economy and supporting its transformation towards total sustainability – including ESG targets and metrics – and driving new behaviours, at institutional, corporate and private levels on this basis. In fact, one of the main challenges we need to resolve is to make sure that private gains (that can be pursued by investing in private markets) do not result in public losses because of their lower level of scrutiny *vis a vis* a public markets investment strategy. An investment strategy in private markets could in fact be subject to a lower or limited enforcement of sustainability policies by huge money managers such as BlackRock, now keen to promote not just ESG investment and the reduction of CO_2 emissions produced by its invested portfolio, but also a new "stakeholders' capitalism" that could be epitomized by the benefit corporation – companies looking to optimize multiple values, including the public good, that makes our community wealthier and happier in the long run.

In our model to support the transformation of countries, private equity investing is the ideal financial and industrial (or economic) tool to drive transformation and innovation. However, it needs to be redesigned and reinterpreted on the basis of a "stakeholders' capitalism" for everybody, well-grounded in the objectives set by benefit corporations and striving to maximize total sustainability. For this we then need to discuss:

- Whether private equity, in its current and most traditional form, is actually good for basic economic performance, as defined by profitability, losses and their volatility through time. And whether its

notorious "illiquidity premium" is particularly relevant and to what extent.
- Whether private equity can actually become an agent of sustainability and inclusion for the shared creation and reinforcement of ethical values for the world of greed investors – almost an oxymoron – and ultra-high net worth individuals.
- Whether it can be truly and safely democratized in efficient and effective ways, allowing an open, easy and economic access to everybody, regardless of their current financial wealth but taking of course into consideration their basic needs and life cycle.
- Whether investment strategies and financial structures that are epitomizing a "hit and run" speculative approach can be innovated and redesigned to support long term transformation, with a truly long term, patient capital approach.
- Whether, eventually, private equity can become the leading front in the social inclusion and green conversion battles (not to mention the one against war in its traditional form), applying the same metrics used in public markets to private companies and projects and with much greater opportunities to act decisively and for a real impact – linking metrics to real decision making, action plans and behaviours – and for even better returns.

6.3 Private equity: a balanced risk/return opportunity

Private markets are becoming fashionable by the day, but mostly because of the relative (or absolute?) unattractiveness of all kinds of other assets. Private equity, that developed as an industry to address these markets, has correspondingly kept growing impressively, with greater and greater "dried powder" available for investments – and with institutional investors (endowments, pension funds, insurance companies and big family offices) investing increasingly in buy-out and opportunistic strategies – using leverage and rapid cost cutting to extract value from their invested portfolio companies and flip them, usually avoiding public markets, retail investors and ESG targets. Before going into more qualitative questions regarding the potential transformation of private equity itself to contribute more to address the Next Gen and sustainability question, it is important to quantify what the risk/return proposition of private equity has been, comparing it with the public stock markets that carry with them their liquidity premium and the high quality and government bond markets, which are bringing with them their safety premium on top of the liquidity one. To address this topic, and consider which target investors private equity could be recommended as investment strategy for a partial allocation of their portfolios, we have carried out an analysis of a basket of over 400 European private equity funds investing in corporations that started to operate between 2010–2015, and, based on a cross section analysis at the same time, we focused on their average returns which were as follows:

- Overall, these funds recorded an average yearly return equal to 18%.
- Just 40 funds lost value – these "losers" lost an average of 26% of their capital.
- The remaining 360 funds recorded average returns at around 19%, with performances of over 36% for the top quartile players.

Our analysis of their historical series, based on quarterly results and for the same basket of funds mostly investing in small–medium corporations (from 2014 to 2021), has shown an average return of around 19%, with a standard deviation of around 21% and a VaR (Value at Risk – measured on the basis of a confidence level of 97.5%) equal to just -7%. The more granular analysis of the performances across the economic cycle has also shown a good resilience during difficult times, including the pandemic's initial year (this also because of the "mark to model" approach of private equity funds in marking their NAV (Net Asset Value) on a quarterly basis. Similar results can be derived through the analysis of Italian private equities, with an average return of 15% during the same period and a standard deviation of 17.5%. With regards to real estate, we considered a basket with over 110 funds mainly invested in Europe. Also in this case, our cross-section analysis has shown results similar to the corporate funds:

- Overall, the real estate funds recorded an average return of more than 8%.
- Just 14 of them lost value, losing just 12% on average.
- The remaining had positive performances at more than 12%, with over 24% for the top quartile.

Similarly, the analysis based on the historical series of these funds, considering the quarterly reports from 2014 to 2021, has shown an average yearly return of around 11%, with a standard deviation equal to circa 13% and a VaR (calculated as above) equal to -17%. They also showed a good resilience during crisis times, with limited losses accrued during the first months of the pandemics. This is certainly a partial analysis and based on a limited, albeit recent, set of data. No matter what the many other limitations are, the overall results show how a well-diversified and long term "buy and hold" strategy in private equity is paying off and with limited absolute downsides. Losses are certainly possible, but the distribution of frequencies highly skewed towards positive performances is making up for most of them. The high granularity of the investments for each single fund is also limiting the number losing capital, with limited expected losses when it happens. They should also perform nominally better during periods of high inflation (differently from the period an-

Figure 6.1 Private equity: a statistical analysis

ANALYSIS OF PRIVATE EQUITY FUNDS Historical quarterly series 2014Q4 - 2021Q3		ANALYSIS OF REAL ESTATE FUNDS Historical quarterly series 2014Q4 - 2021Q3	
Number of European EP funds	400	Number of European RE funds	111
Average annual yield	19%	Average annual yield	11%
Standard deviation	20%	Standard deviation	13%
Annual VaR (97.5%)	−7%	Annual VaR (97.5%)	−17%
FTSE Italy Small Cap Index		FTSE EPRA/NAREIT Developed Europe	
Average annual yield	9%	Average annual yield	8%
Standard deviation	51%	Standard deviation	35%
Annual VaR (97.5%)	−35%	Annual VaR (97.5%)	−35%

FTSE MIB and 10Y BTP comparative analysis

	FTSE MIB yields 2001-2021	10Y BTP yields 2001-2021	Simulation of the loss in value of the 10Y BTP under three inflation scenarios Simulation horizon 10 years		
Average annual IRR	−2%	2%	Yield BTP 10Y	0.971%	18/11/2021
Daily VaR (97.5%)	−3%	−1%	Simulation	Inflation	Expected loss
Annual VaR (97.5%)	−47%	−18%	1st scenario	3%	−24%
Standard Deviation	23%	10%	2nd scenario	6%	−42%
			3rd scenario	9%	−55%

Source: Bloomberg

alysed) and better retain their purchasing power in real terms – exactly the opposite can be said of fixed rate bonds or money. Moreover, an even greater diversification could be attained through "multi-strategy" private equity funds, that are able to strategically allocate across debt, hybrid and equity instruments, multiple asset classes (for example, corporates, real estate and infrastructure) and strategies (growth and buy out, value added and opportunistic, green and brown field). It would also allow a more opportunist focus on the investment strategy throughout the cycle, given the long time-horizon covered and the relative inelasticity of the capital structures and overall set-ups (for closed end, callable funds the capital is committed to a given strategy and asset class and would remain "committed" but "undrawn" and therefore not put at work if that strategy or asset class becomes less attractive for periods in between.

6.4 Three ways to go private

There are potentially three ways to develop a private equity proposition. One entails raising institutional funds, mainly through closed-end structures and with strict time-limits on the use of capital. Capital is called just when the single investments are ready to be made and is returned as soon as divestments are made. Institutional investors are supposed to manage their overall strategic asset allocation and relative treasury and liquidity position and, once the tactical asset allocation is made (with capital assigned to the single counterparts), they give ample discretionary power to the single investment company selected, that is usually managing several funds at the same time, with different vintages – this is the most traditional way and how much of the industry is still managed. In this model, the only "living company" is the investment management one, putting little capital at risk and gaining the most if things go well. The investment company then manages a long list of investment funds, with limited partners that have little or no control at all on the investment management company itself but bearing nonetheless most of the risks if things go bad (whilst paying hefty fees to the investment company for its services and in case of positive returns).

A second model is relatively more innovative, with the emerging trend of "evergreen capital" – i.e. capital which is not returned to shareholders at divestments at all, or just for its capital gain and dividend stream components. This second approach could just be dedicated to institutional investors which, however, could call for stronger governance rights and have a tendency to dislike such structures as (apparently) not maximizing their overall flexibility on the treasury and in future changes in either strategic or tactical allocations. Or it could alternatively try and use retail capital indirectly, e.g. working with a discretionary mandate and an "evergreen" capital structure through the use of insurance companies, or as part of their portfolios of underwritten policies. Several traditional private equities have started acquiring in-force books (life insurance and annuities) for their permanent capital structures. These are something like the "holy grail" of private investment, according to McKinsey,[3] because of the time and effort that managers can save on each successive fundraising and the flexibility it provides to invest at times, like in a crisis, when other forms of capital can become scarce, also allowing for longer or even infinite holding periods, should there be the need or opportunity for it. But still, retail involvement would be "indirect."

There is however a third way, where retail investors can participate directly without being intermediated by a pension fund or an insurance company. This model is now emerging by capitalizing on the equitization need (a need for the economy, an opportunity for the retail investors) that requires its "retailization" because of the different potential of the capital pool directly owned by families through their financial savings. In this model, the investment management companies manage the funds through a single legal structure, allowing more direct alignment and greater participation in the governance by retail investors and with the stronger involvement required on the side of the financial intermediaries (banks, private bankers and independent financial advisors) that are acting in the asset gathering part of the value chain. In this model, the investment company and the investment vehicle often coincide – with a single legal entity that is raising capital, deploying and managing it, and developing through time as a living company (as a typical "ltd" holding company would do) – to also provide greater guarantees and opportunities for *pari passu* treatments to small investors. Because of the evergreen structure of the capital, this "third way" could include the flotation of the company in the stock-market to promote its democratization and transparency and provide an easier way-in (or out) for retail investors to participate as small owners and according to a model that *The Economist* has defined as "capitalism for everybody." Ideally, for such "integrated" investment management companies (quite similar, from a Profit & Loss and Balance Sheet perspective to an actively managed holding company), a mix of institutional and retail investors could co-invest alongside each other as typically happens for all major companies traded in regulated, international stock-markets.

A mix of institutional and retail investors participating alongside each other in the funding of an evergreen and integrated investment management company would provide several advantages with few shortcomings. On one side, the more scientific underwriting of the institutional investors would provide a further level of guarantee to the benefit of retail investors, and a continuous monitoring and active participation in the governance of the company by professional financial analysts and investors. Long term, patient capital institutional investors with an interest to invest in certain themes (e.g. green conversion) or topics (e.g. transformation of the home country) would also provide greater clarity, direction and a signalling effect for retail investors to follow. It would also help in negotiating better terms for the limited partner investors and in keeping a strict control on the operating costs of the holding company. Far from being a retail product that is offered to institutional investors, such an investment company proposition would stand as a sophisticated, well developed investment solution for an institutional that is extended to retail investors as well as an opportunity for better risk/return payoffs, diversification and as a concrete sign of democratization and greater inclusion in the world of finance. On the other side, the presence of retail investors would also be beneficial to institutional investors. It would support the scale-up of the capital being managed by the company and its proper valuation – especially if floated in the stock market. In fact, for public investment companies, having long-term institutional investors would help in reducing its short-term volatility. But liquidity could only be attained through the active participation of a large number of retail investors. And a more proper valuation (with a limited discount on its Net Asset Value, or even a premium on it) could be more easily attained because of the retail investors presence, given their greater appetite to buy stocks for its goodwill and future pattern of growth, and more limited reliance on the static NAV measure (preferred by institutions).

6.5 Are public markets worth a premium?

Public markets allow for greater scrutiny and transparency, supervision and control, hence better protection for the smaller, individual retail investors. They also allow for a quicker and inexpensive liquidation of the investment that is tradeable in very small tranches and with multiple buyers and sellers interacting, following the rules of the regulated markets and hence ensuring an optimal "price discovery." They can be profitable as well, as they can allow the pursuit of trading strategies for the short term – with no long due diligence and negotiation processes required and an easy way out should the company go bust. Overall, the theory goes, all of this allows them to hold on to a liquidity premium (or, *vice versa*, for private markets to suffer an illiquidity discount) and a certain attraction for retail investors as well, as exemplified by the high number of meme-trading strategies registered during the initial years of the pandemic. Leaving aside the all-times high valuations registered recently by stock-markets – influenced by the lax monetary policies of the last years and by the emergency measures taken by governments around the globe to support the recovery after the Covid-19 hit – the legitimate question we should consider when comparing these with private markets regards the very justification of their liquidity premium. In order to answer this, we have considered a similar quantitative analysis to the one just presented, using public market proxies to the corporate and real estate private equity basket ones.

As a proxy of the corporate private equity fund, we have considered the FTSE MIB Small Cap Index for the Italian Stock Exchange, with a very similar focus to the Italian private equity analysed. For this, the analysis of the historical series has shown an average return of around 9% (about half of the private equity funds' performance), and with a standard deviation of circa 51% and a VaR of about -35% (therefore significantly riskier). As a proxy of the real estate private equity funds, we have chosen instead the FTSE EPRA/NAREIT Developed Europe Index, with a broad range of investment strategies covered. Its performance is similar to the corporate proxy, with an average return of around 8%, a standard deviation of 35% and a VaR of -35%, based on the same level of confidence (at 97.5%). It also confirms an overall better performance of private markets, based on both returns and risk profiles. Certainly, we could pose as a counterargument that private equity investments are more rewarding because of their greater inherent risk, which is not fully captured by statistics as they are "marked to model," whilst public markets have market prices that include the vagaries of the "animal spirit" of the market. Not to mention the active trading of hedge funds and of all other kinds of arbitrageurs increasing volatility.

But what about the illiquidity discount that we should price-in as well? There is illiquidity in getting them invested, given the time required to deploy capital, by originating, negotiating and then closing 10–15 deals that are typically required by a fund to get fully invested. And there is illiquidity in getting them divested, as the investors would need to wait for the liquidation of the fund – usually happening gradually after a 5–10-year period. With earlier exits allowed only via bilateral transactions, where the counterparts that need to sell usually start negotiating from a 20% discount basis. We will later discuss how the illiquidity of private equity can be limited and how different legal and financial structures could make them traded in regulated stock markets, making private equity "public" and with the possibility of early exits at much lower discounts or on a par (or even with premium, given certain characteristics – such as the inclusion of the asset management component with the asset managed one and the proper balance of the supply and demand of the shares traded in the market). A large share of public, regulated and highly liquid markets are however also made up by so called "risk free" investable assets, e.g. government bonds that are issued and guaranteed by the state, and therefore usually backed by its ultimate power to extract taxes from domestic citizens and assets, and to print money to pay out that bonds (inflating its way out of debts). Similar to this "risk free" assets there are also quality bonds with issuers characterized by high credit ratings. Should we then consider, for this kind of public market, a very different conclusion *vis a vis* what we just discussed for the equity stock markets? Given their very limited solvency risk as most of their volatility is in fact coming from performance risk, i.e. the risk that their fixed rate coupon will become less competitive, given changes in the level of interest rates in the economy and in the inflation rate. Inflation, more specifically, could eat out a significant portion of the purchasing power attached to a very solid and high quality (from a solvency perspective) debt instrument. For this, we have analysed the historical series of the BTP (the Italian, fixed rate, government bond, with a duration of ten years, similar to the one of private equity funds) from 2001 to 2021. Its

VaR is circa 18% with very limited average returns (less than 4% in the last 20 years, a little more than 1% in the last three).

More importantly, whilst the inflation risk would be well covered by the repricing capacity of the real economy (corporations) and of real assets (real estate and infrastructure), a fixed rate, long term government or high-quality bond would not. As an example, an average inflation rate of around 3% in the next 10 years would reduce the purchasing power of BTP by around 25%, and an inflation rate of 6% would reduce this more than 40%, and a 9% inflation by more than 55%. Finally, we also considered aggregated portfolio analysis, by composing public market indexes and government bonds, or even including private equity benchmarks, with strategies focused on the real economy (corporations) and real assets (real estate and infrastructure). Overall a well-structured mix of a robust private equity exposure on real economy and real assets, a more reduced one on equity public markets exposure and with a limited one in government bonds, showed significant reduction in the overall riskiness, due to diversification effects and their imperfectly correlated performances, and much better average returns, with a much stronger purchasing power hedging capacity in case of future inflation (something that was not obviously incorporated in the analysis of the last 20 years).

6.6   Private equity: barbarians at the gate?

If private equity, and its investment strategies covering the wider range of private markets – from corporations to real estate and infrastructure – is potentially of interest to institutional and retail investors from a risk/return optimization point of view, and useful in promoting the transformation and innovation that countries (such as Italy) strongly require, the same could not be said for the underlying assets it will invest in. In fact, private equity funds have long been described as grasshoppers – as epitomized in the famous investigative 1989 book by Bryan Burrough and John Helyar "Barbarian at the Gates." Buy-out private equities usually take over stable and healthy companies, loading them up with debts using their good assets as collateral. They then proceed in rapid and uncompassionate cost cutting, striving to maximize their EBITDA (Earnings Before Interests and Taxes) in 3–4 years maximum and then flip them to other funds or to a trade buyer on the basis of a sale price that, being usually based on a multiple of the end-year EBITDA, ensures a CoC (Capital on Capital) multiplication of (monetary value) that is usually in the range of 2–4 times bigger, hence guarantying an IRR (Internal Rate of Returns) that are, based on the different strategies pursued, usually positioned at around 15–25%. These returns make the limited partners happy and keen to invest more, and the general partners (the partners of the private equity fund) even happier, as they get a cut of the overall return, usually equal to 20% of the extra return ("carried interest") obtained on top of a given hurdle rate (around 8% for closed funds), and with "catch up" mechanisms (e.g. 80% to general partners of the extra profits generated after a given hurdle rate is achieved, until they get the 20% share mentioned above). The carried interest then comes on top of management fees, set at around 2% of the committed capital (and then of the deployed capital, until the single portfolio companies are divested). The interesting and potentially very rewarding part occurs at the level of the investment management company (the "AIFM" – Alternative Investment Fund Manager"), where the general partners acquire the fixed fees and the performance fees as carried interest. Whilst at the level of the "AIF" (Alternative Investment Fund), the overall capital – usually just from institutional sources – there will be gains but it will also bear the brunt of potential losses, net of the management fees and of the carried interest.

Given the strong alignment of incentives (when the general partners are also asked to co-invest a significant share of their wealth, as usually happens) the model works well in terms of financial value creation, but problems can arise after the exit or, in the case of multiple "flips" between private equity funds, when a company goes through multiple rounds of private equity, ending up with lots of debt and little investment in R&D and on its intangibles for the future as they would not optimize EBITDA. This is certainly a risk of private equity, but a greater clarity needs to be considered. First, different private equity funds pursue different strategies, from "buy out" (buying from the entrepreneur and typically in a highly leveraged way") to "growth" (investing capital in the company, without necessarily requiring a "drag along/ tag along" contractual clause – the entrepreneur, if still shareholder of the company has the right, but also the obligation, to co-sell when the fund does it). And different entry and exit strategies can also make a difference. Funds can pursue "secondary" deals (e.g. buying from or selling to other private equity) or just avoid them, seeking capital increases to support the entrepreneur and then promoting the IPO of the private company they have invested in, usually taking a longer time horizon to fully exit the portfolio company to support its development as "public company," free floating on regulated stock markets and with an independent governance and board. Of greater interest to our discussion, private equity players, once representing the very essence of the inner sanctum, with their secrecy, accessibility to very few "big money" investors and "greed is good" culture, are also opening up to transparency and democratization, ESG targets and stakeholders' approaches and an increasing focus on "making good" whilst performing well or even better. Almost an antithesis of their founders' approach as symbols of the capitalism on steroids of the Anglo-Saxon economies of the last half century, they could become the game changer in the active rebuilding of the economy and societies, based on a different and more holistic definition of private wealth – something that is not purely economically rewarding for the winners Pursuing a total sustainability philosophy and quantitative objectives such as social inclusion and green conversion is certainly something very difficult and new, requiring new governance and financial structures, models and approaches and – more importantly – the pragmatic translation of intangible ambitions into tangible actions: moving from the new theoretical metrics to new real behaviours. For this, in the coming paragraph, we will discuss all these key points in turn, and the implications of these challenges for the successful definition and realization of a private equity for everybody.

6.7   Private equity for everybody

In our view, the best recipe for a private equity that invests in the private markets of a country to support its total sustainability conversion would be one where "growth capital" (through a balanced mix of majorities and minorities investments) is pursued, with a more patient approach (in terms of holding period, even 5–10 years instead of the customary 3–4) and with a capital structure ideally backed by "permanent capital" (e.g. a private equity fund that has a duration of the capital raised of more than 25–30 years, which is typically the tipping point where the NPVs of these years and the remaining infinite ones do not make a real differences anymore). It should also consider, as remarked in our previous statistical analysis, an investment approach that encompasses a plurality of investable assets, from the real economy (where, in the case of Italy, around 80% of the investable value lies) to real assets (where likely 80–85% of the potential investable base is) and based on well-defined investment themes. A few investment themes, such as "digital transformation of manufacturing companies" or "ESG/ green conversion of utility corporates," can then be composed and complemented into a well-rounded investment strategy that highlight where the investment opportunities should lie. They should also highlight the best approach to manage the companies and projects invested, supporting their transformation on the basis of the strategies highlighted in the investment themes and progressively reaching out their performance targets.

But well thought exit strategies would also be crucial, not just to realize financial value, but also to avoid a well-executed and better managed investment striving for total sustainability being mis-sold to some revenant "barbarian at the gate" – seeking a financial trade and a financial gain and not much else. It follows, in our view, that the best investment strategy consistent with total sustainability and a new definition of wealth would avoid flipping the portfolio companies between private equity funds (or even between different funds managed by the same investment company, with the many conflicts of interest that could arise). A private equity proposition based on "evergreen capital" and where the management component (the AIFM) is comprised in the same legal entity along with the managed one (the AIF) would not have such stringent constraints in the time horizon and would better seek the monetization of the company through its IPO and its future trading as a true public company.

This would reinforce the anaemic capitalization of Italian companies on *Borsa Italiana*, for example, and increase the universe of investable equity assets that institutional and retail investors could consider for their pot of allocated capital, as most are still constrained by the "tradability/ liquidity" requirements. It would also be easier for these "public" investment companies to raise further capital on the stock exchange and in turn benefit from financial, commercial and reputational synergies. This could be true for corporations, but the same could also be done, via dedicated investment vehicles, for real estate and infrastructure projects pursuing "core," "core plus" (developed building, offering a rent) but also "value add" (developed building that needs refurbishment – with Grade

A, safety Standards, Leed/Net Zero certifications, adjunct real services to complement the property proposition) and even "opportunistic" initiatives (green field and brown field urban regeneration and development projects). Traded investment companies with a focus on private assets could also pursue mixed strategies, with investment focused or crossing between the real economy and real assets worlds. If private markets can be made liquid, with a private equity proposition as the lead and anchor investor that support their transformation, innovation and everything else, they need to become listed on the stock market. This can also be true for private equity companies themselves, as they are increasingly approaching stock markets to monetize their investment management companies, closed end funds and permanent capital more, and through increasingly innovative capital structures and related governance structures. In fact, we can distinguish three strategies to make private equity liquid and therefore more truly "for everybody" – as the illiquidity risk is reduced they become even more investable for retail investors and, as they can be traded also through small tickets (from € 1K, for example), they become accessible to informed investors that may be long on financial culture but fairly short on money to invest (this could be the case for many Gen Zero and Alpha digital natives and financially savvy young students.)

On one side, the biggest private equity investment managers such as Blackstone, Apollo, KKR, Carlyle, EQT and more recently TPG, Bridgepoint and potentially CVC, have already floated the AIFM on the basis of its asset under management and (mostly) its management fees (the performance fees linked to the carried interest structure are usually left to the management team, because of their inherent unpredictability and high volatility that would be penalized by the stock market). As the AIFM are commission-based businesses, highly stable and with limited capital employed, they tend to be traded at huge premiums, with multipliers of the EBITDA that are typical of the asset management sector.[4] On the other side, the AIF can be floated, usually at a discount, leaving the investment management company independent and private (and hence usually secretive about the carried interest structure and internal governance). In this case, quotes of the funds would be floated, and not shares, as in the case of an investment management company. Still, as in typical real estate and infrastructure private equity deals, such funds would allow retail investors to trade easily and freely on the stock market, and hence get an exposure to risk/return profiles that would be for them otherwise unattainable or very costly, but with a number of information asymmetries and potential value migrations between the AIF and the AIFM at their own peril.

6.8 Private equity "all-in-one"

Based on the first model, when the AIFM goes public it would share its management fee structure in full and a portion of the performance fees. In a way, it would allow retail investors to participate in a financial intermediary operating in the alternative asset management space, whilst they would not invest directly in the funds (the real capital put at work into private markets). Innovation would therefore be limited, as limits on the opportunity of private equity and private markets available to everybody. On the other side, if the AIF goes public, usually sharing the risk/return profile of limited investors, it will not create the transparency and optimal alignment of interests that can be reached when retail investors have direct stakes in the investment management company, ideally through a company that is listed and easily tradeable in the stock market. The AIFM would retain the brain, as well, and the equity brand value, thus limiting the upside potential coming from the build-up of goodwill (hence justifying a discount, rather than a premium, as typically registered for real asset funds). As stated, there is however a third way that can optimally allow investment in both the AIFM and the AIF, when both are part of the same company, as in the case of a "self-managed" AIF. This is easier for AIF with evergreen capital, as a "self-managed" closed-end fund would need to hire people and build an organizational structure destined to be liquidated with the time-limited fund itself. Most of the holding structures are in fact very similar to a self-managed AIF with evergreen capital, with a more flexible approach to define the best investment strategies and holding periods (evergreen capital structures are in fact better at supporting multi-strategy AIF).

They are typically born with a mix of institutional and retail shareholders (and not just institutional), to optimize capital raising capacity but also overall liquidity (for, everyday liquidity can be better achieved with a multitude of retail investors, but the deepness of that liquidity, and the overall stability of the capital structure is better pursued with a core of institutional shareholders that are "long only" patient capital). Also, the evergreen capital structure if almost a prerequisite for listed companies (fixed time funds, with forced liquidation period, are more difficult to trade and can get less synergies from the IPO process, as the equity story would need to be re-built for each new fund and a different brand name). A private equity "all-in-one" structure, with the AIF and AIFM included in the same and only company would then provide the best option given the aim of supporting the transformation and innovation of the country, with the goal of total sustainability and with a very long-term view. It could also become more competitive from both the funds and uses side. It would optimize the capital raising capacity, particularly so when the "all-in-one" company (fully regulated from a financial services perspective) is traded on the stock market – more transparent, liquid, subject to the scrutiny of public markets and easily investable for institutional and retail investors alike. Any new capital raise would not constitute a new fund, but a contribution to the same pot of capital managed, as happens for a Ltd company. It would also optimize the capital deployment capacity, as the shares of the traded company could be used in certain jurisdictions and given other regulatory constraints, as a means to investment through shares swap (as in the case of SPAC – Special Purpose Acquisition Companies) and allow greater flexibility in the choice of investment horizons and exit strategies and a lower cost of capital overall (being liquid, the premium paid for the illiquidity should be mostly eliminated). It could also become more easily well known to the large audience, given the notoriety achieved through the stock market. Eventually, it could also command a premium, or a more limited discount, as the "all-in-one" would include the equity brand based investment management company and the fund itself. It would offer a share of a regulated company and not of a fund. It would build a brand for retail investors and recognized by consumers as well. It would ensure a better continuity in the overall equity story, made up of the track record of the investment team, but also by the technology, processes and procedures, culture and the value of the company – including the portfolio companies, with an enlarged view of the company as a group and a strong commonality on the end pursued.

6.9 Retailization of finance

An evergreen-capital based, stock-market traded, self-managed, all-in-one investment company specializing in private markets through a mix of investment strategies could better support the equitization challenge of many countries, following the long series of Black Swans that have contributed to the financial burdens and hyper-leverage already discussed. Also, given its potential nature as "retail" (i.e. not reserved to institutional investors only), and being open to the ownership of families and private citizens (participating as investors either indirectly – through their pension funds and life insurance companies; or directly – through the intermediation and financial advice of banks and other financial intermediaries), such a structure could be an ideal mechanism to promote an "equitization through retailization." A retailization of finance would mean that private equity investments made in private markets would become increasingly open to citizens, contributing towards the creation of a "capitalism for everybody." This would also be critical for the pursuit of the other targets of a "total sustainability" proposition. With most citizens involved as owner of the investment company and therefore shareholders in the real economy and real assets of their country, it would be easier to develop an investment proposition based on ESG principles and on the mission and core values of the same company as a benefit corporation. With a increasing number of shareholders, no matter what their individual weight but with good enough "skin in the game," a stakeholder's approach would become more easily consistent with the overall targets of profitability and economic value creation of the "for profit" investment company. An army of shareholding citizens would then vote with their feet, deciding which investment vehicle to invest in, given its specific investment policy being pursued and the impact on all the sustainability dimensions. Having long term, mission related institutional investors would also contribute to make the overall proposition more professional, robust and safer, given their signalling effects.

Retailization is eventually the way to go, for the future of private equity and private markets, because of its mostly untapped potential (in terms of asset gathering and management) and the risk/return optimization opportunities it can offer to families and individuals of all generations and financial status, provided that a proper strategic asset allocation is done with the help of a financial advisor. Far from being an exclusive opportunity for UHNWI and private clients, it can now be promoted to mass affluent clients as well. According to Leon Volchyok, managing director at Blackstone,[5] we are today in the early stages of mass affluent investor participation, but with a huge way to go. Retail investors in the USA usually invest minimally in alternative funds, versus a 26% of pension funds and 51% in endowments. In Europe, and Italy specifically, even the share of institutional investors exposure to alternative investments (i.e. private equity investments in private markets) is a fraction of that, falling often below 10–20% for endowments and at less than 5–10% for pension funds. Retail exposure is then almost non-existent, notwithstanding the recent promotion of fiscal incentives and a greater focus paid on the financial education of savers at large. Eventually, with the development of evergreen-capital based, stock-market traded, self-managed, all-in-one investment company that can offer minimum investment tickets as low as € 1,000, the "equitization by retailization" opportunity could be extended to mass market clients as well, following the independent advice of financial advisors (whether high touch or high tech) and the sacred principles of diversification (a €1K bet on a well-diversified investment companies pursuing different strategies in private markets could represent a 5% exposure for a portfolio of €20K, with the remaining savings held in government bonds, liquidity and other money market instruments). What's more, having even a small amount of savings invested into a real asset would provide a strong defence against inflation and an alternative way to get exposure to the equity market without the burden related to the selection, monitoring and active management of a number of bets on SME and real estate assets.

6.10 Is private equity good for stakeholders?

A publicly traded "all-in-one" private equity, targeting both institutional and retail investors, with a multi strategy approach that is targeting corporations, but also real estate and other infrastructural assets, could be a good way to promote a "capitalism for everybody" that closely reconciles the interest of share and stakeholders. If the idea is to provide an easily investable, actively managed, proxy of the wealth of a given country, then such a multi-strategy structure would also happen to include other relevant dimensions of the real economy and assets of that country. The

Figure 6.2 Equity and private markets: towards a retailization

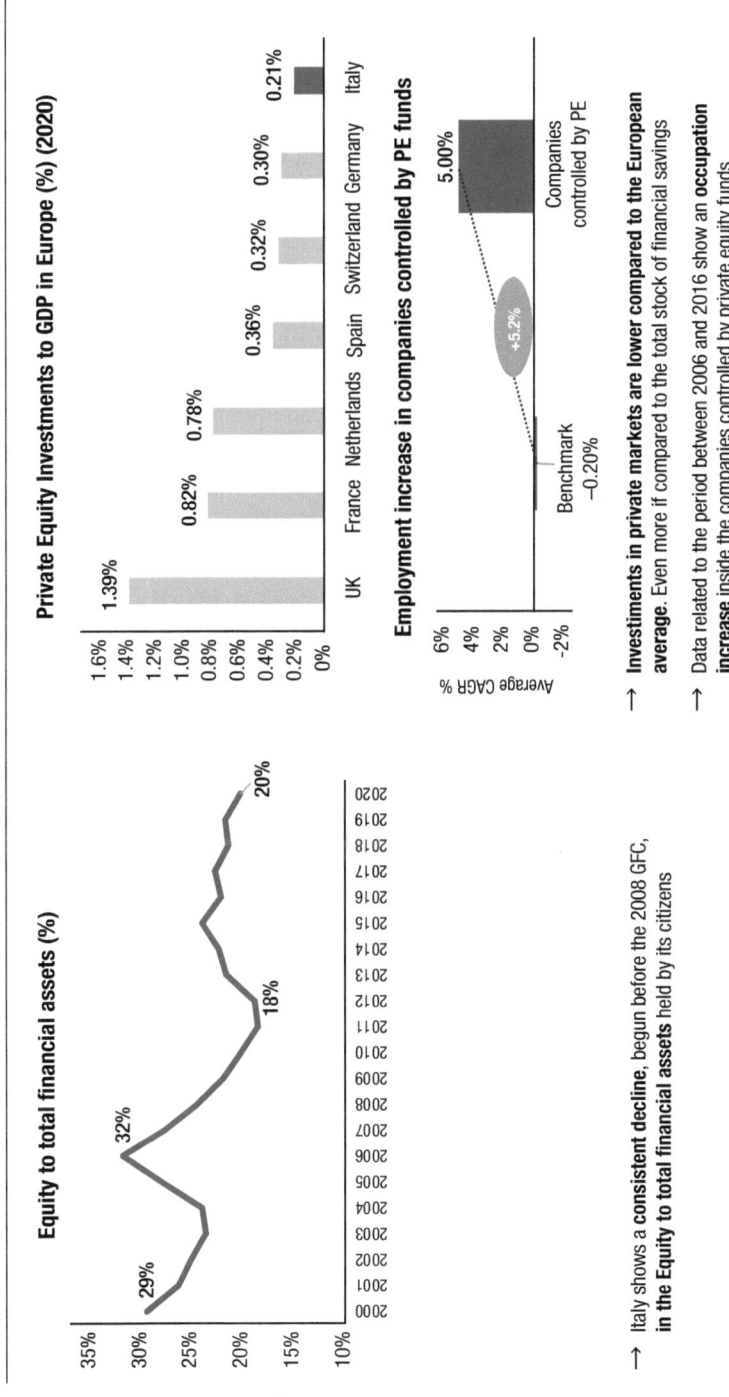

Sources: Eurostat; AIFI

whole investable universe would in fact be a multiple of the investable universe of public corporations (for Italy a rough estimate puts stock market traded SME at around €750 Mn, with private business at around €3 Tn and a real estate stock at around €8 Tn, plus the stock of physical and intangible infrastructure). A structure comprising of different asset classes and investment strategies would also reduce the overall intrinsic risk of any private market bet because of the higher overall diversification effect. If it is true that a limited focalization can imply a less effective approach in investment management, synergies could however be attained if the focus is played at the level of the local value chain and territories of a given country, where competitive corporations contribute to attractive cities and *vice versa*. The overall argument on the potential holding discount that is frequently created by investment companies pursuing diversified bets is also missing a critical point: the entire universe of the private equity funds is also, *de facto*, very similar to a well-diversified holding company. They add real value when they are good at selecting the right investments, in managing them well and exiting them successfully – and they realize the full value produced in due time, as they monetize on their investment cycle. Holding companies should not be any different, if they are designed, structured and managed as private equity ones and not as power-broker plays. In fact, a steady stream of over performances *vis a vis* the stock-market could justify a premium on the same holding by recognising this as an "alpha platform" that is able to consistently beat the market in an uncorrelated way, hence turning new capital raises into higher and higher NAV over time.

Being a diversified investment management company also has further advantages. In fact, for the pursuit of a stakeholders driven, total sustainability approach, the integration of the analysis perspectives of SME, real estate and infrastructure assets become increasingly relevant and *vice versa* – thus justifying positive synergies and therefore a potential premium. In the case of investment companies that are also benefit corporations, the wider view of the main real asset classes and related constituencies can also become a central element of the strategic direction pursued and create a focus on the "impact investing" theme. Even assuming private equity is good for institutional and retail investors alike, and even more so if it is pursued through innovative structures based on evergreen capital, flexible strategies that are multi-asset and cover a wider range of real assets, the question still remains when applied to invested companies. Is, in fact, a private equity shareholder bringing value to the many stakeholders a company or an entire city may have? And would a private equity with an "all-in-one" set up provide a better match as a financial investor and as an operating partner? Or is the grasshopper theory really true, with financial, limited partner investors extracting value from the underlying investments, with a few general partners becoming tremendously rich in the process to the detriment of all the other stakeholders?

6.11 Green is good

The Gordon Gekko of the private equity in the future could well say how "green (as opposed to greed) is good." It is certainly good for the planet and its inhabitants and it should become so even for the investors that bet their capital under management on ESG companies and projects, or invest and try to turn around those that are less so. In turn, it should become good for consumers and citizens as well. In short, if total sustainability is good and actually required for the survival and development of humankind, private equity can be a great force for good, if it raises money from the right counterpart, through the best governance and financial structures and pursuing a better and more comprehensive definition of private (and as a consequence also public) wealth. Not only will private equity be huge as total capital raised, particularly if it can start seriously tapping into the pockets of retail savers. But it can have a much greater investable universe in the (real) economy as earlier exemplified for Italy. Not only that. Private equity, having a sizeable stake in the invested companies as majority or very well qualified minority, could have a much greater say in the governance and future strategies towards total sustainability. Given the increasing role played by private equity players as "operating partners," i.e. contributing their managerial expertise on subjects ranging from finance to IT, from cost management to marketing and sales, they could also have a much greater role in supporting companies in the transformation journey, not just as a supplier of capital and the decision maker, but as factual and decisive agents of change, sharing the international best practices in social inclusion and green conversion across portfolio companies.

Maybe counterintuitively, recent studies have for example shown how private equity may in fact reduce gender pay gaps in their portfolio companies.[6] This may be because of the more accelerated growth in the business and revenues they usually bring along with capital. And it may partly occur because of the rigorous cost management and cutting they usually apply to newly invested companies – hence levelling down average salary and reducing the outliers. It could also be explained by their more economically rational – and less biased – approach to productivity maximization of the labour force. There is also a more virtuous explanation and an inherent ambition: as more and more private equity players and decision makers become converted to total sustainability, the social inclusion and the fair treatment of all internal and external stakeholders will also become an increasingly relevant target, through investment and the following active management decisions. This conversation will off course be driven by the greater demand for corporate responsibility exercised by institutional investors as they start preferring private equity players with a strong ESG rating and, ideally, be set up as benefit corporations. This greater demand will make capital more abundant and cheaper for the converted Gekkos and would imply as a consequence an even greater transparency and ESG-based accountability.

The institutional investors' role in driving this shift should therefore not be underestimated. However, an even greater role would be played if private equity, developed as an open opportunity for everybody – easily accessible and with small tickets of "all in one" investment companies that are traded on stock-markets – would become increasingly invested by everyday retail people, including the new generations and the cohorts of the stakeholders that have been usually overlooked by "capitalism on steroids" private equity finance – women and ethnic minorities, for example, and the large numbers of affluent and mass market people. Not only should they be more sensitive towards the goal of total sustainability, but also part of the active definition of what this should really mean for them as relevant a part of the benefit corporation proposition and voters of modern and vibrant democracies. Not only that, as the real challenge, and potential greater outcome, will still remain linked to the end behaviour of people as consumers and citizens. Well intentioned, "green is good" private equity players, inspired and supported by sustainability sensitive investors, would promote real economy companies and real assets that are keen to promote the sustainable behaviours of the consumers they are trying to reach with their offer, leading the way to transform the metrics that inform their internal decision making into real behaviours

– when we decide what to eat and wear, how to travel and where to live. This transformation will be driven by the offering set up and by pricing decisions. It will also be driven by a mix of communication and marketing, information and training, and by emerging role models that should live like the key decision makers in private equity "walking the talk."

6.12 Ant or grasshoppers?

Are we ants or grasshoppers? The answer to this question should be objective enough, and grounded in hard data, but also more clearly linked to the definition of the wealth-being that for us is worth pursuing. In fact, from a purely financial perspective, the world has behaved as if it were dominated by ants, with diverse forces – including older generation preparing for retirement, oil-exporting countries accumulating sovereign wealth funds, cash-rich big digital and other high-tech companies – helping to generate a stock of money that is mostly sitting idle and not used for consumption. This "saving glut" has kept growing, going from $160 Tn to $510 in the years between 2000 and 2020.[7] Financial savings can remain parked in current accounts or become invested into liquid stock markets. But they are more rarely used for private equity investments in private markets, particularly for the retail savings part. This is not only translating, on the basis of the risk/return analysis previously discussed, into lower returns for the investors, but also in lower growth rates in GDP, where the main productivity gains are expected to be. The opportunity is then to pursue a greater deployment of that idle capital into more productive uses that can secure higher IRR (for the investor) and higher growth rates (for the economy). However, it remains to be seen whether we have behaved as ants with regards to the other many intangibles that are making up our ecosystem and represents the core of values that really matter to our stakeholders. From this perspective, we have not been saving enough truly scarce resources, such as the quality environment or the balancing of the society – behaving as grasshoppers on ESG targets to then play an ant on the purely financial side. This paradox is more evident, and likely promoted, by the huge polarization of fortunes, where a few super-rich people detain most of the financial wealth, and hence behave like a financial ant, as they simply cannot spend enough to avoid a rapid accumulation of financial savings and also overspend on non-renewable resources because the price mechanism expressed by the market is not able to fully capture the negative externality created, or it results in prices that – no matter how high they are – are irrelevant to them. In order to resolve this imbalance, the challenge for private equity is to invest greater shares of the accumulated savings that are owned by the majority of people and not just by the super-rich. Ideally, we should all become more grasshopper-like on the financial side – putting more of our money into private markets and as equity at work – and more ant-like on the other dimension of sustainability, preserving more for the winter to come. The social and ecological dimensions should be of greater interest to the "remaining 99%" that cannot afford to buy everything they want no matter what the cost and would face more directly the negative externalities created. The same should ring even more true for the next generations, which do not have much to save on the financial dimension anyway, and plenty to lose on the side of social and environmental sustainability, and in the scarce resources of the world destined to them.

6.13   Rollercoasting… and long Covid

We all leave in time and space, and our existence, thoughts and actions, or the lack of them, are strongly influenced by the context we live in. We may call it destiny or providence, nemesis or serendipity but ultimately our ideas are relative to our times, and our behaviours are driven by the economy and society of the country in which we raise a family, develop a career, make a living, whilst saving enough for our retirement and to ensure some basic welfare for our children. Nonetheless, we have argued, there are certain core values and corresponding emotions and passions that can transcend the strict time/space dimension that we experience during our lifetime. As we save capital, other assets and durable goods that we can transfer to our future generations, we are also able to live by values that were taught to us by our parents and grandparents, and that we may be able to pass on to our children. We have also argued that no matter what the relative dependency and subjectivity of certain targets or objects, we should always rely on truths that are objective enough to be serviceable. We may use them as invariances that are good enough to make sense of prolonged periods of time, such as economic cycles or a generation or two. Let us consider for example the objective enough truth of the state of the markets after the global financial crisis (2008–2010) and, more specifically, after the Covid-19 pandemic (2020–2022). A state of the market dominated by rollercoasting and long Covid.

On one side, we may find "rollercoasting" markets, dominated by high volatility but still mostly going upward that could support an argument for a world that, on a nominal, purely financial basis, has never been so rich. On the equity side, we can observe price/earnings cyclically adjusted at around 40, according to Robert Schiller of Yale University at the beginning of 2022, with most international stock markets at historical highs. On the debt side, correspondingly, we can point to extra returns for owning high-risk bonds at their lowest value, no matter what level the emerging rises in interest rates planned by Central Banks to fight an already high inflation will be. Even if a distinct chance of financial markets crashing as a result of these factors[8] is considered by global investors, the overall financial system looks today much better capitalized and regulated than after the global financial crisis[9] and therefore able to absorb the potential shock generated by overpriced assets that have been inflated by very aggressive quantitative easing policies. On the other side, we can observe a "long Covid," with a global economy that is just recovering from a couple of years dominated by ill health and social and economic disaster, with economic activity contracting in 2020 in 90% of the world's countries, a much higher proportion than those hit by the two world wars, the great depression and the global financial crisis. This is coupled by global supply chain disruption causing inefficiencies and disruption in real output and relative prices, and by a wave of almost inevitable debt restructuring that could be prolonged and messy, particularly for the poorest countries and populations. The average total debt burden of low- and middle-income countries grew by 9% in 2020. More than half are now at risk of financial distress. With growing polarization and an increase in the number of people living in extreme poor conditions (+80 Mn in 2020, the largest increase of the last three decades[10]), not to mention the further damage caused to the planet and biosphere and the looming risk of some geopolitically motivated regional or global wars. Whatever the future and the ups and downs of the "rollercoasting" and "long Covid" scenarios, the question we have posed at the beginning is whether we can analyse and address these and other challenges with the same definition and theories of wealth management that have dominated modern and contemporary approaches to economics and finance, or whether we just have to think of something new. We believe in the latter: starting from an extended and augmented definition of wealth and a corresponding theory – good for modelling and planning, managing and controlling what we plan to achieve, and sustaining a case for the great changes we need to overcome but also serviceable enough to drive concrete actions.

This new definition of wealth and wealth management is now not only long overdue, but also utterly urgent. Given the high inflation experienced, the equitization needed to rebuild economies that were brutally hit by the financial crisis, the pandemics, the geopolitical tensions and regional wars, and the globalization decoupling and supply chain disruption to come, we need these new definitions and corresponding approaches to drive and inform the long wave of private equity opportunities that we all expect. Traditional asset managers are now all racing to expand offerings in alternative investments to boost profitability and address pent up demand.[11] Globally, more than a dozen are already managing at least $100 Bn in alternative assets in 2021, including the likes of Black Rock, Invesco and PGIM. Some are buying up existing private equity platforms, signalling how private markets are becoming central to their growth strategy. According to a Prequin survey, over 80% of institutional investors want to now invest more in private equity in the coming years. And an increased wave of interest from wealthy retail clients – and not only them – looking for stable and higher long-term returns is widely expected. Their pent-up demand will grow louder as inflation becomes entrenched in the economy, whilst public markets in equities and bonds remain volatile. Globally, alternatives assets topped $15 Tn and around 15% of the total assets under management in 2021. They are expected to rise to $22 Tn and 16% by 2025.[12] As a consequence, they already account for 42% of the industry's revenues according to BCG, rising to 46% by 2025. It represents a huge opportunity that would be a critical miss for any professional asset manager or country. Something to reckon with and address in time, but with a new wealth management model of the future – to ensure first of all wealth management – and countries – have a future after all.

Notes

1 Harriet Agnew, "BlackRock's Fink rejects accusations of being 'woke'," *Financial Times*, January 17, 2022.
2 Katie Martin, "Private markets are a hot topic for 2022," *Financial Times*, January 14, 2022.
3 Ramnath Blasubramanian, Alex D'Amico, "Why private equity sees life and annuities as an enticing form of permanent capital," *McKinsey Quarterly*, February 2, 2022.
4 Antoine Gara, "TPG's IPO cement fee shift for private equity firms going public," *Financial Times*, January 13, 2020.
5 Leon Volchyok, *The Retailization of Private Markets*, ALFI, 2021.
6 Pilita Clark, "Private equity's strange effect on workplace inequality," *Financial Times*, January 15, 2022.
7 "Why the world is saving too much money for its own good," *The Economist*, February 5, 2022.
8 "When the ride ends," *The Economist*, February 12, 2022.
9 "What goes up," *The Economist*, February 12, 2022.
10 Martin Wolf, "The looming threat of long financial Covid," *Financial Times*, February 15, 2020.
11 Brooke Masters, "Fund houses buy up "alts" specialists to move beyond equities and bonds," *Financial Times*, March 20, 2022.
12 Boston Consulting Group, *Global Asset Management 2021: The $100 Trillion Machine*, 2021.

7 HOPE: A Case for Change*

7.1 The serendipity of HOPE

We started thinking of HOPE in the aftermath of the first wave of the Covid 19 pandemics and during the first lock-down, whilst analysing and forecasting the potential economic and social disruption these events brought to Italy. The serendipity of HOPE as an idea was likely the reaction to a dramatic crisis due to an exogenous factor (the virus) but which was actually aiming (even if, initially, almost unconsciously) to address some of the most structural endogenous weaknesses of the Italian economy. This is characterized by high public debt, low growth and productivity and an embryonic development of its stock markets and domestic alternative asset management industry. In fact, the scope and the ambition of HOPE developed further, to include a full rethinking of the concept of wealth being pursued as sustainability targets were included in the analysis and a stakeholders-based approach was considered as a critical component for the project's design and its successful development into a proper alternative investment management company. In fact, HOPE (an acronym, which stands for HOlding di Partecipazioni Economiche) started as an idea of creating a kind of "private" Sovereign Wealth Fund (SWF) for Italy. A provocative oxymoron *per se*, it refers to the fact that Italy does not have any natural resources (like oil or gas) to finance a "public" SWF, but plenty of public debt (reaching almost 160% of GDP at the end of 2021) that makes the country of potentially sub-investment grade. This overly nega-

---

* With the lead contribution of Elisa Galassi, CRO and Head of Total Sustainability of HOPE S.B. SICAF.

tive picture, and the negative representation sometimes given by somewhat superficial outside-in analysis, is balanced by the great potential of its natural and real assets (including the beauty of the country, its historical and artistic heritage, its touristic potential and so on), its talented, export prone and very resilient SME sector, and its underdeveloped, underexploited and likely undervalued real estate and infrastructure sectors. Moreover, it does not take into consideration the much more limited leverage reached by private debt and the significant stock of private wealth that Italians, as keen savers, have been able to put aside since WWII. Given a stock of around €4.8 Tn of financial savings (not to mention the wealth of Italian citizens invested in their own home – around 65% of their total savings), it would be easy to consider the introduction of a "wealth tax" to finance the creation of a "public" SWF or to reduce the €2.5 Tn burden of public debt.

Leaving aside the political costs (and social impacts) of such a hypothesis, a public SWF funded by taxes would have left room to a more Leviathan styled state, with the risk of a looming nationalization of the economy – even more so given the upcoming funds (around €230 Bn) coming from the Next Generations EU fund (Italy is the major beneficiary of this program, which is however adding further debt to the EU Countries and to its future generations, with Italy sharing the pain). Further public sources could distort the proper and optimal allocation of capital, the pursuit of efficiency and effectiveness and further increased the detachment of citizens from the economic destiny of their country (as taxpayers, they have the incentive to avoid contributing and, as recipient, they have the opposite temptation of wasting common resources which are perceived as a "free lunch"). Hence, the idea of a "private" SWF was to try and tap into the financial savings of Italians by their free choice to invest in the country as private equity directed towards its private markets – comprising of its real economy of SME, but also its real assets as a mix of real estate and infrastructure related to its main cities and best territories. Not only would such a strategy make better use of the savings of its citizens and help the re-equitization of the country by the retailization of private equity, but it would also support the development of the Italian stock-market and overall alternative investment management industry. It would also offer a better, market based, realignment of the transformative investments driven by the Next Generations funds and provide a more virtuous realignment of the economic, social and civic incentives and interests of its citizens, as they would feel like shareholders of the country and not just taxpayers, with a clear influence on the direction of travel and sustainability goals sought.

7.2 Capitalism for everybody

If the surrounding idea was to support the creation of a "capitalism for everybody" model, specifically focused on a proposition of private equity open to as many citizens and savers as possible, the next steps were to discuss and define which kind of objectives such a model would try to pursue and with which kind of legal, financial and governance structures. In HOPE's experience, we have envisioned the creation of an "evergreen capital" investment company, with a long term investment horizon and structured as a "living company" (e.g. not designed to close at the end of the first investment cycle) that would be self-managed (hence including the fund and the investment management company in the same legal vehicle) and as investable as possible not only by highly experienced "patient capital" institutional investors, but also by the largest number of retail investors with the required and critical help of financial institutions providing them with advice and on the basis of the principles and constraints indicated by the MIFID 2 Regulations. Such a proposition, to be consistent with the "capitalism for everybody" stated target should in fact provide an easy and safe way for normal citizens to invest in its country's private markets: in small amounts (minimum ticket of € 1 K, for example), cheaply, in a transparent and easy way (under the overall advice of its financial intermediary of choice) and with the opportunity to sell the invested shares if needed, fast and with a small discount. On this basis, HOPE was founded as a limited company and transformed into a self-managed SICAF retail (long term fixed capital investment company, non-reserved hence investable not only by institutional and professional investors but also by common retail investors), multi-asset and multi-strategy (hence going granular in the creation of its invested companies and assets, and comprised of a balanced mix of SME, real estate and infrastructure). The SICAF would also seek its floatation on the Italian stock exchange to give liquidity to its mixed portfolio of mostly illiquid investments and with the presence of specialist banks playing a broker dealer role. It would then be distributed by a large pool of banks and with successive capital raises through time, consistent with the capital deployment timing so as to reach a critical size of capital under management available for Italian based investments. To address the key issue of liquidity and marketability, two further strategic levers would then been considered on top of the above-mentioned distribution capabilities of the main banks and the role of the specialists as market makers:

- The first, a targeted and dynamic mix of investors for the first capital raises, focusing specifically on financial institutions and long term, sustainability-sensitive family offices (and the management team of HOPE) for the first "seed funding" of the company. Followed by a second raise targeting mostly institutional investors (domestic only, in the first wave) – mainly pension and welfare funds, endowments and life insurance companies, with a lighter weight of family offices. The role of retail investors is then deemed to extend and increase in weight in future capital raises and with a dominant role in 5–10 years' time once the stock is fully liquid.
- The second, a target set of capital raises that is planned in advance and based on pent up demand for the investment proposition of HOPE and progressively driven and reinforced by the equity story and brand being built with the investment portfolio – encompassing SME but also urban regeneration and development projects and with sustainability as a *fil rouge*. Differently from other private equity funds, the ambition is to build a values-based retail brand.

The overall investment policy would then be consistent with the requirements to qualify for fiscal incentives (so called "PIR Alternative" tax incentive offered by the Italian state for investment in its real economy: these incentives also suggest investors do not sell their holdings for at least 5 years) and with an internal governance and management that would be "best practice" according to international standards. For this, we have created a Board of Directors with a majority of independent members and non-executives, with an Investment Committee made up by the executive investment partners with an advisory role only (final decisions on investments and divestments are made by the Board) and with a parallel "Sustainability Committee" also advising the Board on matters more closely linked to the total sustainability targets, and comprised of representatives of the civic society, including people from finance, the industries and academia, but also other members involved in non-profit initiatives, social engagement with the target stakeholders (e.g. younger generations) and

7   HOPE: A Case for Change   147

others. In the context of this book, the experience that is most relevant to discuss is not however its overall legal and financial set up, or even its governance and management, but the idea of HOPE positing itself as a benefit corporation (i.e. considering a stakeholders-based approach and seeking also non-financial impacts from its investment policies and decisions) and pursuant of objectives that are consistent with an ex-art. 8 of the FDSR (Financial Directive on Sustainability Reporting). More importantly, the experience of HOPE is to try to pursue its private and for-profit investment management objectives, impact investment targets and others, by also considering an extended definition of wealth-being – something that can mix elements of financial wealth and economic value and also of wellness and happiness, driven critically by social and ecological goals among others. This extended and augmented definition of wealth-being should inform the initial investment decisions and, more importantly, the following active management ones on the basis of a "sustainability compact" that has been agreed with the management of the invested companies or projects. It should also inform the exit strategy that, in the case of HOPE, primarily considers the stock markets (with IPO of private companies invested) or the sale to retail households and long-term investors (for the real estate part). In the HOPE case study, we have tried to do this by logical steps. Specifically, by defining the mission and vision of the company first, then its core values, pay off and claims, and key stakeholders. From there the key objectives for the short, mid and long term as benefit corporation – and to cross reference them with the sustainability and ESG related objectives, taking also into consideration the taxonomy promoted by the EU.

7.3   HOPE's mission and vision of "wealth"

Traditional wealth management models are mostly based on purely financial approaches in the way they define targets *ex ante* and gauge performance *ex post* and, consistently structure models of planning, management and reporting. They define simple targets, such as the return on the capital nominally invested (e.g. ROE and ROA), or risk adjusted (e.g. RORAC or RAROC) and, specifically in a private equity context, they may be expressed in percentage points (e.g. IRR) or volume of money "multiplied" (e.g. CoC – Capital on Capital). Also, they are all based on two, very well-known, key principles of the "dismal science." First, that the "utilitarian" approach which states that, given the "economic agent" taking a investment decision (or for which such a decision is taken), all that really matters is how their own egocentric utility is maximized. Second, that a "time value of money" principle applies, that is "better an egg today than tomorrow" and that given an appropriately high discount rate, an egg today will always be the better choice, no matter how big the chicken tomorrow. All of this is not only bringing to a limited analysis and to the potential risk of one-sided and short-sighted decision making, but also, it may lead to the creation and development of critical burdens, with a potential disruption point of no return that impacts heavily on the wealth-being we want to achieve. Because of this we have tried in our model for a wealth management of the future, to achieve a broader and more consistent definition, to include the key perspectives of the economic, social and ecological sustainability that can contribute to wealth-being and to the preservation – survival and development – of the human species. But in order to do this we have to start by defining exactly the ultimate purpose of HOPE.

HOPE's mission is "to drive the transformation of Italy towards sustainability by making private equity open to everyone" (and shareholders in the country). The vision of HOPE is then "to become the leading, private, long-term investor, empowering people as shareholders of Italy's real economy and assets and promoting a positive change in their behaviour as investors, customers and citizens." A hermeneutical analysis of our aims should provide more clarity on the value proposition that HOPE is aiming to communicate and deliver, and its level of ambition. More specifically, HOPE's initial scope is limited to Italy, and the reference to sustainability is then broken up into three – "financial, social and ecological" – dimensions. From a financial standpoint, HOPE is seeking to support the re-capitalization (re-equitization) of the country's leveraging on the retailization of private equity – aiming to raise, in the long term, mostly from Italian households. Equity capital will be deployed in private markets hence addressing the stakeholders' opportunity to access an investment universe that was previously only on offer to institutional and professional investors. The financial sustainability dimension is then pursued at a macroeconomic level (at the level of the country) and at microeconomic one (at the level of the single portfolio of companies invested). From a social sustainability point of view, the focus is mainly on gender parity and inclusion, and on financial education as a tool to overcome those challenges. Finally, from an ecological point of view, the target is to fight climate change and contribute to the health of residents by reducing CO_2 emissions and other pollutants. The overall mission, short term pursuits and ultimate scope are then captured in the naming and in its pay off ("GenerAzione Italia"). HOPE (an acronym referring to its active management holding status), is also a message of "hope" following the pandemic crisis, and of the passion and emotions that can lead its stakeholders toward better futures. However, it is not a fatalistic hope or wishful thinking of something good that will happen inevitably. But a factual hope that starts from action: a wilful action plan that can lead stakeholders to take their destiny in their own hands, and that of the country by doing so. The pay-off is then supporting this concept: "azione" in Italian means both "share" and "action" – stakeholders take their best hopes back in their own hands by investing in the equity of the country and by taking action themselves. "Generazione," in Italian, means both "generation" (with reference to the alpha generations that will be able to overperform and create huge value), but also regeneration and evolution (referring to the topics of "transformation and innovation" of the country and of "corporate/ urban regeneration" with regards to its SME and cities). The full pay-off "GenerAzione Italia" is implicitly also reminiscent of the anthropological challenge posed by the vision, where HOPE should aim to support people in becoming better investors, but also consumers and citizens, caring about the sustainability of their country as an economic, social and ecological system. The core values of HOPE are then defined to consistently support its mission, vision, brand identity and pay off, as a set of polar stars that guide the behaviour of its employees and stakeholders at large. There are five core values:

- A "search for truth" that should drive every thought and action, in a pragmatic way, hence becoming serviceable for relevant stakeholders and invariant and objective enough, in the Robert Nozick definition, to be acted upon and produce a positive impact on humankind.
- A "passion for sustainability" that should guide behaviours of people, as investors, customers and citizens, for a sustainability that is financial, social and environmental; and in a dynamic way, to support people in becoming better – looking at the end rather than starting point.

- An "action-based entrepreneurship" that should look to innovate and transform, evolving in meaningful and positive ways, with a visionary approach encompassing innovative technology but that is also based on humanism, with humankind are ultimate beneficiary.
- A drive "towards higher futures" that should inform the challenge of the company in leveraging the experience of past generations and in getting back the lost hope of future ones, whilst living up to the challenges of today's and tomorrow's key decision makers.
- A "fair competitiveness," that should always be driven by a search for excellence and for superior performances in everything people do, but in a humble manner with a sense of compassion that makes people feel and care for others, and promoting inclusion.

7.4 HOPE as a stakeholder based, benefit corporation

HOPE was born as a benefit corporation and therefore, according to Italian Law, must pursue targets that may have impacts of a wider nature and include also un-economical objects. This is captured at high level in its statutory foundations and described in greater detail by its board – composed of a majority of non-executives, that takes into consideration the proposals from its Committee of Sustainability, also composed of non-executives – and, from an executive structure point of view, with the support of the Chief Executive Officer and the Chief Risk Officer, that is also acting as Head of Sustainability. These impacts are pursued through a mix of strategies that are consistently part of a "multi-strategy approach" and, as of today, focusing on "competitive corporates and innovative technologies" and "sustainable cities and digital and green infrastructure." For HOPE as a benefit corporation, a number of stakeholders have been defined and named, including:

- Italy, as a country, economic and socio-political entity, but also interpreted as an integrated ecosystem including, for example, its historical and artistic heritage, natural beauty, set of common democratic and liberal values and of course cohesive population. The target is to make it more competitive and compelling, and more sustainable from a financial, social and environmental point of view, for current and future generations alike. Because of the way HOPE was born, Italy is probably its first stakeholder of reference and with long term objectives attached. In greater, more technical detail, the target is to pursue the development of the economic model of reference as a "capitalism for everybody": open and inclusive, market based and liberal but also compassionate and fair, with a keen interest in the pursuit of a wider definition of wealth which include the wellness of its population present and future (wealth-being). For the territories, cities, industrial districts, overall communities of reference, specific sub-focuses can also be developed, interpreting Italy as a united country, but also composed by multiple universes with their own set of wealth and wellbeing targets.

- The other stakeholder of reference is therefore the current population of Italy, which can support the transformation and innovation of the country, and of its economic model of reference, by its own evolution and development. Central to part of this task is the greater and better information and training of all kinds of citizens with regards to their financial preparedness, which is a strict requirement for their direct involvement as investors and shareholders of the country. With no financial knowledge, training or expertise, any exposure to any kind of discretionary investment activity could become not only a hazard that should be mitigated in by the advice of financial professionals from the regulated banking system. But also, with no clear and thorough understanding of what "total sustainability" means there could be limited appreciation of the impact of investing goals pursued as shareholders of a benefit corporation. And, finally, no real change would happen to behaviour at the level of the individual private citizens – as retail investors, workers and consumers. Hence the maieutic challenge recalled in the vision of HOPE that goes well above any ambition purely related to making good investments and returning nice profits to its financial shareholders.
- Within the Italian population, but not limited to it, HOPE as a benefit corporation is then promoting a specific sensibility on the weakest and least protected minorities. They are not just less wealthy and powerful given the *status quo* of the wealth of the country, but also with a greater exposure to the unsustainability introduced by the nemesis of wealth and by the current state of the world, characterized by financial crisis, indebtedness and inflation, pandemics and disruption in the main value chains of production-distribution,

geopolitical tensions and global decoupling between major economic and military blocks. These weakest and least powerful parts of the population are also, incidentally, the ones with the greatest, marginal opportunity to contribute to the creation of wealth (not to mention – quite obviously – wellbeing). Women and younger generations are, for example, typically under-employed, with great talents, energy and willingness to contribute to the transformation of the country. They should also be more aligned with the overall mission regarding the pursuit of "total sustainability" – they have benefited less in the financial wealth dominated world of the post-industrial revolution and, the young specifically, should care more about the long-term future and would be required to take an interest and the lead of the country in the mid-term.

- Being an investment company HOPE is then naturally focusing on its own investors – even more so given that it is also targeting retail investors which may have limited savings and are not professionals in the investment management space as it is typically the case for institutional investors. As HOPE is a long-term investor, it requires a consistently long-term holding period from the investors side, with "patient capital" attitude that is more interested in the capital appreciation in a 5-10 years' timeframe and less in quicker gains generated by short term volatility. As the investment proposition is equity investments and in real economy and real assets in private markets the objective with regards to these stakeholders is also to provide a means to defend their purchasing power for highly inflationary scenarios and robust collaterals (with limited add on leverage) as a protection in case of negative performances. It is of course subject to all the typical risks related to private equity approaches and specifically, the focus on Italy is the most relevant idiosyncratic risk – as the risk return is mostly focused on the Italian economy with some resilience offered by the level of internationalization of Italian companies. Consistent with the proposition of "capitalism for everybody," the entry investment ticket is kept to a minimum and, for retail investors specifically, the planned listing on the stock exchange is meant to offer an easy way out of the investment in case of short-term needs.

7.5 HOPE's framework as a benefit corporation[1]

As a benefit company, HOPE is aiming to pursue a broader set of objectives with a common benefit pay-off for its most relevant stakeholders and as defined in its statute. In short, these include:

- Generating fair and sustainable profits in the medium/ long term for all the relevant stakeholders involved in HOPE activities and for all the companies in the portfolio. HOPE will create a wealth that is widely spread and impacting directly and indirectly on the environment and the community. It is aiming to do this by pursuing a set of well-balanced objectives that relates to financial, social and ecological sustainability (or "total sustainability"), with a particular focus on the creation of opportunities for the new generations.
- Promoting solutions that generate a positive impact on the country, supporting the strengthening of an entrepreneurship of excellence and the urban regeneration of Italian cities.
- Pursuing a positive impact in the communities and territories in which HOPE operates and invests – e.g. with the support of inclusion enhancing initiatives, of third-sector entities and with services offered directly or indirectly to the community and the territory of reference.
- Minimizing the negative impact on natural resources, both coming from its own operations or through the implementation and management of its invested companies, in particular by guiding and accelerating the process of "green" transition for its portfolio companies.

Matching the three pillars of the sustainability – financial, social, environmental – and its target stakeholders, HOPE has detailed the main impact objectives, which are pursued through the two core investment strategies "competitive corporates and innovative technologies" and "sustainable cities and digital and green infrastructure."

In the sphere of financial sustainability, three objectives have been identified:

- *Equitization* – HOPE aims to support the recapitalization of Italy,

investing equity/equity-like in the real economy of the country and without discrimination of territories or regions.
- *GDP growth* – HOPE is committed to contributing to the growth of the Italian GDP through its investments in real assets, thus supporting the transformation and development of the Italian economy and society sustainably, and adopting an investment policy consistent with the objective ex-art. 8 of the SFDR.
- *Tax* – Complete fiscal transparency and contribution to the welfare state and to the rebalancing of the deficit and public debt. Act as a proxy of paid dividends to shareholders, salaries to employees and fees to suppliers.

In the context of social sustainability, HOPE has set its goals by looking specifically at some of the country's weakest and least protected segments of the population. In particular, women and the young generation, for which it focuses on social inclusion and participation in civil society and economic markets:

- *Gender Parity* – the SICAF pursues minimum gender parity targets for itself and its portfolio companies, both in terms of workforce composition and compensation at different levels of seniority.
- *Next Generation* – HOPE is committed to the valorisation of young people (Generation Zed) in the world of work through dedicated training and education programs aimed at increasing financial knowledge, civic awareness and interest in Italy.
- *Job Creation* – the SICAF supports accelerated growth of its portfolio companies, injecting equity and acting in an operating partner role, thus stimulating economic opportunities and job creation in HOPE and its portfolio companies, in different sectors and geographic areas.

Regarding environmental sustainability, the SICAF aims to protect ecosystems and biodiversity that will ensure the survival and prosperity of humankind:

- *C02 emissions* – HOPE pledges to reduce carbon emissions of its portfolio companies in line with Cop 26 objectives, so contributing to fighting climate change.

7 HOPE: A Case for Change   155

Figure 7.1 Hope sustainability framework

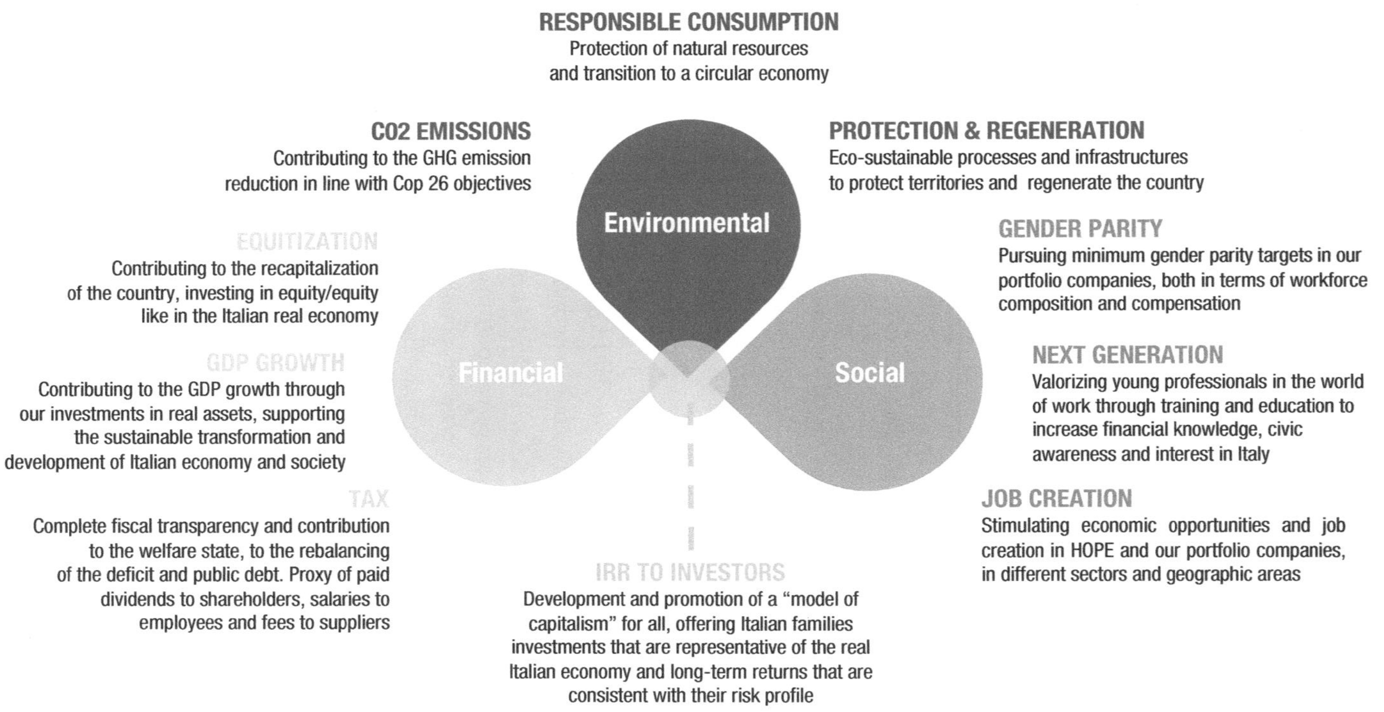

RESPONSIBLE CONSUMPTION
Protection of natural resources and transition to a circular economy

PROTECTION & REGENERATION
Eco-sustainable processes and infrastructures to protect territories and regenerate the country

GENDER PARITY
Pursuing minimum gender parity targets in our portfolio companies, both in terms of workforce composition and compensation

NEXT GENERATION
Valorizing young professionals in the world of work through training and education to increase financial knowledge, civic awareness and interest in Italy

JOB CREATION
Stimulating economic opportunities and job creation in HOPE and our portfolio companies, in different sectors and geographic areas

CO2 EMISSIONS
Contributing to the GHG emission reduction in line with Cop 26 objectives

EQUITIZATION
Contributing to the recapitalization of the country, investing in equity/equity like in the Italian real economy

GDP GROWTH
Contributing to the GDP growth through our investments in real assets, supporting the sustainable transformation and development of Italian economy and society

TAX
Complete fiscal transparency and contribution to the welfare state, to the rebalancing of the deficit and public debt. Proxy of paid dividends to shareholders, salaries to employees and fees to suppliers

IRR TO INVESTORS
Development and promotion of a "model of capitalism" for all, offering Italian families investments that are representative of the real Italian economy and long-term returns that are consistent with their risk profile

Environmental · Social · Financial

- *Responsible Consumption* – HOPE wants to adopt processes and measures aimed at the reduction of pollution, waste management and conversion to a circular economy, with particular reference to the protection of scarce natural resources and animals, reducing the conditions of cruelty to which they are subjected in the various production cycles.
- *Protection & Regeneration* – eco-sustainable processes and infrastructure to protect territories and regenerate the country the SI-CAF selects, investments in businesses and projects of urban regeneration and development, which recover natural resources and enhance the natural and artistic beauty of the country, in balance and synergy with its economic and financial systems, to reduce the contribution of pollution in the protection of biodiversity and with a positive impact on the welfare of the community.

Ultimately, at the centre of total sustainability HOPE places its investors, to whom it is accountable through the results achieved by its economic activity.

- *IRR to Investors* – At the centre of the total sustainability framework HOPE places its investors, to whom HOPE offers investments that are representative of the real Italian economy and guarantees long-term returns that are consistent with their risk profile.

These main objectives have been outlined further for the principal areas of the impact analysis: governance, clients, community, providers and the environment and specific medium/long-term KPIs have been identified. Annually, HOPE defines short term objectives for the following year as well as the related action plan, and continuously monitors activities to identify any corrective actions.

Governance

The governance dimension relates to internal practices and policies that lead to effective decision making and in full alignment with compliance. HOPE aims to develop innovative and best practice governance models for itself and its portfolio companies, adopting a common ethical code, similar core values and ensuring transparency and fairness with regards to all stakeholders. In the following table, a summary of governance, ESG criteria and stakeholders' engagement is described with its relevant KPI.

Objectives	Description	Key Performance Indicators
Governance of benefit company	Adopting a consistent policy, spreading the culture of the Benefit Company and the recommendations of the Sustainability Committee	• Development of the HOPE Benefit Company Policy • Annual designation of the Sustainability Committee members • Periodic HOPE management meetings to plan strategy and take decisions • Periodic training for HOPE employees on the objectives set for a positive impact • Educating portfolio company management teams on the Benefit Company's purpose and objectives
ESG criteria integration	Incorporating environmental, social and governance factors into business and investment processes	• Investment processes integrated with ESG factors and Benefit Company's objectives • Co-creating impact measurement and management plan with portfolio companies • Ongoing monitoring of the progressive achievement of the ESG objectives defined for our investments
Stakeholder engagement	Taking into account the needs of stakeholders in order to direct investment toward their well-defined common benefit	• Regular meetings of the Sustainability Committee and of the Strategic Advisory Board to receive guidance on HOPE investments and strategy • Development of a platform to provide the market with transparency on investments in execution and collection of feedback • Framework for direct stakeholders' engagement on specific investments
Tax	Complete fiscal transparency and contribution to the welfare state and to the rebalancing of the deficit and public debt. Proxy of paid dividends to shareholders, salaries to employees and fees to suppliers	• Existence of a robust tax policy/strategy for governance, internal control of taxation of HOPE and all Portfolio Companies

Workers

The wellbeing of employees is an increasingly important factor in the success of a company and can influence their behaviour and results both positively and negatively. HOPE takes the wellbeing of its own employees and those of its portfolio companies seriously, drawing inspiration from the most advanced policies to guarantee adequate gender representation and non-discrimination, pursuing an overall objective of fully enhancing the value of employees, both from a professional and human point of view, helping everyone to become "better people" and not just "better investment professionals." This objective is translated into HOPE's corporate values, which are meant to lay the foundations of the behaviours that are desirable and instrumental for the benefit corporation to effectively pursue its long-term objectives. HOPE supports the development of competitive packages in terms of remuneration and benefits, training and opportunities for personal growth, for the quality of the working environment, its own inclusion and respect for diversity, relevant transparency and kindness in internal communication, also looking to providing flexibility and job security.

Objectives	Description	Key Performance Indicators
Decent work	Fostering the creation of a healthy and stimulating working environment, where the ideas of each employee are considered	• The constitution of a "shadow committee" composed of young employees with advisory and propositional functions for the Board of Directors • An Ethical code for all Portfolio Companies inspired by HOPE ethical guidelines • The definition of an ESG Compact on decent, respectful working policies for all Portfolio Companies • Policies to improve work-life balance (e.g. smart working) and increase the sense of belonging of portfolio companies' employees
Training and professional development	Plan and deliver training aimed at career development and sustainability awareness	• Planning and delivery of training on sustainability, whistleblowing, health and safety and specialized training for HOPE and portfolio companies
Remuneration policies	Offering fair pay to employees, according to anti-discrimination and work-life balance policies	• HOPE remuneration policy, including mechanisms for participation in medium-term results, carried interest with long-term claw backs to offer better protection to retail investors

Objectives	Description	Key Performance Indicators
		• Fair remuneration policies in line with the market, including employee participation in company results, to develop a sense of ownership for the portfolio companies and a keenness on performance
Sustainability objectives	Motivating the board and management to pursue objectives of common benefit	• Inclusion of ESG sustainability factors in HOPE remuneration policies for its own and the management of portfolio companies • Induction sessions for HOPE board and management on sustainability issues • Annual evaluation of top management employees conducted with the integration of ESG criteria and performance factors in their variable compensation
Health, welfare & social protection	Ensuring security in offices and promoting welfare policies for employees and their families, as well as protection for whistleblowing	• Welfare policies for HOPE and its portfolio companies • Whistleblowing policy for HOPE and its portfolio companies • Adoption of Health and Safety Management System for HOPE and its portfolio companies

Customers

For its customers – i.e. institutional and retail investors – HOPE aims to offer medium/ long-term economic objectives and impact-investing actions and results. Objectives may for example include:

- *Equitization.* A contribution to the recapitalization of the country, through equity investments in the real economy and without discriminating between territories or regions.
- *GDP Growth.* Contributing to the growth of Italian GDP through investments in real assets, supporting the transformation and development of the Italian economy and society in a sustainable way, pursuing an investment policy consistent with the ex-art. 8 of the SFDR.
- *IRR to investors.* Contributing to the development and promotion of a model of capitalism for everybody inspired by total sustainability, offering most Italian families a simple way to access investments that are representative of the real economy and with absolute, risk-adjusted returns over the long term that are consistent with their risk/ return profile.

Objectives	Description	Key Performance Indicators
Equitization	Bringing equity into the real economy through HOPE core investment strategies	• Fundraising of at least EUR 3 billion in 10 years • Over 70% of investments in Italy
GDP growth	Contribute to GDP growth through HOPE core investments, supporting social inclusion and environmental transitions	• Portfolio Companies' turnover growth in the long term equal to three times the growth of Italian GDP • At least 60% of investments that promote social and environmental characteristics • Over 10% of investments with social and/or environmental objectives
IRR to investors	Mitigating risk through a diversified and granular portfolio (multi-asset, multi-strategy)	• Investment concentration ratio below 15-20% of total assets, with strong diversification at multi-asset, multi-strategy level
	Ensure maximum transparency and low management costs	• Transparent, understandable, truthful reporting • Management costs less than 100bp on AUM collected
	Ensure stable and increasing dividend pay-out over time and an attractive IRR in the medium/long term	• Stable NAV appreciation • Dividend distribution from the fifth year onwards
	Ensure easy access to the investment with minimum thresholds and relevant liquidity obtained through the stock exchange	• Listing on the Milan stock exchange (Borsa Italiana) Milan with daily pricing
	Ensuring anti-inflationary characteristics and following non-speculative approach	• Definition of a sound and responsible investment policy, aimed at obtaining economic results in line with the risk profile and with around 80% of Italian investments in real economy/ real assets
	Enabling Italian households to invest in the real economy	• 10.000 retail shareholders by the end of 2023 • Shareholders who hold the investment for 5 years are eligible to fiscal incentives (PIR Alternative)

Community

HOPE is aiming to make a positive impact on the community of reference and, more specifically, on women and young people (Generation Zed and Alpha) by achieving the following objectives:

- *Job creation.* HOPE is looking to create new jobs, both as part of HOPE and its portfolio companies, in different sectors and different geographical areas of Italy.
- *Gender parity.* HOPE is pursuing gender parity targets in its portfolio companies, both in terms of workforce composition and remuneration, reducing gaps with an incremental approach.
- *Next Generation.* HOPE is striving to enhance the value of young professionals and introduce them to the job market, also supporting the information, training and development of civic awareness and conscience and a keen interest in Italy among the new generations.
- *Inclusive communities.* HOPE aims to promote solutions to protect the interests and support the inclusion of weaker population groups that are at risk of being marginalized, such as pensioners or people preparing to retire who still have a strong potential active place in society.

Objectives	Description	Key Performance Indicators
Job creation	Creating new jobs in different sectors and geographic areas through the growth of HOPE portfolio companies	• Creation of new jobs in different sectors and geographical areas • Conversion of employment relationships, 30% post temporary contract hiring
		• At least 30% recruitment after temporary employment contracts
Gender parity	Pursue minimum gender parity goals Composition of the corporate population for HOPE and its portfolio companies	• At least 40% of women in the boardroom • At least 30% of women in top management • At least 40% of women in the workforce
	Pursue minimum gender pay gap realignment goals	• At least 25% reduction in gender pay gap for portfolio companies
	Supporting the inclusion and professional growth of women	• Training on issues of inclusion and professional growth
	Developing solutions to safeguard women's health, safety and welfare	• Policies to support working mothers (e.g., breastfeeding support, subsidized childcare) • Development of infrastructure to increase women and family wellbeing

Objectives	Description	Key Performance Indicators
Next generation	Foster young workers for HOPE and for its portfolio companies	• HOPE population composition: 25% workers under 30 years old given budget of workforce growth
	Develop training courses for young people to develop professionalism	• At least 30% of training plans to young workers out of the total number of plans promoted to employees • Training courses on financial investments to guide the less experienced to conscious investments • Training on pension provision issues
	Develop training courses for young people to develop civic awareness and interest in Italy	• Increased awareness of sustainability issues for employees of portfolio companies • Training for young workers through university/ executive and training courses held by HOPE team • Production of position papers, books, podcasts, articles on sustainable investing
	Develop infrastructure dedicated to the mental and physical development of young people	• Development of sports facilities dedicated to young people • Development of spaces to facilitate relationships between people, training and enjoyment of the arts
Inclusive communities	Promote services and facilities aimed at fighting social isolation and improving the well-being of individuals through active aging and self-esteem	• Senior and social housing and other services dedicated to them in urban regeneration projects • Investments in the silver economy (e.g. health, pharmaceuticals, new technologies)

When considering the community, HOPE is also including suppliers as an additional subcategory of stakeholders. In fact, the concept of "total sustainability" must necessarily go beyond the scope of the company and extend throughout its value chain. In this way, the sustainability must be extended from the individual good or service produced by the company to the way in which this good or service was produced and, from there, to the entire supply chain, involving aspects that until a few years ago were little considered but that today have taken on a significant importance. These include, for example, the economic conditions of workers and suppliers, health and safety, the full alignment with the rule of law and all kinds of compliance procedures, and the full transparency on procurement selection choices. The latter is an increasingly important point as sustainability in supply chain management is gaining increasing attention in both academic literature and industry practice as an area of opportunity and potential risk. In fact, more and more companies are implementing sustainability initiatives in their supply chain in response to pressures from consumers, investors, and even employees. HOPE is therefore aiming to promote responsible supplier management for itself and for its portfolio companies, in order to extend sustainability throughout the supply chain, and in particular for strategic suppliers, whose relevance and influence on the benefits generated require a medium to long-term partnership.

Objectives	Description	Key Performance Indicators
Engagement of strategic suppliers	Responsible selection of suppliers who respect human rights and ensure decent working conditions	• Compliance with UN Global Compact principles and OECD Guidelines for Multinational Enterprises
	Selection of strategic suppliers who share similar core values	• Policy for the selection of strategic suppliers that have a code of ethics and care about the protection of workers' rights and show respect for the environment and the overall community • Mandatory minimum certifications aimed at guaranteeing the safety and quality of the supplier's product/ service

In addition, HOPE is planning to sponsor charitable initiatives through volunteer and philanthropic activities that will be identified annually by considering the historical context of reference to achieve environmental and/or social impact, and without endangering its financial targets. In in its own communication initiatives, HOPE is also aiming to contribute to the information and sensibilization regarding the most pressing financial, social and environmental issues the country is facing, as a current set of concerns and challenges to address in the present and as an ambition to move towards better futures, to support next generations and the development of Italy in the long term.

Objectives	Description	Key Performance Indicators
Philanthropy	Volunteering by HOPE employees and portfolio companies and donations	• Annual planning of a volunteer program directed to all employees and voluntary participation • Annual selection of philanthropic initiatives with an impact on the community and the environment

Environment

For the territories and the environment, HOPE is also setting medium/long-term objectives and impact action plans, for each of its main investment strategies and overall. Specific targets may include:

- *Reduction of CO2 emissions.* HOPE is pursuing CO2 reduction targets, for itself and its portfolio companies, based on the COP 26 guidelines, through the reduction of Scope 1, 2, 3 emissions.
- *Responsible consumption.* HOPE is adopting processes and measures aimed at reducing pollution, waste management and facilitating a conversion towards a circular economy, with particular reference to the preservation of scarce resources of natural origin and of animals, reducing the cruel conditions to which they are subjected in the various production cycles.
- *Protection and regeneration.* HOPE is selecting investments in businesses and urban regeneration projects that support the recovery and re-usage of natural resources and enhance the country's natural and artistic beauty, with a positive impact on the community's wellbeing.

Objectives	Description	Key Performance Indicators
CO2 emissions	Raise awareness of climate risks and develop a formalized environmental policy	• Assessment of physical and transition climate risks exposure for the portfolio companies • Definition of a formalized environmental policy for all portfolio companies
	Implement effective carbon footprint reduction solutions for portfolio companies	• Calculation and monitoring of the carbon footprint of portfolio companies • Definition of carbon footprint reduction targets and action plan for the portfolio companies • Reduction of the carbon footprint for the portfolio companies, by adopting specific solutions
	Promote choices and solutions aimed at the efficient use of energy	• Measurement of energy consumption for different energy sources and definition of consumption reduction targets for portfolio companies • Reduction of energy consumption by improving the efficiency of plants/processes • Increased use of renewable energy sources

Objectives	Description	Key Performance Indicators
Responsible consumption	Reduce emissions of pollutants into the atmosphere, water and soil	• Measurement of pollutant emissions and definition of emission reduction targets for portfolio companies • Measurement of recycled and non-recycled waste and assessment of hazardous waste management for portfolio companies • Reduction of emissions of harmful substances into water and air
	Promoting the transition to a circular economy	• Optimization of waste management, especially hazardous waste
	Promote choices and solutions aimed at the efficient use of water	• Measurement of water consumption and definition of reduction targets • Reduction of water consumption
	Promote construction processes that minimize the impact on land and the ecosystem	• Definition of operational plans for the eco-sustainable management of the site (e.g. suppliers, logistics, materials)
Protection and regeneration	Protect biodiversity – local fauna and flora	• Adoption of plans for biodiversity protection and sustainable land management • Specific certifications to protect biodiversity, including origin of raw materials
	Regeneration of areas and territories through sustainable cities projects	• Re-qualified areas (sqm)
	Create buildings resilient to climate change	• Design of climate-resilient properties (new construction/renovations)
	Implementation of eco-efficient solutions for the community aimed at regenerating relationships	• Creation of spaces dedicated to community services in square meters (bike paths, parks, spaces for exhibitions, events, etc.)

7.6 HOPE framework as pursuant of ESG[2]

HOPE is aiming to integrate ESG criteria into its overall investment decision-making process. This chapter describes the approach, practices and tools HOPE uses to integrate ESG factors into its investment policies – from screening to underwriting, from management to the final exit and valorisation. As a start, when screening potential investment opportunities, HOPE aims to assess the potential contribution of the selected company to the overall, incremental total sustainability that could be attained. In particular, the selection process includes a preliminary ESG assessment that is conducted by HOPE's internal team. This is mostly aimed at verifying that the potential investment is in line with HOPE's main strategy and objectives, and is typically followed by a proper ESG due diligence which is used to deepen the relevant themes that emerged in the first preliminary "scoping" phase. The preliminary ESG assessment involves three main screening steps:

1. Exclusion principles.
2. Presence of controversies.
3. Internal ESG assessment.

The first screening provides the information necessary to exclude investments in certain sectors of activity which are not considered socially or ecologically responsible. These include:

- *Fossil fuels.* Including exploration, extraction of fossil fuels (coal, oil and gas), power generation from fossil fuels and provision of related services (e.g. transport, storage and pipelines), the construction of new structures for the extraction, storage, transport or production of fossil fuels.
- *Nuclear energy.* Including the production of energy from nuclear power plants and the production of equipment for nuclear energy production and usage.
- *Non-conventional weapons.* Development, production, use, maintenance, distribution, storage, transport or sale of armaments or parts thereof (nuclear weapons, cluster munitions, anti-personnel mines, chemical and biological weapons).
- *Tobacco.* Production and/or distribution of tobacco and other related processed goods, provision of products/ services related to tobacco and its processed products.
- *Gambling.* Management of online-gaming platforms, running of businesses in the gambling sector (e.g. casinos, betting agencies), distribution of related products/services.
- *GMO products.* Production of genetically modified organisms for industrial use, including animals for food and tobacco companies.
- *Pornography.* Production, distribution, diffusion, or advertising of pornographic material.

7   HOPE: A Case for Change   167

The analysis of the exposure of the potential target in one of the above-mentioned sectors is carried out based on the actual economic and financial data retrieved by the investment team in the preliminary discussions with the management. The risk management function then carries out the appropriate checks on the exclusion principles based on the information gathered from the investment team and from other third party-sources if available. After the first screening, the management then assesses the presence of relevant disputes and controversies related to the investment, which may involve also ESG issues or potential negative social and environmental impacts (e.g. legal proceedings, serious environmental damages, violation of human rights). The information is obtained by the investment team from the dialogue with the management of the potential target and from the related documentation provided (e.g. accounting schedules, where it is possible to observe the presence of any provisions dedicated to possible liabilities arising from existing social and/or environmental disputes). The risk management function is informed by the investment team about the results of the interviews and provided with the necessary data for this second preliminary screening. The CRO reserves the right to request further details on specific issues necessary for the assessment. Based on the results achieved, the CRO and investment team may then evaluate whether to proceed with further analysis.

ESG Assessment for "competitive corporates and innovative technologies"

For the first "competitive corporates and innovative technologies" strategy, HOPE management proceeds with the first ESG assessment of the policies, strategies and processes adopted by the target company according to the internal ESG framework, retrieving data from the potential target through a dedicated questionnaire. This assessment identifies the main ESG issues to which the potential target is exposed and can guide the HOPE management team in understanding its strengths and areas for improvement. The ESG framework is based on HOPE environmental objectives and the company's strategic priorities, and takes into account the SDG goals, the requirements on the principal adverse impacts defined by the Regulatory Technical Standards of the SFDR, the topics tackled by the European environmental taxonomy, as well as the topics recently identified in the final report of the European social taxonomy. The reference framework is then based on a balanced scorecard which includes 216 indicators both quantitative and qualitative, but objectively measurable, considering environmental, social and governance aspects. More specifically:

- Environmental indicators include the target companies carbon footprint, the efficiency of energy sources, pollution control and transition to a circular economy
- Social indicators include, among others, metrics related to workforce composition and promotion of diversity, occupational health and safety, and staff training.
- Governance indicators cover, among others, aspects related to sustainable corporate governance, data protection and cybersecurity.

Figure 7.2 ESG Framework for Competitive Corporates and Innovative Technologies

The framework is then further detailed and tailored, in terms of ESG indicators and weights, for each of the individual potential investment opportunities and based on a materiality analysis, which considers the characteristics of the company, the relevant ESG factors of the sector (identified using the SASB materiality matrix) and the type of activities it is mostly involved in. For example, an investment in the biotechnology and pharmaceuticals industry does not have material issues related to GHG emissions, whilst it might present issues related to product quality and safety. All main indicators of the ESG framework are then linked to the UN SDGs and to the EU taxonomy and can be quantitative, qualitative or descriptive. Each indicator is also assigned a weight based on the relevance of the topic for the specific industry and given HOPE goals as a benefit corporation. The answers that are provided by the potential targets are then transformed into a rating (from one to five): for quantitative indicators, the rating is based on a comparative analysis with the industry average (with a rating equal to 3 in case of alignment to the industry/market standard). For qualitative indicators the rating can be one, three or five depending on the presence of the requested item and certifications, whilst for descriptive indicators the rating is applied discretionally based on the answer provided. The final rating is obtained as a weighted average of the individual indicators, allowing results to be aggregated at different levels: i.e. as ESG evaluation criteria, as individual E-S-G pillars, and as an overall, synthetic rating.

Regarding the *environmental topics*, the framework has been organized in categories covering the following:

1. Climate change & decarbonization, which includes:
   - Environmental management, which evaluates the presence, completeness and efficacy of formal policies tackling the impact of the company in the different environmental aspects and defining practices and actions to protect and conserve environmental resources.
   - Carbon footprint, aimed at measuring the company's emissions for the different scopes, the overall carbon footprint and assessing the company's exposure to physical and transitional risks related to climate change.
2. Efficient energy use, which evaluates not only the company's energy consumption and production, but also the use of renewable energy

sources, as well as policies and procedures in place to optimize the overall energy efficiency.
3. Water use and optimization, which examines the company's water consumption and pollutant emissions to water from its production processes and the optimization policies in place.
4. Pollution control, which analyses the practices in place to reduce emissions of air pollutants, the use of plastic and other environmentally harmful non-hazardous products, the noise pollution from the economic activity and the ecological footprint due to travel/ commuting.
5. Transition to a circular economy, including the evaluation of waste management policies of the company and the measurement of hazardous waste and non-recycled waste generated as well as the use of recycled raw materials.
6. Environmental quality and biodiversity, targeted at evaluating negative impacts of the economic activity on flora and fauna, as well as policies and actions to protect and conserve impacted species.

Table 7.1 ESG questionnaire and KPI for Environmental topics

Category	ID	ESG Evaluation Criteria	ID_1	Key Performance Indicators	Type
Environmental management	E.01	Adoption of a formal environmental policy (if yes, request a copy)	E.01.1	Enter a description	Descriptive
	E.02	Adoption of initiatives to reduce the company's environmental impact (e.g. energy/water consumption, waste reduction or recycling, consumption of raw materials, eco-design, protection of biodiversity)	E.02.1	Enter a description	Descriptive
	E.03	Incidents or disputes over environmental issues during the year. If yes, please ask for details in the comments (reason, possible sanctions, etc.).	E.03.1	Enter a description	Descriptive
			E.03.2	Impact of environmental costs on total costs in the last three years	Quantitative
Carbon footprint	E.04	Adoption of internal policies to reduce GHG emissions	E.04.1	Management system for GHG emissions (indicate in the notes field if the management system is certified e.g., ISO 14064)	Qualitative

7 HOPE: A Case for Change

Category	ID	ESG Evaluation Criteria	ID_1	Key Performance Indicators	Type
			E.04.2	Definition of targets for improving performance related to GHG emissions	Qualitative
			E.04.3	Mechanisms for reporting violations of the measures adopted for GHG emissions reduction	Qualitative
			E.04.4	Internal/external audits on compliance with the adopted GHG emission controls	Qualitative
	E.05	Assessment of exposure to physical and transitional risks related to climate change, and processes implemented to manage such risks. If yes, please provide details	E.05.1	Enter a description	Descriptive
	E.06	Carbon footprint of the company (for Scope 1, 2 and 3)	E.06.1	CO2 emissions (scope 1)	Quantitative
			E.06.2	CO2 emissions (scope 2)	Quantitative
			E.06.3	CO2 emissions (scope 3)	Quantitative
			E.06.4	Carbon footprint	Quantitative
Energy efficiency use	E.07	Adoption/intention to adopt internal policies aimed at improving energy efficiency and reducing energy consumption	E.07.1	Adoption of an energy management system (indicate in the notes field if the management system is certified e.g., ISO 50001)	Qualitative
			E.07.2	Definition of targets for improving energy consumption performance (e.g., quantitative reduction targets)	Qualitative
			E.07.3	Mechanisms for reporting violations of energy consumption controls	Qualitative
			E.07.4	Internal/external audit of compliance with adopted energy consumption controls	Qualitative
	E.08	Intensity of energy consumption during the year by high impact sector	E.08.1	Energy consumption in GWh during the year	Quantitative

Category	ID	ESG Evaluation Criteria	ID_1	Key Performance Indicators	Type
	E.09	Total non-renewable energy consumption (kWh) and % of renewable energy over the year	E.09.1	Total non-renewable energy consumption (kWh) during the year	Quantitative
			E.09.2	% of renewable energy consumed during the year	Quantitative
	E.10	Total non-renewable energy production (kWh) and % of renewable energy over the year	E.10.1	Total non-renewable energy production (kWh) during the year	Quantitative
			E.10.2	% of renewable energy produced during the year	Quantitative
Water usage optimization	E.11	Water consumption management policy (alternatively specify adoption of internal procedures)	E.11.1	Definition of targets for improving water consumption performance	Qualitative
			E.11.2	Mechanisms for reporting violations of water consumption controls	Qualitative
			E.11.3	Internal/external audits of compliance with adopted water consumption controls	Qualitative
	E.12	Water usage and recycling	E.12.1	Water consumption during the year (m^3)	Quantitative
			E.12.2	Percentage of water recycled and reused	Quantitative
	E.13	Policy for the management of harmful emissions to water (alternatively specify adoption of internal procedures)	E.13.1	Water consumption and purification efficiency management policies (e.g., monitoring systems, definition of roles and responsibilities)	Qualitative
	E.14	Purification efficiency in terms of residual chemical substances in post-purification wastewater ([IN] − [OUT]) / [IN]). Possible distinction for each polluting factor	E.14.1	Purification efficiency in terms of residual chemical in post-purification wastewater ([IN] − [OUT]) / [IN]) [NITROGEN]	Quantitative
			E.14.2	Purification efficiency in terms of residual chemical in post-purification wastewater ([IN] − [OUT]) / [IN]) [CHROME]	Quantitative

7 HOPE: A Case for Change

Category	ID	ESG Evaluation Criteria	ID_1	Key Performance Indicators	Type
			E.14.3	Purification efficiency in terms of residual chemical in post-purification wastewater ([IN] − [OUT]) / [IN]) [SUSPENDED SOLIDS]	Quantitative
			E.14.4	Purification efficiency in terms of residual chemical in post-purification wastewater ([IN] − [OUT]) / [IN]) [SULFUR]	Quantitative
			E.14.5	Purification efficiency in terms of residual chemical in post-purification wastewater ([IN] − [OUT]) / [IN]) [SULPHATES]	Quantitative
			E.14.6	Purification efficiency in terms of residual chemical substance in post-purification wastewater ([IN] − [OUT]) / [IN]) [COD].	Quantitative
			E.14.7	Purification efficiency in terms of residual chemical in post-purification wastewater ([IN] − [OUT]) / [IN]) [CHLORIDE]	Quantitative
			E.14.8	Purification efficiency in terms of residual chemical in post-purification wastewater ([IN] − [OUT]) / [IN]) [AMMONIA]	Quantitative
	E.15	Emission of harmful substances into water (T). If the value is greater than 0, please provide clarification	E.15.1	Tonnes of emissions to water generated	Quantitative
			E.15.2	Consumption of chemicals per unit of product	Quantitative
Pollution control	E.16	Adoption of internal policies to reduce emissions of air pollutants and tools to measure them (inorganic pollutants, air pollutants, ozone-depleting substance)	E.16.1	Management system for air pollutants (e.g., monitoring systems, definition of roles and responsibilities)	Qualitative

Category	ID	ESG Evaluation Criteria	ID_1	Key Performance Indicators	Type
			E.16.2	Performance improvement targets for air pollutants (e.g., NOx, SOx, PM)	Qualitative
			E.16.3	Mechanisms for reporting violations of air pollutants controls (e.g., NOx, SOx, PM)	Qualitative
			E.16.4	Internal/external audits of compliance with adopted air pollutant controls (e.g., NOx, SOx, PM)	Qualitative
	E.17	Amount of air pollutant emissions (inorganic pollutants, air pollutants, ozone-depleting substances)	E.17.1	Tonnes of inorganic pollutants equivalent emitted	Quantitative
			E.17.2	Tonnes of volatile organic compounds emitted (VOCs)	Quantitative
			E.17.3	Tonnes of ozone depletion substances equivalent	Quantitative
	E.18	Internal policies to limit the use of plastics	E.18.1	Presence of internal policy on plastic usage	Qualitative
	E.19	Policies to reduce the use of environmentally harmful non-hazardous products	E.19.1	Enter a description	Descriptive
	E.20	Green procurement practices (purchase of sustainable raw materials and optimisation of logistics in the procurement phase)	E.20.1	Green procurement policies	Qualitative
	E.21	Processes to control and reduce noise pollution	E.21.1	Enter a description	Descriptive
	E.22	Policies to reduce the ecological footprint due to travel/commuting (incentives to use public transport, bicycle facilities, virtual meetings, etc.)	E.22.1	Enter a description	Descriptive
Transition to a circular economy	E.23	Types of waste generated by the activity (hazardous and non-hazardous)	E.23.1	Enter a description	Descriptive

7 HOPE: A Case for Change

Category	ID	ESG Evaluation Criteria	ID_1	Key Performance Indicators	Type
	E.24	Waste management policy (alternatively specify adoption of internal procedures – incl. hazardous waste)	E.24.1	Waste disposal (e.g. monitoring systems, definition of roles and responsibilities)	Qualitative
			E.24.2	Definition of targets for improving performance related to waste production	Qualitative
			E.24.3	Reporting mechanisms for violations of waste production controls	Qualitative
			E.24.4	Internal/external audit of compliance with adopted waste generation controls	Qualitative
	E.25	Quantity of hazardous waste generated during the year (T)	E.25.1	Amount of hazardous waste generated during the year (T)	Quantitative
			E.25.2	Amount of radioactive waste generated during the year (T)	Quantitative
			E.25.3	If the value is higher than 0, please provide details on their management	Descriptive
			E.25.4	% of hazardous waste generated during the year / total waste	Quantitative
			E.25.5	% of hazardous waste not recycled during the year / total waste	Quantitative
	E.26	Internal policies to promote the use of recycled or recyclable raw materials	E.26.1	Presence of an internal policy for the use of recycled or recyclable raw materials	Qualitative
	E.27	Non-recycled waste during the year and use of recycled raw materials	E.27.1	% of recycled raw materials used	Quantitative
			E.27.2	Quantity of non-recycled waste generated during the year (T)	Quantitative
			E.27.3	% of non-recycled waste during the year / total waste	Quantitative
	E.28	Adoption of innovative sustainable materials in the production process	E.28.1	Economic and product sustainability certification	Qualitative

Category	ID	ESG Evaluation Criteria	ID_1	Key Performance Indicators	Type
Environmental quality and biodiversity	E.29	Policies to protect biodiversity and to sustainably management of land, including forests	E.29.1	Enter a description	Descriptive
			E.29.2	Presence of a Policy to address deforestation	Qualitative
	E.30	Negative impacts of the activity on biodiversity (yes/no). If yes, please provide details	E.30.1	Enter a description	Descriptive
	E.31	Actions and/or initiatives implemented to protect and conserve biodiversity. If yes, please provide details	E.31.1	Enter a description	Descriptive
	E.32	Geolocation in non-biodiversity-sensitive areas, where activities negatively impact these areas	E.32.1	Property sites in or near protected areas	Qualitative
	E.33	Existence of specific certifications aimed at protecting biodiversity, also considering the origin of raw materials	E.33.1	Presence of certifications, e.g. FSC, PEFC, DCFL	Qualitative

The ESG framework for the *Social pillar* is structured in the following thematic categories, which also reflect the EU social taxonomy:

1. Social dialogue, workforce and living wages, focusing on people in their working lives or as workers.
2. Human rights and working conditions, including aspects related to health and safety for workers, lifelong learning, social protection, human rights and child labour.
3. Integration, inclusion, diversity, addressing equal opportunities for women, in terms of policies supporting non-discrimination and diversity, the promotion of gender parity and reduction of gender pay-gap, as well as job creation for young generations.
4. Adequate living standards and wellbeing for end-users, which focuses on consumers of products and services, safeguarding them from high risks to health or safety, protecting personal data, ensuring responsible marketing practices, ensuring durability and repairability of products.
5. Inclusive & sustainable communities and societies, adopting processes to promote equality and inclusive community growth and policies to involve stakeholders to guide decision making processes and avoid potentially negative impacts.

7 HOPE: A CASE FOR CHANGE

6. Philanthropic initiatives, including volunteering and donations to NGOs and/or local institutions.

Table 7.2 ESG questionnaire and KPI for Social topics

Category	ID	ESG Evaluation Criteria	ID_1	Key Performance Indicators	Type
Social dialogue	S.01	Organization and quality of social dialogue	S.01.1	Enter a description	Descriptive
	S.02	Social disputes during the year (e.g. number, reasons, outcome, etc.)	S.02.1	Enter a description	Descriptive
	S.03	Presence of internal policies respecting the fundamental rights of employees (examples: freedom of association, right to strike, exercise of trade union rights in the workplace)	S.03.1	Presence of internal policies for the respect of fundamental rights of employees	Qualitative
			S.03.2	% Of employees who are union members (second level bargaining)	Quantitative
	S.04	Percentage of the workforce covered by collective bargaining agreements on working conditions	S.04.1	% Of employees covered by NCBA	Quantitative
	S.05	Presence of initiatives to develop a sense of belonging at work (e.g., working groups/advisory committees)	S.05.1	If yes, Enter a description	Descriptive
Living wages	S.06	Presence of fair and adequate remuneration policies	S.06.1	% Of workers with a wage above the minimum subsistence wage	Quantitative
			S.06.2	Ratio between average annual salary and average industry salary	Quantitative
	S.07	Presence of incentive mechanisms/corporate participation/profit-sharing	S.07.1	Brief description of the incentive mechanisms adopted	Descriptive

Category	ID	ESG Evaluation Criteria	ID_1	Key Performance Indicators	Type
			S.07.2	% of employees, not counting founders and managers, who received a bonus during the last fiscal year	Quantitative
			S.07.3	% of profits distributed as bonuses to non-executive employees in the last fiscal year	Quantitative
			S.07.4	% of employees who received shares, stock options or stock equivalents	Quantitative
Workforce	S.08	Total number of employees	S.08.1	Total number of employees	Descriptive
	S.09	Geographical distribution of employees (% in Italy, Europe, Worldwide)	S.09.1	Enter a description	Descriptive
	S.10	Types of employment contracts in place (fixed-term and permanent) and % of employees with permanent contracts	S.10.1	% employees hired with permanent contracts compared to sector average	Quantitative
			S.10.2	% temporary contracts converted into permanent contracts	Quantitative
	S.11	Staff turnover: provide the number of entrants, leavers, average workforce for the year	S.11.1	Employee turnover compared to the sector average	Quantitative
	S.12	Net job creation	S.12.1	New jobs generated during the year	Quantitative
	S.13	Absenteeism: provide the average number of workers absent per year	S.13.1	Average number of workers absent during the year	Quantitative
	S.14	Adequate staff composition to ensure inclusion and required specialization	S.14.1	% highly specialized employees	Quantitative
			S.14.2	% of workers employed in R&D	Quantitative
			S.14.3	% employees with more than 10 years of experience in the sector	Quantitative

7 HOPE: A Case for Change

Category	ID	ESG Evaluation Criteria	ID_1	Key Performance Indicators	Type
			S.14.4	% employees from a country other than the country of the company	Quantitative
Working conditions – Health and safety	S.15	Adoption of internal OSH policies (including protection of workers from hazardous chemicals)	S.15.1	Occupational health and safety management system (indicate in the notes field if the management system is certified e.g. ISO 45001, OHSAS 18001)	Qualitative
			S.15.2	Definition of targets for improving performance on health and safety in the workplace	Qualitative
			S.15.3	Mechanisms for reporting breaches of adopted occupational health and safety arrangements	Qualitative
			S.15.4	Internal/external audits on compliance with the health and safety at work measures in place	Qualitative
	S.16	Frequency rate of occupational accidents	S.16.1	Rate of accidents at work [total number of accidents* 200,000/ number of hours worked]	Quantitative
	S.17	Severity rate of the occupational accidents	S.17.1	Number of days lost due to injury, accident, death, or illness	Quantitative
			S.17.2	Severity ratio (days lost/ total working days)	Quantitative
			S.17.3	Average duration ([days off work]/[number of accidents])	Quantitative
			S.17.4	Presence of recognized occupational diseases (number of employees)	Quantitative

Category	ID	ESG Evaluation Criteria	ID_1	Key Performance Indicators	Type
Working conditions – Life-long learning	S.18	Adoption of employee training programs	S.18.1	Training programs on sustainability issues	Qualitative
			S.18.2	Training programs on anti-bribery/anti-money laundering/code of ethics/whistleblowing	Qualitative
			S.18.3	Health and safety training programs	Qualitative
			S.18.4	Career development training programs	Qualitative
			S.18.5	Number of planned training hours per employee	Quantitative
	S.19	Resources dedicated to employee training	S.19.1	Average cost of training per employee	Quantitative
	S.20	Employee engagement in training	S.20.1	Percentage of employees trained in sustainability issues	Quantitative
			S.20.2	Percentage of employees trained in anti-corruption/anti-money laundering/code of ethics/whistleblowing	Quantitative
			S.20.3	Percentage of employees trained in health and safety	Quantitative
			S.20.4	Percentage of employees trained in career development	Quantitative
	S.21	Youth policies and projects	S.21.1	Enter a description	Descriptive
			S.21.2	Training plans for young people/Total training plans for employees	Quantitative
Working conditions – Social protection	S.22	Presence of a whistleblowing policy for reporting wrongdoing and discrimination	S.22.1	Presence of a whistleblowing policy	Qualitative
	S.23	Adoption of welfare policies (e.g. healthcare, health insurance, pension schemes etc.)	S.23.1	Presence of a welfare policy	Qualitative

7 HOPE: A Case for Change

Category	ID	ESG Evaluation Criteria	ID_1	Key Performance Indicators	Type
			S.23.2	% Of employees covered by a company health care plan	Quantitative
			S.23.3	Presence of private pension schemes	Qualitative
			S.23.4	Policies in support of working mothers (e.g., breastfeeding support, subsidized childcare, day-care on company premises)	Qualitative
			S.23.5	Presence of additional benefits (e.g. company canteen, meal vouchers, company conventions, subsidy for sports activities)	Qualitative
	S.24	Actions and/or initiatives aimed at the well-being of employees (e.g. smart-working, flexible working hours, team-building events, ergonomic offices etc.)	S.24.1	Enter a description	Descriptive
	S.25	Presence of employee satisfaction survey systems	S.25.1	Definition of targets for improving employee satisfaction	Descriptive
Human rights	S.26	Presence of processes and/or policies for handling complaints/incidents related to the principles of the UN Global Compact or the OECD guidelines for multinational enterprises	S.26.1	Declared adherence to the principles of the UN Global Compact or the OECD Guidelines for Multinational Enterprises	Qualitative
			S.26.2	Presence of a Human Rights Policy	Qualitative
			S.26.3	Policy to monitor compliance with the UNGC principles or the OECD Guidelines for Multinational Enterprises or complaint handling mechanisms to address such violations	Qualitative

Category	ID	ESG Evaluation Criteria	ID_1	Key Performance Indicators	Type
	S.27	Ethical incidents or incidents relating to non-compliance with the principles of the UN Global Compact or the OECD Guidelines for Multinational Enterprises	S.27.1	If yes, Enter a description	Qualitative
	S.28	Adoption of internal policies for selecting suppliers based on the presence of a code of conduct within the code of ethics	S.28.1	Presence of supplier selection policies adopting a code of ethics (on strategic suppliers)	Qualitative
Decent Work – *Child labour*	S.29	Exposure to a significant risk of accident for underage workers	S.29.1	Exposure to activities and/or suppliers at significant risk of child labour incidents, exposed to hazardous work in terms of geographical areas or type of activity	Qualitative
Integration, Inclusion, Diversity	S.30	Presence of internal policies supporting non-discrimination and the promotion of diversity in the workplace (examples: maternity and paternity benefits)	S.30.1	Enter a description	Descriptive
			S.30.2	Presence of equal parental leave policies for primary and secondary figures	Qualitative
	S.31	Incidents of discrimination	S.31.1	Number of incidents of discrimination	Quantitative
			S.31.2	Number of incidents of discrimination leading to sanctions	Quantitative
	S.32	Gender Parity: Percentage of women in the workforce at the end of the year	S.32.1	Number of women among total employees at end of the year	Quantitative
			S.32.2	Percentage of women in the top management	Quantitative
	S.33	Gender Pay Gap: Ratio between the average salary of women and men	S.33.1	Gender pay gap ratio	Quantitative
	S.34	Pay Gap: Ratio between the average salary of managers and other workers	S.34.1	Ratio between the average salary of managers and other workers	Quantitative
	S.35	Presence of young workers	S.35.1	% workers under 30	Quantitative

Category	ID	ESG Evaluation Criteria	ID_1	Key Performance Indicators	Type
	S.36	% of disabled employees at the end of the year: provide the number of disabled employees at the end of the year	S.36.1	Number of disabled employees at the end of the year	Quantitative
Adequate living standards & Well-being for end-users	S.37	Safety and quality of products and services provided (certification, recall management, disputes)	S.37.1	Presence of mandatory minimum certifications to ensure product safety and quality	Qualitative
			S.37.2	Number of product recalls issued due to product safety/quality defects	Quantitative
			S.37.3	Costs incurred because of legal proceedings related to product safety and quality/legal fees	Quantitative
	S.38	Design of durable and repairable products	S.38.1	Avoiding the use of harmful chemicals in products or in the provision of services when less harmful alternatives are available	Qualitative
			S.38.2	Prompt, effective and transparent recall procedures in case products develop defects that endanger the safety of users	Qualitative
			S.38.3	Offering extended warranty periods for product defects	Qualitative
			S.38.4	Design of durable and repairable products (availability of spare parts, interoperability with competitive parts) and offer of services enabling a seamless multimodal experience (e.g., in transport)	Qualitative

Category	ID	ESG Evaluation Criteria	ID_1	Key Performance Indicators	Type
			S.38.5	Commitment to applying European safety legislation also to imported products	Qualitative
			S.38.6	Disclosure of chemicals present in products (toys, paints, furniture) or used for services such as house painting, hairdressing)	Qualitative
	S.39	Protection of customers' personal data, respect for privacy and cybersecurity	S.39.1	Design IT interfaces in a responsible way, avoiding exposing users to 'dark paths', with particular attention to preventing any kind of discriminatory algorithms	Qualitative
			S.39.2	Designing privacy terms and conditions in simple, short and understandable language	Qualitative
			S.39.3	Offering connected products that maintain their primary function even if the software is switched off or outdated	Qualitative
	S.40	Responsible marketing practices (e.g., profiling, non-discrimination, diversity, promoting sustainable behavior)	S.40.1	Adopting data collection policies that avoid profiling users for commercial purposes	Qualitative
			S.40.2	Promotion of non-discrimination and diversity in marketing practices	Qualitative
			S.40.3	Promoting healthy food options proactively, especially when targeting children	Qualitative

Category	ID	ESG Evaluation Criteria	ID_1	Key Performance Indicators	Type
			S.40.4	Dissemination of information on social and environmental impacts in the product supply chain	Qualitative
	S.41	Access to quality health products and services, including care services	S.41.1	High standards of quality and safety of these products, which must be easily accessible. Enter a description	Descriptive
	S.42	Access to healthy and highly nutritious food especially for children	S.42.1	High standard of quality of these products. Enter a description	Descriptive
	S.43	Access to education and life-long learning	S.43.1	Organization of forums/webinars/events aimed at raising "public" awareness about sustainability issues	Qualitative
Inclusive & Sustainable communities and societies	S.44	Adoption of processes to promote equality and inclusive community growth	S.44.1	Access to basic infrastructure for stakeholders (e.g., transport, telecommunications, financial services, electricity)	Qualitative
			S.44.2	Childcare and child support	Qualitative
			S.44.3	Inclusion of people with disabilities	Qualitative
			S.44.4	Initiatives/plans for retraining staff to support the environmental and digital transition	Qualitative
			S.44.5	Promotion of policies to recruit local workers (including suppliers)	Qualitative
			S.44.6	Promotion of equality and non-discrimination through community-based initiatives. If yes, please describe	Descriptive

Category	ID	ESG Evaluation Criteria	ID_1	Key Performance Indicators	Type
	S.45	Policies to support sustainable livelihoods and land rights	S.45.1	Involvement of stakeholders to guide decision-making processes	Qualitative
			S.45.2	Plans and actions to avoid negative impacts on the communities impacted by business operations	Qualitative
			S.45.3	Continuous dialogue with stakeholders to obtain consensus before starting new activities with potentially negative impacts	Qualitative
	S.46	Respect for the human rights of affected communities by carrying out appropriate risk-based due diligence	S.46.1	Involvement of stakeholders on issues related to the defence of human rights and restrictions on civil liberties and the rule of law	Descriptive
Philanthropic initiatives	S.47	Philanthropic activities (volunteering, donations to NGOs/local institutions)	S.47.1	Existence of volunteering schemes directed at employees	Qualitative
			S.47.2	Volunteering hours provided by employees last year	Quantitative
			S.47.3	Donations to non-profit organizations/ local institutions or other initiatives with an impact on the community and the environment	Qualitative

The assessment of the aspects related to *corporate governance* has been organized into six main categories:

1. Corporate governance in terms of adequate composition, participation and presence of a control model.

2. Ethics and compliance, which includes the presence of a code of ethics, as well as policies and procedures for fighting corruption, money laundering and protecting human rights.
3. Remuneration policies, aimed at reducing the gender pay gap, ensuring adequate compensation and including ESG criteria in the establishment of the variable component of compensation.
4. Risk Assessment, in terms of data protection safeguards and cybersecurity, and operational risk management, including whistleblowing policy and internal control and audit processes.
5. Sustainability in action, addressing objectives and safeguards on ESG topics, and corporate social responsibility, verifying sustainability competencies and commitment at the highest corporate body.
6. Transparency and reputation in reporting, including fiscal transparency and reporting.

Table 7.3 ESG questionnaire and KPI for Governance topics

Category	ID	ESG Evaluation Criteria	ID_1	Key Performance Indicators	Type
Corporate governance	G.01	Board composition: presence on the board of members of the less represented gender	G.01.1	Presence of minority representatives on the board	Qualitative
	G.02	Board composition: % of women on the Board of Directors	G.02.1	Percentage of female representatives on the board members	Quantitative
	G.03	Presence of independent directors on the Board of Directors	G.03.1	Percentage of independent directors on the board of directors	Quantitative
	G.04	Attendance at board meetings	G.04.1	Average percentage attendance at board meetings	Quantitative
	G.05	Independence of auditors	G.05.1	Presence of independent auditors	Qualitative
	G.06	Adoption/intention to adopt an organization, management and control model pursuant to Legislative decree 231	G.06.1	Presence of a control model	Qualitative
	G.07	Identification of incremental levels of protection concerning those provided for in Legislative decree 231 concerning the management of influence (lobbying and political engagement)	G.07.1	Enter a description	Qualitative

Category	ID	ESG Evaluation Criteria	ID_1	Key Performance Indicators	Type
Ethics & Compliance	G.08	Presence of offices/activities in countries at risk in terms of corruption and/or human rights. Refer to countries deemed at risk by official sources (e.g., Transparency International for corruption and Global Risk Profile for human rights)	G.08.1	Enter a description	Qualitative
	G.09	Adoption of internal practices aimed at combating corruption and money laundering	G.09.1	Presence of internal practices aimed at combating corruption and money laundering	Qualitative
	G.10	Presence of a code of ethics	G.10.1	Presence of a code of ethics	Qualitative
	G.11	Presence of a Human Rights Policy	G.11.1	Definition of improvement targets related to safeguarding fair working conditions (e.g., diversity, human rights)	Qualitative
			G.11.2	Mechanisms for reporting violations of adopted safeguards related to fair working conditions (e.g., diversity, human rights)	Qualitative
			G.11.3	Internal/external audit of compliance with adopted safeguards related to fair working conditions (e.g., diversity, human rights)	Qualitative
	G.12	Possible cases of corruption/anti-money laundering	G.12.1	Expenses incurred because of legal proceedings related to corruption and money laundering compared to total litigation expenses	Quantitative
Remuneration policies	G.13	Adoption/intention to adopt internal policies for the alignment of male/female remuneration	G.13.1	Presence of internal policies for the alignment of male/female remuneration	Qualitative
	G.14	Adopt/intend to adopt internal policies to ensure adequate remuneration (e.g., at industry average)	G.14.1	Presence of internal policies to ensure adequate remuneration	Qualitative

Category	ID	ESG Evaluation Criteria	ID_1	Key Performance Indicators	Type
	G.15	Adoption/intention to adopt remuneration policies whereby the variable component is also dependent on the achievement of specific ESG objectives	G.15.1	Presence of remuneration policies whereby the variable component is also dependent on the achievement of specific ESG objectives	Qualitative
Risk assessment – Data protection and cybersecurity	G.16	Access to personal and/or sensitive data	G.16.1	Enter a description	Descriptive
	G.17	Access to personal and/or sensitive data	G.16.2	Average number of customers subject to data breach incidents/ total customers	Quantitative
	G.17	Presence of formalized processes and/or policies on data protection (GDPR compliance)	G.17.1	Privacy management system. Describe in the notes field and attach documents	Descriptive
			G.17.2	Definition of privacy security performance improvement objectives	Qualitative
			G.17.3	Mechanisms for reporting breaches of adopted privacy security safeguards	Qualitative
			G.17.4	Internal/external audits of compliance with adopted privacy security safeguards	Qualitative
	G.18	Technological measures in the field of IT security	G.18.1	Investments for the enhancement of technological structures in the field of information security/Total Capex in the year	Quantitative
	G.19	IT security incidents	G.19.1	If yes, Enter a description	Descriptive
			G.19.2	Delta data breach compared to the previous year	Quantitative
Risk assessment – Operational risk management	G.20	Adoption of a system/process to protect whistle-blowers – wrongdoing and discrimination	G.20.1	Presence of legality rating: if yes, please provide a rating	Descriptive
	G.21	Adoption of internal control and audit processes	G.21.1	Presence of internal control and audit processes	Qualitative

Category	ID	ESG Evaluation Criteria	ID_1	Key Performance Indicators	Type
Sustainability in action – Corporate social responsibility	G.22	ESG issues discussed in boardroom at least once a year	G.22.1	Enter a description	Descriptive
	G.23	Presence on the board or in senior management of personalities with experience in sustainability issues	G.23.1	Enter a description	Qualitative
	G.24	Presence of person(s) dedicated to CSR issues (ex. transversal function, part-time, full-time)	G.24.1	Enter a description	Qualitative
	G.25	Actions and/or initiatives implemented on CSR issues (e.g. reporting, goal setting, etc.)	G.25.1	Enter a description and attach documents	Qualitative
Sustainability in action – Sustainability goals	G.26	Integration of sustainable development objectives in strategic/industrial plans	G.26.1	Presence of sustainable development objectives in strategic/industrial plans	Qualitative
	G.27	Adoption of policies to ensure minimum ESG standards throughout the supply chain (upstream and downstream)	G.27.1	Presence of policies to ensure minimum ESG standards throughout the supply chain (upstream and downstream)	Qualitative
	G.28	Adoption of processes/tools to assess and improve customer satisfaction	G.28.1	Presence of processes/tools to assess and improve customer satisfaction	Qualitative
	G.29	Allocation of adequate resources for the sustainable transformation of processes/products/services	G.29.1	Investment in innovation to improve environmental performance and reduce atmospheric emissions from business processes/ Total CAPEX	Quantitative
	G.30	Adoption of systems/processes for measuring and managing social and environmental results (ESG KPIs)	G.30.1	Presence of systems/processes for measuring and managing social and environmental results (ESG KPIs)	Qualitative
Transparency & Reputation	G.31	Adoption of a Non-Financial Statement (DNF) or annual sustainability report	G.31.1	Preparation of a Non-Financial Statement (DNF) or annual sustainability report	Qualitative
	G.32	Adoption of an external governance certification system (process and product certification)	G.32.1	Presence of an external governance certification system (process and product certification)	Qualitative

7 HOPE: A Case for Change

Category	ID	ESG Evaluation Criteria	ID_1	Key Performance Indicators	Type
	G.33	Transparency and completeness of fiscal reporting	G.33.1	Adoption of international accounting standards in tax matters	Qualitative
			G.33.2	Number of fines and/or penalties received in tax matters	Quantitative
			G.33.3	Presence of litigation by shareholders and/or directors on tax issues	Qualitative
	G.34	Existence of a robust tax policy/ strategy for governance, internal control of taxation of the company (alternatively specify adoption of internal procedures)	G.34.1	Management system in the field of fiscal transparency (e.g., Tax Control Framework)	Qualitative
			G.34.2	Mechanisms for reporting violations of the adopted controls relating to tax transparency	Qualitative
			G.34.3	Internal/external audits on compliance with adopted tax transparency controls	Qualitative

The results of the preliminary ESG assessment, together with the verification of the principles of exclusion and controversies, are summarized by the investment team in a report, which includes the Risk Manager's opinion and that will be presented both to the Investment Committee and to the Sustainability Committee.

Any shortcomings found during the preliminary screening phase may lead to a waiver of the investment opportunity or to the identification of potential items of concern that will need to be further investigated in subsequent phases of analysis and subject to decision by the Board of Directors.

Having gathered all information and opinions, the Board decides whether to proceed with the due diligence, which includes a proper ESG due diligence, conducted by specialized providers.

In particular, ESG due diligence is designed to conduct an in-depth and detailed analysis of significant ESG risk factors, on which it is possible to define strategic objectives and ESG indicators for monitoring these objectives over time.

The ESG due diligence aims to:

- understand the context and the sector and assess specific ESG issues, related for example to climate change risk (both transitional and physical risks), production processes, business model and supply chain complexity;
- analyse the ESG policies already implemented by the target company and assess its ability in terms of methodologies, tools and processes to address these issues;
- identify the ESG objectives for the investment, which represent the key success factors for a competitive advantage over peers and the reference industry;
- request, if necessary, the development of a corrective action plan to achieve ESG objectives for significant incremental improvements that may lead to competitive advantage.

Results from the due diligence are analysed by the Investment Team and by the Risk Management Function (which formulates its opinion on the investment risks) and synthesized in the Investment Memorandum. After examining the contents of the Investment Memorandum and acknowledging the opinions of the Sustainability Committee, the Board of Directors deliberate on the investment execution.

An ESG Compact, including the specific objectives (and KPIs) that are intended to be achieved with the investment, is agreed upon.

ESG Assessment for "Sustainable Cities and Smart/Green Infrastructure"[3]

As far as the "Sustainable Cities and Smart/Green Infrastructure" strategy is concerned, the ESG Assessment is carried out through the ESG Cities Framework, developed by HOPE together with a working group of experts in the field of real estate: strategic advisors, consultants and engineers (ARUP), designers (PLANET Smart City), contractors (Borio Mangiarotti S.p.A.) and software developers (TECMA). In particular:

- ARUP is a global company composed of designers, planners, engineers, architects, consultants and technical specialists, working across 140 countries and covering most aspects of today's built environment, and with a primary goal to develop a truly sustainable

- built environment, balancing the needs of a growing world population, and the finite capacity and health of our planet.
- PLANET Smart City is an innovative proptech company, focussed on smart affordable housing, with expertise in smart solutions integration, digital services and social innovation to enhance citizens' quality of life. The society pioneers new standards for affordable housing worldwide and also works in partnership with developers to revitalize existing communities through smart technologies.
- Borio Mangiarotti is a real estate development company, active as a developer and general contractor, with an extensive track record in the real estate sector in Milan, Italy.
- TECMA is a public company listed on the Italian stock market, specialized in the business innovation components of the real estate sector. It develops technology and marketing strategies for new development markets. It is focussed on an original business model in real estate investments.

The ESG Framework developed by HOPE and its partners is the result of a process of sharing expertise, know-how and experience of a variety of actors playing different roles along the value chain of an urban development project. This process has made it possible to look at sustainability issues from different perspectives to develop an ecosystem of knowledge and a common language to aim at sustainability in real life projects.

This ESG Framework is designed to be applied to different projects and has the ambition to become a benchmark and standard practice in the market. The model is structured as a balanced scorecard of indicators, selected following law requirements, national, European and international standards (e.g. UN SDGs, EU taxonomy, SFDR, GRI, GRESB; Leed, Breeam, Well, etc) whose weights are defined according to three scenarios:

1. Standard Practice – performance compliant with local/national regulatory requirements and on the average level of the sector or of the area considered.
2. Best Practice – performance in line with the most recent and future European policies and standards, such as the EU Taxonomy; this scenario includes a proactive attitude of anticipating regulatory requirements and developments.
3. Pioneering/innovative practice for most innovative and best in class

developments (e.g. Net Zero Carbon buildings, Carbon-Storing Buildings, Circular models – DFMA and DFD – and Ecological and Biophilic approach)

This approach allows the framework to be applied flexibly and dynamically at the different contexts and projects, and it can be used as a decision support tool in every phase of an urban regeneration project:

- the investment phase, which includes all necessary analyses for the investment decision (i) the preliminary project analysis, (ii) the ESG due diligence, (iii) a Fit Test;
- the project planning and construction phase which covers (i) the strategic planning and the definition of ESG policies and targets, (ii) the ESG monitoring, (iii) the reporting to all the relevant stakeholders both internal and external;
- the final evaluation in the Valorisation phase, to assess the achievement of ESG targets defined for the project, and final reporting for potential investors.

This ESG Framework is in the process of being digitalized through an innovative software platform, providing centralised data gathering, data insights, continuous monitoring and assessment of KPIs to report on projects' ESG performance in a streamlined digital process. The platform can also allow for the activation of checkpoints and early warning systems to predict and manage potential critical issues in the implementation phases. The digital framework is capable of evolving and adapting to the evolution of the market's needs and to the sustainability policies and regulatory requirements evolution.

The ESG Framework for Sustainable cities consists of three pillars – environmental, social and governance – 18 thematic categories, 58 sub-categories and 166 KPIs.

For each KPI a reference benchmark has been identified. Each benchmark is then articulated into three levels that reflect the scenarios just introduced (standard, best/better/pioneer). The comparison between the specific KPI and its benchmark highlights the area of improvement of the project performance.

Environmental indicators have been organized into six categories, covering aspects related to:

7 HOPE: A Case for Change

Figure 7.3 ESG Framework for Sustainable Cities and Smart/Green Infrastructure

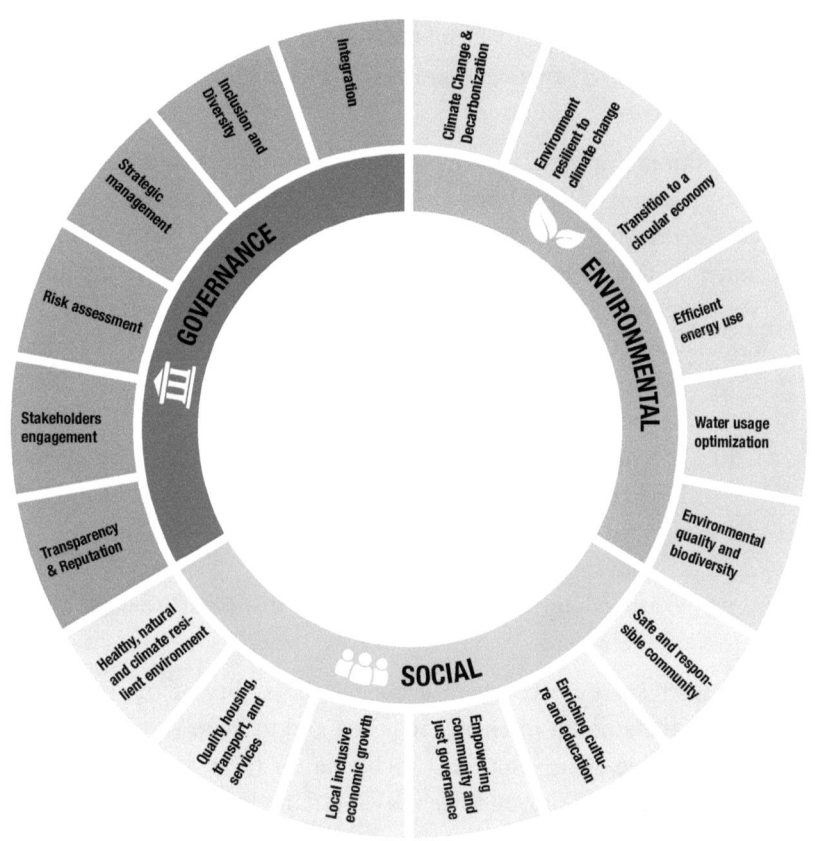

1. Climate change and decarbonization, focusing on strategies to meet targets (+1.5°C) set at international levels and to measure the carbon intensity of each development/project in details. This includes the three following subcategories:
    i. Climate change adaptation – climate change risk assessment.
    ii. Carbon/GHG emissions (embodied/operational).
    iii. Net-zero/carbon neutral design.
2. Creation of an environment resilient to climate change, which takes into account strategies deployed in order to anticipate, prepare for, and respond to hazardous events/catastrophes. These strategies will have to deal with different timeframes (30-50-100-200 years), proj-

ect specificities in terms of land use and urban functions involved, and constraints/opportunities linked to specific geographical locations. This category covers the three following subcategories:
   i. Resilience to catastrophe/disaster.
   ii. Effectively managed protective ecosystems.
   iii. Urban microclimate.

3. Transition to a circular economy which involves designing, testing, and applying of circularity principles to different phases of a project, identifying materials responsible for the largest share of energy and resource consumption within the built environment, finding strategies and alternative materials to reduce their impact and foster circular processes. This includes the following five sub-categories:
   i. Life-cycle assessments.
   ii. Responsible sourcing of materials.
   iii. Circular design (Design for Adaptability and Longevity, DFMA – Design for Manufacture and Assembly, DFD-Design for Disassembly).
   iv. Digital tools to improve circularity.
   v. Waste Management strategies with a specific focus on operational waste.

4. Efficient energy use, which evaluates the ability of the project to reduce the amount of energy required and to increase the adoption of renewable energy sources. Focussing on these aspects from the design phase has proven to be relevant in implementing energy-saving strategies and achieving the expected targets in the operational phase. This includes the following four sub-categories:
   i. Energy consumption.
   ii. Energy consumption metering.
   iii. Renewable energy.
   iv. Commissioning.

5. Water usage optimization through better management of water resources, minimising water consumption in particular of potable/drinking water and design of efficient systems to reduce and monitor water consumption, allowing periodical control on the proper functioning of the water-related systems. This includes the four following subcategories:
   i. Indoor water consumption.

ii. Outdoor water consumption.
iii. Water quality.
iv. Water consumption metering.

6. Environmental quality and biodiversity refer primarily to the ecological connections and to the creation or restoration of green and blue infrastructures to support local biodiversity, landscape quality and visual amenity. This category also focuses also on responsible use and management of soil and land, fostering remediation of polluted soils, the use of already used or disturbed soil and avoiding the use of greenfield areas. This can be pursued considering the following sub-categories:
   i. Biodiversity and habitat (Ecological Networks and Nature-based solutions).
   ii. Landscape value and visual amenity.
   iii. Air pollution prevention.
   iv. Quality land use.
   v. Soil preservation and restoration.

Table 7.4 ESG Framework and KPI for Environmental topics

Category	ID	Sub-category (ESG Evaluation Criteria)	ID_1	Metrics/KPIs
Climate Change & Decarbonization	E.01	Climate change adaptation and risk assessment	E.01.1	Screening and Vulnerability Assessment of climate-related physical risk [0-1]
			E.01.2	Adaptation solutions that can reduce physical risk related to climate change [0-1]
			E.01.3	Design building considering global warming in the future [0-1]
	E.02	Carbon/GHG emissions	E.02.1	Assessment on Embodied carbon [kg CO_2e/m^2]
			E.02.2	Assessment on Operational carbon [kg CO_2e/m^2y]
			E.02.3	Perform LCA in accordance with Level(s) [0-1]
			E.02.4	GHG emissions (Scope 1) [t CO_2e/y]
			E.02.5	GHG emissions (Scope 2) [t CO_2e/y]
			E.02.6	GHG emissions (Scope 3) [t CO_2e/y]
	E.03	Net-zero/carbon neutral design	E.03.1	Commitment to net zero carbon [0-1]

Category	ID	Sub-category (ESG Evaluation Criteria)	ID_1	Metrics/KPIs
			E.03.2	Commitment to partial net zero carbon [0-1]
			E.03.3	Building passive strategies [0-1]
			E.03.4	Natural ventilation [0-1]
			E.03.5	Building active Strategies [0-1]
			E.03.6	Electric Vehicle Supply Equipment Provisions [%]
			E.03.7	Electric Vehicle Supply Equipment Infrastructure [%]
			E.03.8	Refrigerant Management [0-1]
			E.03.9	On-site renewable sources – roofs [0-1]
			E.03.10	On-site renewable sources – facade [0-1]
			E.03.11	Energy storage [0-1]
			E.03.12	Environmental certifications – EU Level(s) [0-1]
			E.03.13	Environmental certifications – Optimized buildings [0-1]
			E.03.14	Environmental certifications – Neutral buildings [0-1]
Creation of an environment resilient to climate change	E.04	Effectively managed protective ecosystems	E.04.1	Urban forestry interventions (0-1)
			E.04.2	Plant species most effective in reducing pollutants (0-1)
			E.04.3	Plant species with minimal content of allergen (0-1)
	E.05	Urban microclimate	E.05.1	Outdoor Passive strategies [0-1]
Transition to a circular economy	E.06	Responsible sourcing of materials	E.06.1	Environmental certification of materials
			E.06.2	Regional origin of materials
			E.06.3	Natural materials
			E.06.4	Design out hazardous/pollutant materials
			E.06.5	Recycled, reused or remanufactured content
	E.07	Circular design	E.07.1	Design for disassembly, flexibility & adaptability
			E.07.2	Material and resource efficiency

7 HOPE: A Case for Change

Category	ID	Sub-category (ESG Evaluation Criteria)	ID_1	Metrics/KPIs
	E.08	Digital tools to improve circularity	E.08.1	Maintenance schedule
			E.08.2	Detailed material specification records
	E.09	Waste Management Strategy	E.09.1	Waste reuse and recyclability
			E.09.2	Construction waste prevention
			E.09.3	Waste data collection
			E.09.4	Operational waste
Efficient energy use	E.10	Energy consumption	E.10.1	EPC Rating [non-renewable kWh/m2]
			E.10.2	Energy saving [%]
			E.10.3	Perform Energy Modelling [0-1]
			E.10.4	Optimize Energy Performance [%]
			E.10.5	CRREM Compliance Prediction
	E.11	Renewable energy	E.11.1	Renewable coverage of primary energy consumption related to heating and DHW and cooling [% in P.E.]
			E.11.2	Renewable coverage of overall building consumption [% in cost]
			E.11.3	Off-site renewable sources
	E.12	Energy consumption metering	E.12.1	Whole Building metering [kWh/monthly]
			E.12.2	Metering of final uses (heating, cooling, DHW, ventilation, lighting, fans, pumps, etc) [kWh/monthly]
			E.12.3	Sharing of consumption with tenants/users [0-1]
			E.12.4	Peak loads analysis (passive Demand Response)
			E.12.5	BMS system to manage peak loads (active Demand Response)
	E.13	Commissioning	E.13.1	Commissioning of envelope [0-1]
			E.13.2	Commissioning of building services/HVAC systems [0-1]
			E.13.3	Commissioning of Building Energy Managing System (BEMS) [0-1]

Category	ID	Sub-category (ESG Evaluation Criteria)	ID_1	Metrics/KPIs
Water usage optimization	E.14	Indoor water consumption	E.14.1	Implementation of low-demand fixture and flushing devices [l/min]
			E.14.2	Commitment to overall consumption reduction [litre/ppl*day]
	E.15	Outdoor water consumption	E.15.1	Minimisation of water consumption for irrigation
			E.15.2	Retain on site runoff [%-th]
			E.15.3	Commitment to overall consumption reduction [l/m2]
	E.16	Water quality	E.16.1	Monitoring of water quality during construction [0-1]
			E.16.2	Operational water quality
			E.16.3	Rainwater discharge quantity [0-1]
			E.16.4	Rainwater discharge quality monitoring [0-1]
	E.17	Water consumption metering	E.17.1	Whole Building metering [litre/monthly]
			E.17.2	Services metering [litre/monthly]
			E.17.3	Sharing of consumption [0-1]
Environmental quality and biodiversity	E.18	Biodiversity & habitat	E.18.1	Connection of ecological networks (index)
			E.18.2	Diversity of native plant species (index)
	E.19	Air pollution prevention	E.19.1	Commitment to the avoidance of fossil fuel onsite for heating, cooling, cooking [0-1]
			E.19.2	Continuous monitoring of outdoor air quality and sharing with occupants [0-1]
			E.19.3	Commitment to use material to reduce pollutants [0-1]
	E.20	Landscape value and visual amenity	E.20.1	Landscape diversity index
	E.21	Quality land use	E.21.1	Level of territorial fragmentation (mq/m)
			E.21.2	Urban agriculture [0-1]
			E.21.3	Soil permeability (%)
	E.22	Soil preservation and restoration	E.22.1	Remediation strategies need (0-1)
			E.22.2	Strategies for minimisation of dust creation in external areas [0-1]
			E.22.3	Soil sedimentation in discharge/drainage networks [0-1]

Social indicators embrace six main categories related to the:

1. Creation of a healthy and climate-resilient environment, in terms of resilient, pleasant and high-quality indoor and outdoor spaces to promote people's health and wellbeing. This includes the three following subcategories:
    i. High-quality indoor and outdoor spaces.
    ii. Community health and wellbeing.
    iii. Sustainable green-blue infrastructure.

2. Development of accessible and quality housing, transport and services, to support and respond to citizens' needs, which include the following categories:
    i. Inclusive social infrastructure.
    ii. Sustainable local mobility.
    iii. Cities for all ages and abilities.

3. Generation of an environment stimulating local and inclusive economic growth, a thriving environment where quality work, sustainability and innovation can develop. This includes:
    i. Quality job and social protection.
    ii. Attractive business environment.
    iii. Green, sustainable and innovative job creation.

4. Empowerment of communities, just governance and partnership, providing mechanisms and tools to promote community support, awareness and participation. This covers the three following subcategories:
    i. Integrated support at the individual, household and local community level.
    ii. Data monitoring and community awareness.
    iii. Effective and transparent mechanisms of participation.

5. Development of a representative and enriching culture and education, valorising the local heritage and favouring quality education and an upskilling environment, which comprises of:
    i. Local heritage, knowledge and culture enhancement.
    ii. Adequate, affordable, and quality education.
    iii. Widespread playful and upskilling environment.

6. Building of a safe and responsible community, pursuing:
    i. Reduced vulnerability of citizens and critical assets.
    ii. Effective stewardship of regulating ecosystem services.
    iii. Security by design.

Table 7.5 ESG framework and KPI for Social topics

Category	ID	Sub-category (ESG Evaluation Criteria)	ID_1	Metrics/KPIs
Healthy, natural and climate resilient environment	S.01	High-quality indoor and outdoor spaces (design)	S.01.1	UTCI – Universal Thermal Climate Index (°C or %)
			S.01.2	Urban Tree Canopy (%)
			S.01.3	Noise pollution (dB)
	S.02	Community health and wellbeing (design)	S.02.1	Open public and community space (sqm)
			S.02.2	Biophilia (%)
			S.02.3	Air quality (μg/m3)
	S.03	Sustainable green-blue infrastructure (design)	S.03.1	Urban Greening Factor (factor)
			S.03.2	Green proximity (sqm within a radius)
			S.03.3	Water infiltration and retention (percentile)
Accessible and quality housing, transport, and services	S.04	Inclusive social infrastructure (design)	S.04.1	Social infrastructures (index)
			S.04.2	Services standards (sqm/inh)
			S.04.3	Basic goods accessibility (0-1)
	S.05	Sustainable local mobility (design)	S.05.1	Public transport accessibility level (grade)
			S.05.2	Pedestrian network connectivity (n.)
			S.05.3	Bicycle network continuity (contiguous km)
	S.06	Cities for all ages and abilities (design)	S.06.1	Universal design principles (0-1)
			S.06.2	Social housing (%)
			S.06.3	Elderly-friendly urban spaces (0-1)
Local and inclusive economic growth	S.07	Quality job and social protection (corporate/design)	S.07.1	Recreational and restorative spaces at work (sqm)

7 HOPE: A Case for Change

Category	ID	Sub-category (ESG Evaluation Criteria)	ID_1	Metrics/KPIs
			S.07.2	Policies to respect rights at work (0-1)
			S.07.3	Wellbeing initiatives at work (0-1)
	S.08	Attractive business environment (design)	S.08.1	Active frontages (%)
			S.08.2	Diverse and mixed land uses (n.)
			S.08.3	Large scale attractors (0-1)
	S.09	Green, sustainable, and innovative jobs creation (corporate/design)	S.09.1	New total jobs (0-1)
			S.09.2	Innovative start-ups (0-1)
			S.09.3	Spaces for co-working (0-1)
Empowering community and just governance and partnership	S.10	Integrated support at individual, household and community level (design)	S.10.1	Local welfare hubs (0-1)
			S.10.2	Social neighbourhood concierges (0-1)
			S.10.3	Active third sector organization (0-1)
	S.11	Data monitoring and community awareness (design)	S.11.1	Sensors (0-1)
			S.11.2	Data-driven smart tools (0-1)
			S.11.3	Citizens science (0-1)
	S.12	Effective and transparent mechanisms of participation (design)	S.12.1	Participatory processes (0-1)
			S.12.2	Spaces for events and meetings (sqm)
			S.12.3	Public spaces activation programs (0-1)
Representative and enriching culture and education	S.13	Local heritage, knowledge and cultures enhancement (design)	S.13.1	Arts and cultures centres (0-1)
			S.13.2	Landmarks (0-1)
			S.13.3	Cultural and natural heritage protection (0-1)
	S.14	Adequate, affordable, quality education for all (design/corporate)	S.14.1	Schools and universities (sqm/inh)
			S.14.2	Youth and learning support services (0-1)
			S.14.3	Lifelong learning opportunities (0-1)
	S.15	Widespread playful and upskilling environment (design)	S.15.1	Space and facilities for play (sqm)
			S.15.2	Sports spaces and facilities (sqm)
			S.15.3	Urban gamification strategies (0-1)

Category	ID	Sub-category (ESG Evaluation Criteria)	ID_1	Metrics/KPIs
Safe and responsible community	S.16	Reduced vulnerability of citizens and critical assets (design)	S.16.1	NbSs and protective design strategies (0-1)
			S.16.2	Safe emergency spots (0-1)
			S.16.3	Citizens emergency and prevention guidelines (0-1)
	S.17	Effective stewardship of regulating ecosystem services (design)	S.17.1	Soil permeability (%)
			S.17.2	Plants for pollinators (index)
			S.17.3	Disturbance regulation (0-1)
	S.18	Security by design (design)	S.18.1	Design strategies for safer spaces for women and girl (0-1)
			S.18.2	Street furniture as protective barriers (0-1)
			S.18.3	Safe pedestrian sidewalks (%)

Governance indicators were selected having as their main focus the application of the ESG Framework to projects. They also address the issue of governance at corporate level because a special purpose vehicle (SPV) may be proposed. In this case the SPV is the entity that accountable for the governance issues of the project. The proposed indicators cover aspects related to the following six categories:

1. Integration, which refers both to the adherence to specific sustainability standards or principles and to the definition of project ESG goals and their integration into the business strategy. International references are: the United Nations Sustainable Development Goals the Task Force on Climate Related Financial Disclosure (TCFD) or the World GBC's Net Zero Carbon Buildings Commitment. Integration is thus viewed from a dual perspective, external and internal, and is, articulated in two subcategories:
    i. commitment to the application/adherence to global sustainable development standards and principles.
    ii. definition of specific ESG goals and their integration in the business strategy.
2. Inclusion and diversity, which describes the efforts made to ensure adequate levels of inclusion and diversity protection, through both

monitoring these aspects and setting specific targets for improvement. The two subcategories provided are in fact:
   i. monitoring of issues related to inclusion and diversity at board, committee and general workforce levels;
   ii. setting targets for increasing the presence of women and for a more equitable age distribution of workers.
3. Strategic management, from a governance perspective, does not specifically refer to the formulation and implementation of ESG objectives but focuses on how these objectives are set and how they are monitored and reviewed. The main categories that will be considered are:
   i. responsibility distribution for ESG management;
   ii. definition of ESG policies;
   iii. definition of ESG targets;
   iv. reporting on ESG issues (that includes reporting on critical issues such as disputes, accidents, fines and conflict situations that may have arisen in the project life cycle.
4. Effective management refers to the activities performed to implement the project and is specifically related to:
   i. the definition and updating of the project's programme of implementation and development;
   ii. the definition of milestones and deliverables;
   iii. monitoring of time and costs (prompt identification of delays or unforeseen costs in the design and implementation phases and adoption of corrective actions).
5. Project Risk assessment, which will ensure that risks are identified and properly addressed. This involves:
   i. commitment to conduct a Due Diligence on ESG issues;
   ii. climate risk management which in turn includes the identification and assessment of transitional risks and physical risks that the project may be facing as it unfolds;
   iii. detailed environmental and social risk assessments.
6. Stakeholders' engagement considers actions that will be implemented to engage internal stakeholders, represented by workers and supply chain entities, but also, and above all, the community within which the project is located. This category of actions includes:
   i. training and growth opportunities related to ESG matters;

ii. requirement on ESG issues aimed at the supply chain;
iii. definition of a formal grievance mechanism;
iv. community engagement actions starting from the monitoring of positive and negative impacts that the project may potentially have on the community.

7. Transparency and reputation include aspects related to:
   i. compliance with law and regulations requirements including, if relevant, voluntary agreements;
   ii. other forms of disclosures beyond what is required by the law (e.g. gender pay gap or fiscal transparency).

Table 7.6 ESG Framework and KPI for Governance topics

Category	ID	Sub-category (ESG Evaluation Criteria)	ID_1	Metrics/KPIs
Integration	G.01	ESG Commitments	G.01.1	Commitment to ESG leadership standards and or principles [0-1]
	G.02	ESG Objectives	G.02.1	Definition of specific ESG objectives [0-1]
			G.02.2	Integration of ESG objectives in business strategy
Inclusion and diversity	G.03	Monitoring inclusion and diversity	G.03.1	Monitoring protocol for inclusion and diversity (considering boards, committees and work force in general) [0-1]
	G.04	Tackling inclusion and diversity	G.04.1	Gender diversity: Commitment to increase the percentage of women in boardrooms [0-1]
			G.04.2	Age group diversity: Commitment to increase the percentage of younger people in boardrooms [0-1]
Strategic management	G.05	ESG Decision making	G.05.1	Allocation of responsibility for implementing ESG objectives [0-1]
			G.05.2	Allocation of responsibility for implementing climate-related objectives [0-1]
	G.06	ESG policies	G.06.1	Definition of policy/policies on environmental issues [0-1]
			G.06.2	Definition of policy/policies on social issues [0-1]
			G.06.3	Definition of policy/policies on governance issues [0-1]
	G.07	ESG targets	G.07.1	Definition of performance improvement targets on ESG-related matters [0-1]

Category	ID	Sub-category (ESG Evaluation Criteria)	ID_1	Metrics/KPIs
	G.08	Reporting	G.08.1	ESG actions and performance disclosure [0-1]
			G.08.2	Monitoring of ESG related controversies, misconduct, penalties, incidents, accidents or breaches against codes of conduct/ethics
Risk assessment	G.09	ESG Due Diligence	G.09.1	Commitment to perform asset – level environmental and/or social risk assessment as a standard part of a due diligence for new acquisitions [0-1]
	G.10	Climate related risk management	G.10.1	Identification transition risks that could have a material financial impact [0-1]
			G.10.2	Assessment the material financial impact of transition risks on business and/or financial planning [0-1]
			G.10.3	Identification physical risks that could have a material financial impact [0-1]
			G.10.4	Assessment of material financial impact from physical climate risks on business and/or financial planning [0-1]
	G.11	Risk Assessment	G.11.1	Asset level environmental and/or social risk assessments [0-1]
Stakeholders' engagement	G.12	ESG training	G.12.1	Training and development opportunities for employees on ESG-related issues [0-1]
	G.13	supply chain engagement	G.13.1	Definition of specific requirements in procurement processes [0-1]
	G.14	Stakeholder grievance process	G.14.1	Definition of formal process for stakeholders to communicate grievance [0-1]
	G.15	Community engagement	G.15.1	Definition of a community engagement program that includes ESG- specific issues [0-1]
			G.15.2	Monitoring impacts on the community [0-1]
Transparency – reputation	G.16	Law and regulation compliance	G.16.1	Reporting on significant instances of non-compliance [0-1]
			G.16.2	Data protection Management System [0-1]
	G.17	Other disclosures	G.17.1	Commitment to disclosure beyond law requirements [0-1]

Application of the ESG Framework

Hope's ESG framework is designed to be a digital, flexible tool for the ESG assessment of an urban regeneration project during all its life cycle

Figure 7.4 Application of the ESG Framework

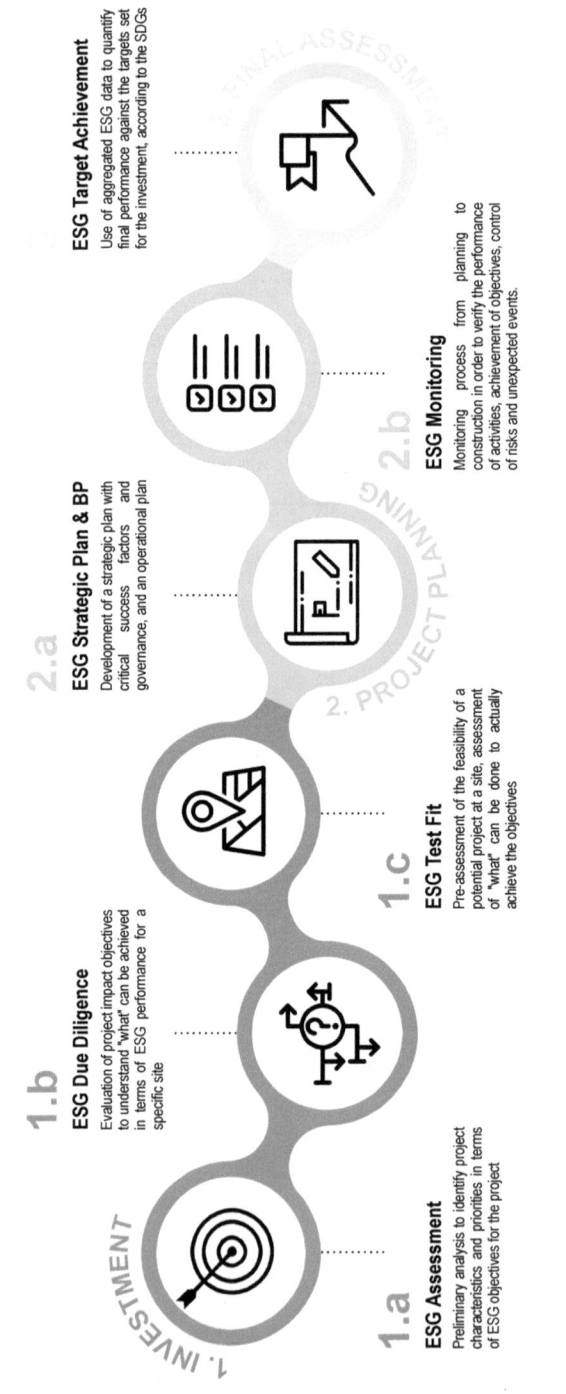

phases: starting from the decision on the investment, through project planning and construction, and ending with the appraisal of the project's outcomes.

In the preliminary analysis of an investment decision, the ESG framework will be used to analyse the characteristics of the project and of the site in which it is located, and to identify the priorities in terms of the objectives to be achieved.

As the first phase ends with the investment decision, it is important that the ESG framework is able to highlight critical success factors and potential threats. In order to achieve this objective, the ESG framework should be accompanied by an ESG technical due diligence and a Test FIT.

The ESG due diligence will be carried out by specialized providers and aims to:

- Understand the context and identify the main ESG issues related to the project, such as the geographical location, the physical and climate transition risk, and finally the social impact.
- Analyse the risks and opportunities related to the project considering the impacts on the environment/community (SWOT analysis).
- Estimate the value creation process from the as-is analysis of the green/brownfield.
  - Define methodologies for future ESG analysis/monitoring and verify the needs arising from regulatory compliance.
  - Prepare a final report containing the results of the analysis and an assessment of the project's ability to achieve a common benefit.

The ESG due diligence will therefore be essential to the assessment of the project's impact objectives, which will be outlined in the ESG framework in terms of objectives and weights. This analysis will be empowered by a Fit Test conducted by a specialized provider. The Fit Test preassess the feasibility of a potential project, evaluating a site and verifying the possibility that it may effectively achieve the objectives foreseen. ESG due diligence and Fit Test are aimed at assessing investment opportunities and defining strategies that can be effectively implemented on-site and can be sustained over time. The focus of this phase of analysis is to understand "what" can be achieved in terms of ESG performance for a specific site (ESG due diligence) and a preliminary assessment of "how" it can be done (Fit Test).

The results of the ESG assessment analysis are summarized in the final investment memorandum for the investment decision. The Board of Directors, after gathering the opinions of the Risk Manager and the Sustainability Committee, make the go-no-go decision. The Board may also require the inclusion of specific ESG objectives and/or the development of dedicated project solutions to strengthen the environmental and social impact commitments to be generated through the investment.

Once in the project planning phase, HOPE will play an active role, with participation in governance and active management as an operating partner leading toward sustainable objectives.

In this regard, the ESG project planning plays a critical role in the success of the urban regeneration project. HOPE will support the development of a strategic plan aimed at defining the critical success factors and the governance to assure the achievement of the ESG Goals, as well as the operational plan, aimed at defining the guidelines to manage the project for the creation of long-lasting value.

In particular, the strategic plan includes the following steps:

1. Analysis of stakeholders' needs: identification of the target stakeholders and their needs, and how they can benefit from the project to steer the design in this direction. For example, the regeneration project could offer new destinations for all city users, return an enhanced/restored area to the neighbourhood, infuse a sense of belonging to the community, and offer a valuable and sustainable lifestyle to the users of the facility.
2. Outlining of the ESG framework to tailor the specific project and its objectives. This is achieved through the construction of an ESG matrix that will be the link from the ESG framework to the particular features of the project, and will help define the options/ solutions/ opportunities to be explored and exploited, and the infrastructure required to manage the service. By way of example, on the ESG Goal of developing a community and promoting sports, the solutions must be aimed at creating places to practice sports, connect parks and promote community, through the development of infrastructure such as parks, running tracks, fitness trails, event areas and multifunctional aggregation centres.

3. Definition of critical success factors: identification of the distinctive elements of the project that generate a positive impact on the environment and the community.
4. Creation of project governance: establishment of three committees to manage all the phases of the project:
   - A "Steering Committee," consisting of Hope and the investment partners, to define the guidelines and oversee the project development, ensuring the pursuit of the defined objectives.
   - An "Operational Committee," consisting of consultants in various capacities (engineers, implementers, specialized ESG consultants) involved in defining the strategy of the project, in particular the project's specifications, contents and implementation activities.
   - A "Feasibility Committee," consisting of contractors/suppliers involved in the material implementation of the project, to verify the technical feasibility of the project against the objectives set.

The ESG framework and in particular the governance of the project will depend on the coordinated action of these committees within its competencies and specific functions. At the beginning of the project planning phase the governance categories and KPIs in the framework will be specified, defining for example:

- Criteria for the selection of committee members or for the selection of constructors and suppliers (for example to fulfil specific needs or specific constraints of the site or the project).
- Communication/participation objectives as a result of the stakeholders' analysis and of the goals of the project itself.
- Commitment to achieve a project certification (selecting the most suitable certification scheme).

The operational plan includes the following steps:

1. ESG planning: which defines the end-to-end guidelines of the project from the selection and procurement of raw materials to efficient site management and project management throughout the project's life cycle.
2. Supplier selection, which aims to select suppliers that ensure the pursuit of the goal of sustainable standards. By way of an example,

parameters used are related to the adoption of internal policies and systems to control and reduce pollution, energy and water consumption, to ensure the health and safety of workers, as well as the presence of a strong governance structure that ensures decent working conditions.
3. Site management, developing processes for optimizing procurement and efficient site management, selecting and managing contractors responsibly while respecting working conditions, and implementing data collection for ESG reporting purposes.
4. Future management, which defines the reporting system at the end of the development before the valorisation of the investment and the monitoring of the long-term performance after the valorisation.

During the development of the project, HOPE will use the ESG Framework, where the project's ESG KPIs and related weights were detailed, to monitor the achievements of the project objectives, leveraging the ESG digital solution developed by TECMA.

The development of a digitalized process will allow for the achievement of three key aspects in the use of data: (1) being aware of all the available information and demonstrate that they can be collected in an organized and structured manner; (2) make use of verified and approved data, meaning that all the underlying datasets will be the 'single source of truth' to be used for the ESG assessment as approved data from relevant managers; (3) data sharing with all relevant stakeholders, both internally and externally as part of a dedicated reporting structure.

Monitoring ESG results

Irrespective of the investment strategy being pursued, from the initial due diligence through to the investment decision being taken and executed, and until the closing of the deal, a common approach to monitor the actual management of the invested company will be followed. During the active management phase, the Risk Management Function will carry out periodic assessments of the investment riskiness, also from an ESG point of view. In particular, the analysis of the many sustainability risks is carried out using the internal ESG framework, the results of which are constantly updated and integrated into the overall risk model. The monitoring activity will be carried out in all the phases of the project development – from planning and designing, to execution – to verify that all the activities are performed as planned (and the objectives are met), that risks are under control, but most importantly, that any unforeseen occurrence is promptly taken care of. An unforeseen event may result from a number of factors, for example, due to an incomplete assessment of site constraints or project requirements, but may mostly arise from unpredictable events. The ability to cope with such events will be a strategic competence built and strengthened thanks to the "lessons learned" from every project and every assessment performed.

With regard to the Sustainable Cities and smart/green Infrastructure Strategy, the monitoring activities will be performed through a digital platform that will translate the single KPIs values into comprehensive assessments from a single pillar view (environmental, social, and governance) and for the project as a whole. During this phase it is likely that a large amount of data and data sources will come into play in subsequent iterations of information updates, thus increasing the complexity of the data collection and management. The digital solution may be connected to external databases along the project phases to transfer data and information at the required time step (daily, monthly, yearly). For this reason, a data strategy will need to be set up at the beginning of the Engagement phase to customize data flows with the specific project needs and include all stakeholders, defining duties and tasks for each of them.

For both strategies, the ESG data gathered from time to time are used to quantify indicators both for regulatory requirements (PAI) and to monitor and control the progressive achievement of the specific sustainability objectives. These were set at the beginning of the investment as a critical and integral part of the overall investment decision. These objectives, their progressive achievement or lack of it, are then organized in a specific reporting, reflecting the progressive evolution of the KPIs that have been identified for each individual objective, and the aggregate performance according to the UN SDGs. The monitoring phase will exploit a set of aggregated data to describe the portfolio performance and the progress of the portfolio ESG results against targets, including the identification of risk categories (i.e. via RAG assessment) at both portfolio and investment/asset levels, and highlighting where major opportunities may arise. High-level information and aggregated data will be as precise, complete and reliable as the underlying datasets will be.

In urban regeneration projects, the value of the digital solution will become reality through the best possible analysis of a large amount of data and information that will be synthesized into user-specific interfaces and visualizations for immediate take up and use in the decision making.

Furthermore, the risk model adopted by HOPE to evaluate the investment on an ongoing basis includes periodic stress test to evaluate the impacts of those sustainability risks on the IRR of the single investment and of the overall portfolio. The stress scenarios should include assumptions relating to the most relevant ESG factors for the portfolio company, such as investments required to reconvert machinery and gradually replace plastic packaging, or an adjustment of employee salaries and working hours in line with the relevant National Collective Labour Agreements. The investigation will reflect not just the IRR (hence financial) impact, but also the social and environmental dimensions, to monitor the risk of not achieving the main goals stated across these three dimensions and accordingly to a more extended definition of wealth being created ("wealth-being").

ESG Valorisation Phase

In the valorisation phase, HOPE conducts a final assessment (so-called "ESG target achievement assessment"), aimed at evaluating the achievement of the set ESG objectives and the impact generated by the pursuit of those objectives.

The analysis will also contain an assessment of how relevant (and material) ESG factors have been managed over time, providing evidence of actions taken and empowering investors to do proper due diligence on the issue.

In particular, HOPE intends to provide evidence of revisions made to long-term objectives and ensure continuity even in the exit phase. Indeed, the ESG investment will need to have affected the company's culture and processes in a way that is permanent over time.

The exit strategy will be carefully defined in order to verify adherence to ESG criteria by potential buyers to ensure continuity in the management of environmental, social and governance aspects.

Finally, in order to promote continuous involvement in the pursuit of sustainable impacts, investors as well as the target's management are incentivized to join the "Hopers Community" in order to share ideas and experiences through periodic meetings, podcasts, and interviews.

7 HOPE: A Case for Change 215

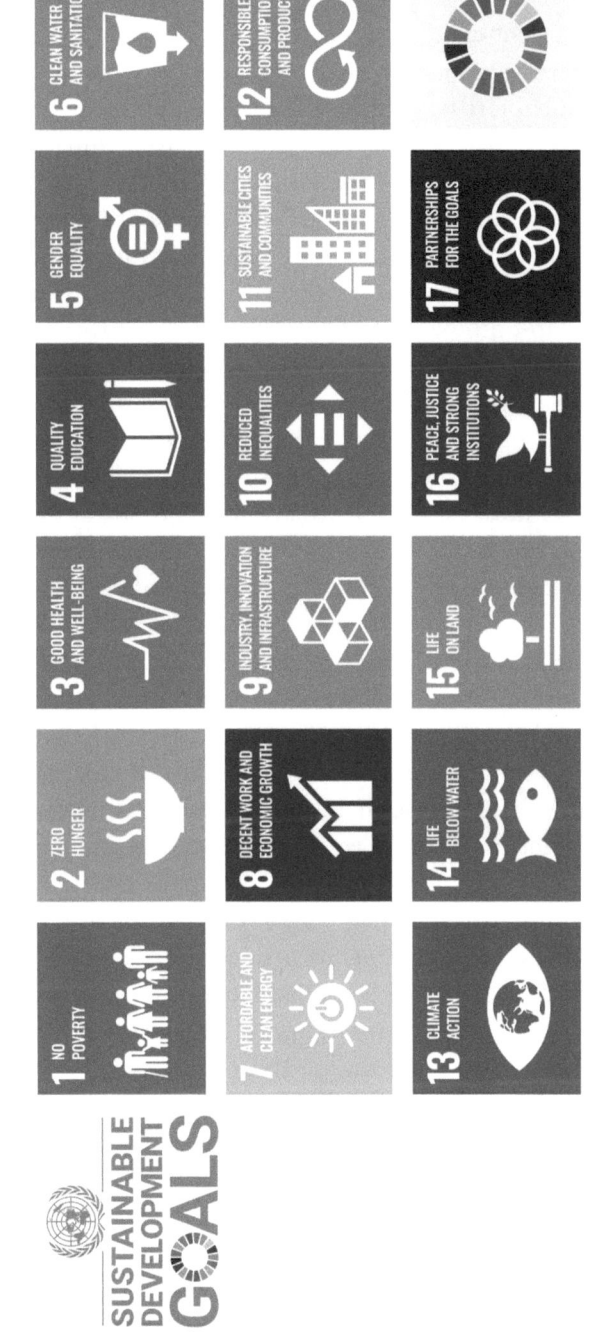

Figure 7.5 Example of the monitoring of the achievement of ESG objectives according to the United Nations' "2030 Sustainable Development Goals"

7.7 Black swans and Russian bears

Based on our recent experience, black swans are not a scarce resource anymore. After the global financial crisis, Brexit, Donald Trump and his wave of global tariffs, the Covid-19 pandemic, the Ukrainian war and the looming crisis that is widely expected from climate change, a number of things have gone wrong for globalization.[4] Leaving aside all the other strategic discussions on the key purpose of finance and economics, it turns out that the very basic idea of each nation specializing in what they do best is less and less operationally viable – hence leading to an overall sub-optimization of the financial wealth that the world can create each year. More importantly, according to *The Economist*, for countries, their firms and citizens, a new-trade off has become apparent: between the business opportunity to trade freely with everybody, no matter what their stance on key issues such as respect for the individual and minorities, use of violence to quell domestic or international adversaries and care of the ecosystem; and the willingness to pursue all other values which are negated by these very counterparts, at the cost of reduced wealth, either as direct effect (as bilateral business waved) or indirect one (as overall suboptimization in the global allocation of resources). *The Economist* has extended this argument, describing the dichotomy and the potential full decoupling occurring between the Sino-Soviet axis (the autocracies – led by China and Russia, plus a handful of smaller countries associated with them) and the rest of the more liberal and democratic world (led by the USA, the UK and Europe, Japan, Australia and Canada and likely India). This was already under way before the Russian invasion, but since it has brutally accelerated. In the last 10 years, the international trade relative to GDP was already down by 5% at a global level, and long-term investments halved in the last 3 years. After the invasion, the Russian bear has projected itself onto global markets (getting to "bear territory," from equities to bonds), strengthening a number of financial and economic imbalances – from higher public debts (to finance the war, and then to build back whatever was destroyed in the process), to higher inflation (spurred by new inflationary fiscal policies and, most importantly, by hikes in the price of energy and on other scarce resources), to the devaluation of certain currencies (starting from the Russian ruble) and to the further debasement of traditional currencies to the benefit of alternative crypto currencies and other defensive proxies (such as gold) during times of high inflation.

The real economy will be negatively impacted for all these reasons and, even more gravely, for the further, dramatic and long-lasting disruption of the global supply chain – with scarce resources becoming rarer and rarer, and rare ones becoming non-existent – not to mention the many things going missing (destroyed, lost or robbed) in between. Leaving aside the chances of a far more dangerous military escalation, even this kind of sanctions-led decoupling is introducing severe damage to an already fragile financial and economic recovery, with expansionary fiscal measures already exhausted. Even more tragically, by creating new urgent priorities, the winds of a new global cold war are making us forget other critical issues – from Covid to climate change. Sustainability is therefore at risk of extinction itself as a topic of interest – who cares about a few more degrees if bombs are destroying cities? And what about rare species, if children are dying in urban warfare? And gender or race parity, if entire populations are at war? And the focus on the next generations if it's not obvious that people can survive into the next week, if some miscalculation happens, followed by some nuclear accident at scale? If the Russian bear is going to impact negatively on all kinds of financial and real economy markets, the canary of total sustainability and ESG seems destined for an early death in the coal mine. In fact, we could even talk of a perfect storm, if we had not used this expression a few times already, for events that, negative as they already were, have been followed by more negative ones in turn. Should we then give up hope and just focus on the basics? Leaving aside the fancy notions of extended and augmented wealth to be driven just by our ego-centric, utilitarian sense of survival?

In fact, we like to think that all these challenges, and the very stream of uninterrupted black swans, by posing unprecedented challenges, are also giving us the chance to reconsider the overall meaning of life – or at least of its economic dimension. It is easier to understand why wealth is not just about money during a pandemic or a war, and how peace and safety, freedom and democracy are greater, overwhelming values to consider in our definition of total sustainability. In our ESG definition, we care about the environment, with its quality and stable climate and the survival of rare species, simply because we take for granted that it is safe from nuclear radiation and bombs, and that species at risk of extinction are not at risk, obviously including humans. We care then about inclusion and gender parity, because we assume that basic freedoms and liberal and democratic regimes are also taken for granted. And we focus on the best governance for institutions and corporates, assuming there is no major geopolitical confrontation between highly militarized counterparts that could lead to war. In short, a new definition of wealth-being and of its management is even more critical during times of crisis and its optimization leads not just to higher GDP, lower CO2 and greater happiness, but to saving lives as well. Although great amounts of financial wealth are made or destroyed during times of war and typically for the benefit of a few, it is easier to understand how relative this is and how many other dimensions are worth considering and prioritizing, working across geographical and political barriers. Rediscovering the ultimate purpose of wealth, which is not just financial – a financial tool and not an end it itself – is now more urgent than ever. Something we should not be ready to trade or give up in answer to other basic, more mundane needs, even if we are ready to recognize its multiple trade-offs.

7.8 A balanced scorecard for total sustainability

In our approach to support and promote a new, extended and augmented definition of wealth, we have suggested a rigorous and detailed approach, to define the key drivers for measurement and control in an "objective enough" way. We have also discussed, through our case study, the work in progress and the experience of HOPE SICAF, articulated between its impact reporting as benefit corporation, and as investment company pursuing an ex-art. 8 SFDR target of sustainability (which framework was drilled down and differentiated for its main investment strategies: "competitive corporates" and "sustainable cities"). However, in our view, what is mainly missing with this approach, and even more with the one promoted by regulatory bodies and policy makers across the globe, is the idea of simplicity. Impact investing and total sustainability should be based on a very simple, clear and direct message – something that most people would be able to grasp in a couple of minutes and remember – at least most of it – through time. A sort of "decalogue" that, in fact, should have not more than ten KPI to remember, ideally articulated into three dimensions (the one of the "total sustainability" – readers will appreciate a certain reference to the numbers deemed "perfect" by the Ancient

Greek philosophers). At HOPE we have also been working on creating our own "balanced scorecard," with no more than ten indicators, articulated along three dimensions that each stakeholder should have in mind when thinking or acting, and communicating to others what "HOPE is really all about."

The three dimensions identified are obviously the "financial," "social" and "environmental" ones, each with three KPI, as a fourth, overarching (and very traditional) dimensions making up the tenth KPI – which is IRR. As a "for profit" investment management company, the first duty of care for HOPE is to be able to originate, deliver and sustain a compelling internal rate of return for the Institutional and retail investors which have chosen to invest in it, allocating part of their savings to its investment policies. It may be obvious to say, but without a positive and competitive IRR there will be no opportunity for HOPE to raise further capital and pursue with great efficacy and efficiency the goals of all its other stakeholders – the realization of economic gain and profitability is at the basis of a benefit corporation and of any stakeholders' approach that should reinforce and not limit this. IRR for investors is then pursued by developing and promoting a "model of capitalism for everybody," open and inclusive, fair and transparent and that is able to offer easy and cheap access to investment opportunities in its private markets (including the real economy and the real assets) to most Italian families, and with expected long term returns that are consistent with their risk/ return profiles, investment/ consumption cycles and overall wealth. For the other three dimensions, we have defined:

- For "financial sustainability," we have identified the amount of equity capital invested (as a contribution to the equitization and transformation of the country); the contribution to the GDP growth of the country and finally (and maybe counterintuitively) the tax paid – certainly as a contribution to the balancing of the fiscal deficit of the country but also (and more importantly for the stakeholders of HOPE) as a proxy of the taxable income that generates the paid dividends (as unrealized gains – e.g. higher NAV that is not paid as dividends – are not taxed. The unrealized gains are however fully captured in the IRR that includes everything).
- For "social sustainability," we have then identified the gender parity target (as referred to both HOPE as a company and to all its port-

folio companies); the overall job creation in the economy (mostly referred to its portfolio companies – but also indirectly on their network of stable business partners), and finally the focus on our next generations, as a mix of valorisation of their potential, information and training, and with a specific focus on financial education and on their interest and involvement in the many topics related to the Italian sustainability agenda.

- For "environmental sustainability," we have eventually referred to the most obvious CO_2 emissions targeted reduction (as HOPE but, most importantly, as portfolio companies and including our real estate and infrastructure portion of the invested portfolio); the responsible consumption that each of us (and through our portfolio companies) can pursue, to optimize sustainability through the protection of natural resources and the transition towards a circular economy; and, finally the protection and development of our territories, through investment in processes, real assets and infrastructure, to support a more resilient and regenerated country.

7.9 Death of globalization and the return of autarky?

The long list of black swans are all potentially pointing to the slow death of globalization. Even climate change is suggesting a greater use of renewable energies, more effectively used on site; and the development of circular economy, banning the oil-guzzling huge flows of material goods across the globe and supporting the recycling of any good produced against consumerism and indiscriminate international trade. Certainly, we should distinguish between the digital and physical dimension of globalization, with more and more data, information and intelligence flowing through the net (at least within each geopolitical block) and with less and less people and raw materials going around the planet – not just in response to pandemics and the quest for Net Zero targets – but also because of sanctions and military blockades that are further crippling our global supply chains. Just consider energy, agri-food, the defence and military, innovative technologies (starting from AI – Artificial Intelligence), media and communication and a few others. They are all now subject to a return to autarky, after the bottlenecks and shortages experienced during the pandemics and then the

Ukrainian war. If Smith's precepts are good during peace time, it may be good for nations to become a bit more self-sufficient when things are tense, to ensure their survival and right to determine their destiny – which could be at risk if critical food supplies, arms, or rare earth that are needed for high tech products and electrification become scarce or utterly unavailable. The slow death of globalization and the progressive return to autarky could suggest a focus on its own turf, leaving aside the total sustainability targets for the whole planet. In fact, in this case, the very opposite could also be true, with nations and citizens more aligned in the pursuit of their ultimate wealth-being, but also keener to contribute to the overall global ecosystem as the crisis of a single, small component (whether led by the emergence of a new virus in an exotic country, or the start of a regional conflict in some other far-away place) could lead to the destruction of values for multiple stakeholders and of a tangible and intangible nature. We like to think this is the case, and that a global compact, based on a new definition of wealth, should now be defined – with even more urgency and critical, almost existential, relevance. Consistent with our previous discussion, the key points that such a compact should advocate are the following, addressing the strategic de-globalization and tactical re-autarkization trends, but keeping the goal of total sustainability and the pursuit – via the intelligent use of finance – of a higher purpose for humankind:

- Given the increased volatility in the global financial system and the overall financial burden driven by excessive public debt, monetization and inflation, and the overall debasement of traditional "fiat" currencies, an even stronger economic opportunity and "case for change" should drive the re-equitization of countries, starting with Italy. This can happen by limiting the growth of leverage and by accelerating and sustaining the investment of private saving by institutional investors and private citizens in the real economy, and as "shareholders" and "stakeholders" of the country. This re-equitization can happen only if capital markets and private equity in particular is made open and easily, cheaply and safely available to everybody. Hence, the re-equitization of the country can happen through the retailization of finance, with a different model of wealth management of the future based on a "capitalism for everybody."

- Given the urgent need of strategic and operational independence (and even some autarky) for certain industrial sectors, vertical integrations of critical value chains would need to happen in the future and, in the case of Italy, likely starting with the agri-food, energy, digital technologies and other manufacturing sectors. A high-level vision and consistent economic policies could be defined by the government of reference but would be better left to market forces for its detailed definition and implementation, promoting the creation of domestic private players of excellence and at scale, traded on the stock exchange as public companies and directly owned by a large majority of local citizens (or indirectly via private institutional investors). A certain degree of "sovereignty" and freedom of self-determination and procurement independence could also be targeted, as part of a domestic policy or in liaison with the other parties of the geopolitical block of reference, for the pursuit of a safer or more stable form of globalization.
- Finally, given the tactical need to pursue autarky and even austerity, certain transformational investments and behavioural changes should also be pursued, with a focus on the development of a shared and circular economy, of renewable sources of energy and on the reduction of carbon emission also pursued by the reduction in the total level of resources consumed (starting from temperature and air conditioning, mobility and travel and even dietary based ones). In short, virtues can be found and pursued during dire times, modifying our lifestyle not necessarily for the worst. A meaningful change in the energy we burn to keep our home warm or cold, or to travel could hardly be noticeable, and different eating habits could lead to healthier and more productive lifestyles (and reduce costs of the health services) as a by-product. A motivated change in the way we invest, work, consume and live as private citizen would therefore be the ultimate reflection of a liberal and democratic society, where optimization happens in the market but on the basis of a fairer, more inclusive and cognitive society made up of people that vote with their actions – starting from how they invest, work, consume and behave as citizens – to ultimately drive total sustainability and wealth-being.

7 HOPE: A CASE FOR CHANGE   223

7.10   The force of a new generation

In "Don't look up," an American apocalyptic black comedy film promoted by Netflix and starring an ensemble cast, including Leonardo Di Caprio and Meryl Streep, two low level astronomers go on a giant media tour to warn mankind of an approaching comet that will destroy planet earth and human civilization. The story is an allegory of climate change and a satire of government, political, celebrity and media indifference to the climate crisis, or to any other crisis for that matter. As such, it is also another story representative of our "nealth," the nemesis of wealth that is reflected in a society that allows us to bypass scientific facts and evidence, and ignore the threat (by "not looking up") of our own self destruction for rich people's short-term gains. The story is inspiring as, eventually, the first step to promote change and revert to a path of sustainability is all about "looking up," going well and above what typical, short-term indicators, based on a traditional definition of wealth, would show us. In fact, for all their merits, ESG and the green movements are still too unclear and far from the qualities of the veritable, objective enough truth that Nozick was suggesting as a serviceable starting point able to support us in moving from ideas to actions, from good intentions to realized fact. In fact, ESG is a "category error" – something that, according to the *Financial Times*, needs unbundling.[5] More clarity is also required for the individuals that take decisions and then pursue courses of action based on them. We all eventually (most of us, at least) want to "do the right thing," but – as in the eponymous movie by Spike Lee – it is unclear what that should be and how we should be doing it.

According to Reuters, the current wealth management model was – for all its limits – able to channel €3.2 Tn into equity funds that claim to have environmental, social and governance objectives. No matter the lack of clarity regarding the many category errors of such ESG labelling, the case for an ethical approach to investment management remains strong – although the "search for truth" is also worth a bit more. The biggest taxonomic mistake in ESG, according to Guthrie, is the category itself and its tendency to become a meaningless marketing tool. It is worth unpicking and going deeper into each and every category to find what really is the "right thing to do." The environmental aim is simple and clear as it relates mainly to decarbonization. But that could also become quite partial by the day, as other imbalances are found in the environment. And it is posing other trade-offs with the other dimensions of our "total sustainability" definition (this is aimed at being more comprehensive and less ideological, being also grounded in the financial and economic dimension, whilst retaining its holistic nature as well). Negating any trade-off in the pursuit of sustainability and maximum returns on capital could otherwise sound hollow, if not hypocritical. In the real world, it is not uncommon to find plenty of people speaking positively about ESG initiatives and suggesting others invest, whilst they put most of their money into bad hands that will almost certainly reach superior financial returns (even more so if they have a relaxed attitude to following the rule of law and in cutting corners).

Managing lots of complex trade-offs does not, however, necessarily mean low returns or the lack of them. Consistently pursuing lower returns could in fact become a weaker and weaker point targeted by critics of ESG and they could relegate this marketing fad to a premature and imminent death. Unprofitable ESG investments should not be pursued with private capital (unless the owners of the capital decide to do so) as an attractive return on capital and economic value creation should be considered as a prerequisite for any other "total sustainability" consideration. But an ESG or "total sustainability" perspective could influence decisions on very profitable investment opportunities. For example, a definition of wealth and wellbeing that includes the perspective of the next three generations could potentially reverse decisions that are currently being taken on investments and projects. And an inclusion of (for example) taxes on all kind of negative externalities created in the economy by unsustainable products or services would also change their market price equilibrium and the corresponding behaviour of economic agents. These taxes could in turn fund public initiatives designed to promote and accelerate the transition, or make up for some of the intergenerational arbitrage that we have discussed and defined as one of the most unfair and massive value migrations (and destruction) of recent times. Specifically, we have argued, that the new definition of wealth and wellbeing strategies, policies and management processes should be reoriented to make sure they are not only extended and augmented, but also farsighted, so as to recreate and sustain hope in the next generations, and a case for the change for the current ones. Generation is indeed a very powerful term as it relates to the creation, or recreation (re-generation and recovery, through a re-birth) of something new for an all-new range of stakeholders that may be too young to count today, or not even born yet, but that nonetheless will be in positions of power in a few years. Generation is also the act of creation as opposed to destruction. And a positive legacy that benefits the young, an act of faith and a statement that is supportive of the survival of humankind and for the development of civilization. It is for us, the baby boomers and the few other middle generations to ensure "generation" remains a positive term for the future and a force to progress towards higher futures that will be determined in time by the future generations. We all bear a great responsibility and the odds for this change back to sustainability are not great.

Ultimately, however, it will be for the new generations to really drive and implement the change, by defining and sharing a new definition of wealth-being, and corresponding strategies, policies and management processes. Alas, new generations seem also subject to extreme polarization. On one hand, people with no vision and ambition, little or no awareness of sustainability, uninformed and uninterested on the many issued related to the economic, social and ecological burdens discussed. They almost behave as the short-sighted people of the Netflix blockbuster – by avoiding looking up at all costs, or just not attempting anything – let alone stopping their new negative contribution to the "nealth" already capitalized by previous generations. On the other hand, there are incredibly mature and sensible young people uninterested in financial wealth, as they are keen to leave a mark on the extraordinary challenges humanity is facing and must overcome. There is also a fine line between those who understand the issues, attack and attribute blame to the people in charge, but add little more than further bluster. And others that are less keen on attributing faults to others and more on taking their own share of responsibilities, with little monetary rewards but a greater than life retribution if what they feel they are doing is for the benefit of others. The more polarized these extremes become, the more uncertain and potentially disruptive the process of change will be, leading to a fight within a single generation. This situation will be for the real "alpha" to win, leading the evolution that failed so many of their predecessors. Contributing to the transformation of the economy and society that so many have promised before them. Leading the future of wealth and wellbeing towards a wealth-being that they will define, craft and realize for the benefit of many others and with the thought that they will also become, in turn, a mid and then old generation worrying about future ones to come. Isn't this eventually the ultimate purpose of existence and the intimate meaning of the total sustainability we advocate?

Notes

[1] Paragraph and framework developed with the lead contribution of Elisa Galassi, CRO and Head of Total Sustainability at HOPE S.B. SICAF.

[2] Paragraph and framework developed with the lead contribution of Elisa Galassi, CRO and Head of Total Sustainability at HOPE S.B. SICAF.

[3] Paragraph and framework developed with the contribution of ARUP.

[4] Economic freedom v political freedom, *The Economist*, March 19, 2022.

[5] ESG is a category error that needs unbundling, Jonathan Guthrie, *Financial Times*, April 4, 2022.